THE LABEL MACHINE

Build Your Music Career With The Record Label Model

NICK SADLER

First published by Velocity Press 2021.
This edition published 2025.

velocitypress.uk
thelabelmachine.com

Printed and bound in Great Britain by Clays Ltd, Elcograf S.p.A.

Cover design
Hayden Russell

Typesetting
Paul Baillie-Lane

PRINT ISBN: 9781913231989
EBOOK ISBN: 9781913231996

GPSR
Publisher: Velocity Press, London, United Kingdom
EU Authorised Representative: Easy Access System Europe - Mustamäe tee 50, 10621 Tallinn, Estonia, gpsr.requests@easproject.com

"I really wish I personally would have had something like it a few years ago when we first started, because I think it really does do a great job of guiding you through the system."

Scott Bell - Label Manager - Cat Family Records

"We've just hit over 500,000 streams. We've had numerous press articles. Our monthly listeners for all the artists that we represent on the label on Spotify has tremendously grown. And I can't stress enough at how important having a resource like the Label Machine really is"

Freddie Harb - Founder and CEO - NOS Recordings

"The Label Machine program and my sessions with Nick were incredibly valuable. His clear and structured guidance gave me the confidence to navigate every step of the Sonic/Panic Vol. 2 release, and I learned so much in the process. We surpassed all our targets, over a million streams and more than a hundred media features, and his support was key to that success."

Ewa Wojkowska - Co-founder - Alarm Records

"With our first campaign, we were able to reach some significant milestones. We saw a 50% increase in monthly Spotify listeners, doubled the number of playlists the artist was added to, and experienced an 80% increase in our email contact list. It's incredibly rewarding to see such tangible growth."

Jose Medina - Label Manager - Damaged Halo Records

"The Label Machine gives you a clear, step-by-step process to help you carve out your personal career path in today's music industry. While many timeless rules still hold true, the breakdown of traditional labels means artists need new tools and this book delivers. It gives you the system, helping to clear your mind, letting you see your music and what you're really trying to say with fresh clarity. It helps you use your limited time more effectively and stay focused on the bigger picture."

Markee Ledge - Artist Kosheen / Substance / Zonal on Sony-BMG, Island, and Universal

"I'd really encourage anyone who started this journey and who's genuinely interested in running a record label properly and getting their music out on their own terms to sign up to The Label Machine. It has been absolutely amazing for me."

Damien O'Reilly - Founder - Scrape & Delete Records

"The Label Machine has been the best possible companion I could have had on my journey building my record label. It gave me clarity, structure, and confidence at every stage of the process. Every time I felt overwhelmed, this book gave me the guidance I needed. It's like having a mentor in print and has turned what felt like a mountain into a mapped-out path. It's easily the best investment I've made in my music career."

Phil Cleeves - Label Manager - Dub From The Ruins

CONTENTS

PART TWO: MUSIC COPYRIGHT

PART THREE: THE PROCESS

PART FOUR: BECOMING ESTABLISHED

Dedicated to my son, Rory River

PREFACE

Congratulations on deciding to read this book. No matter what stage you are in your music career, simply reading this book will enable you to become more successful in all the music industry's essential business elements.

What do I mean by business elements? These elements allow you to make money from your music, such as distribution, marketing and music promotion, fan growth and management, and managing multiple royalty streams.

In recent years, I've seen a growth of music gurus, music success masterminds, and online music courses that teach different ways to do each of the elements. And some of them are great. And some of them even say you don't need a record label anymore. And they are right.

We are living in a world where you don't need a record label in the traditional sense. You don't need to 'sign' to a record label. You can do it yourself. However, if you want to build a successful music career, you need to make sure you have your music business elements in order.

These business elements fall under the services and responsibilities of one particular entity in the music industry. The record label. Both traditional and modern-day record labels are structured to provide these business elements.

So why reinvent the wheel when there is already a framework that ensures all your important business elements work together in harmony giving your music the best possible chance of success?

So whether you are looking to launch an independent record label or launch your own musical career professionally, this book is for you. By looking at the business of music through the lens of a record label, you can learn how to use a record label blueprint to build and grow your professional music career.

INTRODUCTION

Why am I writing this book? Well, this edition you are reading is my second edition. The first one sold out so my publisher signed me again to write this follow-up. However, there were two original reasons for writing the first edition, which still ring true today.

One. I have found no comprehensive resource relevant for the last fifteen years of the music industry that puts everything you need into one place for artists wanting to set up and run their own record label. That covers every detail and gives practical information on how to do it all. No roadmap, so to speak.

Two. I've set up and managed many record labels, and I love helping artists and music entrepreneurs do the same. However, I was limited by my time and wanted a way to help the many instead of the few.

Now a bit of history. When I started Never Say Die Records with Tommy Dash (aka Skism), we didn't know how to run a label. I had a little experience with music publishing through getting a few of my tracks in video games, and Tommy had experience building his career as a breakbeat DJ and producer.

As we knew so little about starting and running a record label, I researched extensively. I bought and read all the popular music business books on Amazon, read endless blogs on the music industry, filed hundreds of internet bookmarks, and wrote massive lists on what we needed to do.

We met with other record label heads to ask them for advice. The very first label manager to help us was Asad Rajia, who ran Funkatech Records. We also met Tim Binns from New State Records, a great help in the early days. And Chris Goss of Hospital Records, who to this day is still a constant source of inspiration.

As we slowly built the label and learnt what we were doing, I compiled all this information into operating manuals or what we called 'Bibles'. We named these bibles after biblical texts. The Koran was for merchandise, The Torah for social media. Well, you get the picture.

These bibles became the template for Never Say Die Records, Disciple Recordings, Get Hype Records and No Tomorrow Recordings. Five years later, and over a million record sales, I had a pretty good grip on how to run record labels.

We also started an artist management company, which I still run to this day, a PR company, a publishing company, and even had our own merchandise printing machines. Some of these ventures worked, and some didn't, and we certainly learnt plenty!

At The Label Machine we currently work with over 300 artists and labels today in growing their music careers. Where I'm happiest is helping creative people build businesses around their art.

I've expanded further into the entertainment world working with filmmakers to produce over 20 award-winning films, including the BAFTA and Oscar-winning live action short 'An Irish Goodbye' on which I was an executive producer.

As well as DJing, producing, remixing and releasing music as Mobscene and Kyries with my writing partners Bruce Gainsford, and Michael Unwin, I've been fortunate to work with some incredibly talented artists. Artists such as The Freestylers, Flux Pavilion, The Prototypes, Foreign Beggars, Three Laws, Markee and Memtrix.

But the biggest name I worked with was Skrillex, who is one of the nicest guys in the industry. When he won his three Grammys, he name-checked our label in his first acceptance speech, which at the time was a very special moment for me.

In short, I've got plenty of experience in bringing success to independent career artists.

Whilst many of my early career experiences have been in running electronic record labels, in recent years I have been working with label owners from all genres of music from jazz, country & western, singer-songwriters, and rock bands. I have seen that the fundamentals for successfully releasing records don't really change between genres.

If you are beginning your journey and think this seems too much, don't worry, I was there once too. By simply making small steps every day, you can achieve what you want from your music career. Just reading this book will give you a HUGE advantage and a step in the right direction.

It doesn't matter where in the world you decide to run your music label either. You can run a label from a laptop in your bedroom, studio, shared office, or anywhere with a good internet connection.

So good luck, and let's begin this journey!

HOW TO USE THIS BOOK

When I wrote this book, I didn't want it to be generalist or just theory-based. I wanted to make it full of detailed practical steps. To show exactly how to set everything up. And by that I mean, what software to use, what websites to visit, what companies to work with, what words to write in emails for PR.

So while I have included a vast amount of detailed information, I also realised it's a pain to manually copy website addresses or copy the text over from a book. You want to point and click, copy and paste. Work fast and efficiently!

This inspired me to take all the practical information of this book, which is essentially everything in parts three and four of the book and create a website platform that has all this information available to easily use. The platform's website address is thelabelmachine.com, and it has allowed me to work with hundreds of artists and music entrepreneurs to build and grow their own record labels.

As you read this book, you will find references to downloadable resources and checklists for the book sections. When these are available, you can download them for free by visiting the Book Resources tab on The Label Machine website.

Buying this book also gives you a 50% discount to The Label Machine's online platform. Simply email a copy of your book receipt to book@thelabelmachine.com, and I will send a special link to sign up. This also includes receipts for buying the book second-hand on Amazon.

The platform also gives you access to the Marketing Machine, which is a full-stack marketing solution which includes website builder, fan management system, contract organiser, funnel automation, social media scheduler, and AI automation builder for all your music marketing needs. Any template you see in the book, will be available there.

We also have integrated music distribution that delivers your music to all major platforms such as Spotify, Amazon, Apple Music and specialist stores such as Beatport. With the community resources, Marketing Machine and distribution, you have everything you need to build and run a music empire.

If you are relatively new to the music industry or have been out of the game for a while, then I suggest reading the entire book from start to finish and then going back over part three when you are ready to take action. If you already understand how the industry and music copyright works, skim read parts one and two and then jump into parts three and four.

Note: When I mention money, I use an average currency exchange of 0.80 £UK to 1.00 $US and will list it in £UK / $US format for easy reference for readers on both sides of the Atlantic.

Note: I use the terms record label and music label interchangeably. They are the same thing.

PART ONE

THE INDUSTRY

OVERVIEW

Part one of the book aims to give you an overview of the music industry to see where the running of a record label fits in with the other aspects of the industry. It will introduce other industry professionals such as artist managers, booking agents, distributors, and publishers and how everyone works together to create successful artist careers.

The following diagram summarises the different relationships in the music industry. This is by no means perfect, and there are lots of indirect relationships across the industry, but this is a good starting point from a music label's point of view.

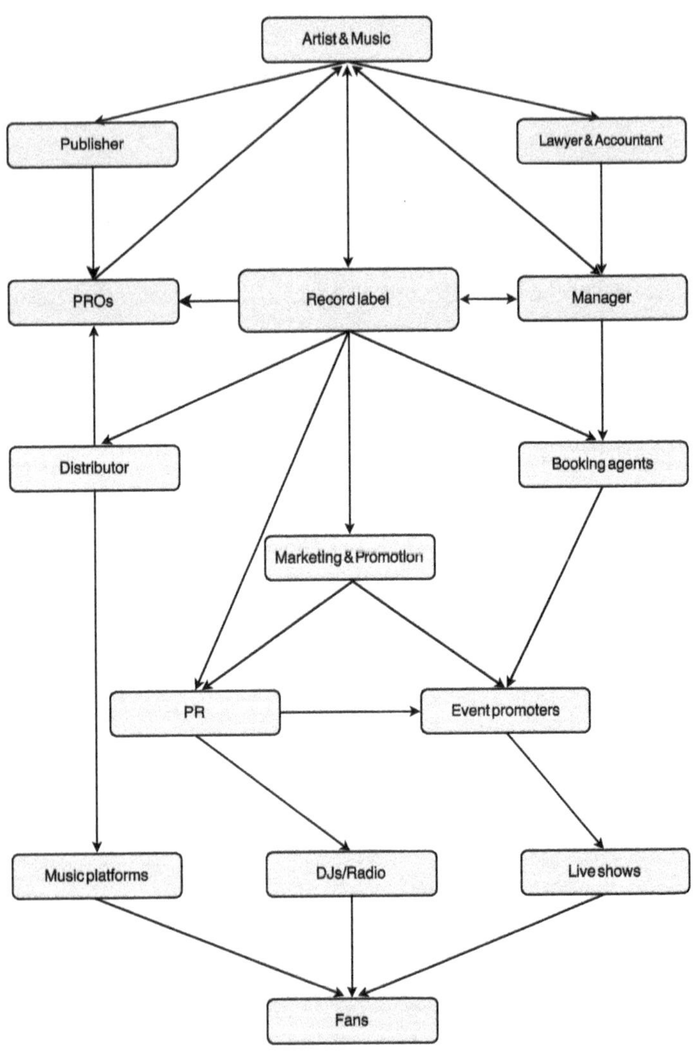

Let's look at each of these roles and activities in more detail, starting with where everything begins, the artist and music.

THE ARTIST

In this book's context, we define the artist as the musician, producer, or collectively the band or producer outfit that creates the music that will be released as a single, EP or album.

But let's dive a little deeper and look at musicians and artists. Is an artist a musician? Is a musician an artist? Or are they the same thing?

A musician is someone who plays music on an instrument that they may or may not have written.

An artist creates art. In the context of music, they make the music either by playing and recording musical instruments and/or producing and composing music on a studio computer.

From a traditional point of view, record labels and publishers often use the term 'recording artists' to describe musicians that play and record the music. And the term 'songwriters' is used to describe artists that write the music and lyrics but don't necessarily play or record the music.

We go into more detail about these differences in Part Two – Music Copyrights.

From a label's point of view, when I talk about artists in this book, I'm referring to all the people who collectively make up the band, producer outfit, or the individual that creates the music masters released as a single, EP or album. You would expect to see the artist live if you went to a gig to see them play as a band or as a DJ playing their own music.

THE MUSIC

"All the good music has already been written by people with wigs and stuff" – Frank Zappa.

It all starts with the music. You need to have great music if you really want to have a successful record label and career in the music industry. While there are mediocre music artists that do well with great marketing and PR plans behind them, ultimately, if you want a long and successful career, you've got to get the music right.

Music ultimately connects the artist to the fans. The music is what we hear on Spotify, a vinyl record, or a live show. It is the one constant that connects all the other parts of the industry together.

This book will mostly refer to recorded music, which is the final recording of a single song, EP, or album. This may have been recorded in a music studio, with a producer and mix engineer, or someone producing beats in a home studio, or a mixture of both. It might be your music you have made yourself, or it may be another artist's music you want to release on your label.

STUDIOS & SOFTWARE

While a good deal of independent music is made in home studios, the software and developers shape a big part of the sound that is produced. It's the studios that create the master recordings of the composed music that artists write.

Recording and producing software include the DAWs (Digital Audio Workstations) such as Logic, Pro Tools, and Ableton Live. Then there are the plugins that recreate the outboard equipment created by companies such as iZotope, Universal Audio, and Waves. Likewise, there are virtual replications of synths and instruments available as well, such as Native Instruments' Kontakt, Spectrasonics' Omnisphere, and Arturia's V Collection. And, of course, there are all the manufacturers of musical instruments that are used in the studios too.

The studios are run by producers, mixing engineers, and mastering engineers, who collaborate closely to bring the artist's vision to life. Producers oversee the entire project, making critical decisions about the arrangement and overall sound. Mixing engineers focus on balancing the individual elements of the track, ensuring clarity and cohesion, while mastering engineers finalize the track, enhancing its sonic quality to meet industry standards for distribution.

AI is making the biggest impact here as I write this edition. It is revolutionizing the industry by providing tools that enhance creativity and efficiency. AI-powered software like Sona and Udio can analyse tracks for optimal mixing, generate realistic instrumental tracks, and even assist in mastering.

These AI tools can also compose entire songs from just a few words or a simple melody, significantly speeding up the songwriting process. As these technologies continue to evolve, they will undoubtedly reshape the music production landscape, making high-quality production more accessible and transforming how music is created and produced in the coming years.

A&R

A&R means Artist and Repertoire. This is traditionally the person responsible for selecting and signing the music for a record label and is often someone that is or was previously a successful artist. If you're looking to get signed to a label, this is the person you need to impress. A good A&R will help shape your music, give you mix pointers, sometimes even sit in the studio and show you little tricks to make your music sound the best it can.

If you are an artist running your own label with your team, you are essentially already the head of A&R. You need to trust your ears to review and provide constructive feedback to other artists you intend to sign and release.

And you don't have to be an acclaimed music artist to be good at A&R. You just have to know what good music sounds like and to have an understanding of the current cultural musical landscape, so you understand what styles and trends in music are working in your particular genre(s) of music.

We will go into more detail on reviewing music and mastering music for distribution in part three of the book.

GREAT MUSIC CHECK

How do you know if you have great music? There is one thing I've found to be a good indicator of great music.

It's a technique taken from a book called 'Mixing With Your Mind' and the author Michael Paul Stavrou explains that the best way to see if a song is GREAT is to simply pick up a very heavy object, such as a large book, and try moving it up and down in rhythm while you listen to the music.

The easier it is to move the book up and down with the music indicates it's good. It's the same principle in action when your head naturally nods along easily to a great song.

We assume you know how to recognise great music in your style of music and as an artist and label owner, you will do your best to make sure you only release great music that you will be proud to put out into the big wide world.

MUSIC MANAGERS

"A manager's job is long, hard, often thankless, but very rewarding" – NS.

Typically, a music manager guides the artist's career, which is essential at the beginning of their career. They often have contacts and experience to help the artist get their first break in the industry.

I also like to say that the music industry is the only industry when the term 'manager' doesn't mean you're the boss. In music, the artist is ultimately the boss, and I believe a manager's job is to help them realise their dreams and aspirations.

An independent music manager often wears many hats. A manager is expected to be a bit of everything and, most importantly, create opportunities for your artist's career.

Once a manager knows the artist's dreams and aspirations, it's their job to create a strategy and to execute that strategy. It's about connecting artists to the right people to develop an overall plan that the artist can easily follow.

It's about building a team around them, such as finding a record deal or setting up their own record label, finding a publishing deal, finding a relevant PR team, and getting them signed to a good booking agency.

It's also the manager's job to make tough decisions and give the bad news that the artist sometimes doesn't want to hear.

Managers come in all shapes and sizes. Some managers are well-connected and will often just introduce an artist to the right people to get the right deals.

More hands-on or administrative type managers ensure the day-to-day running of the artist's career is done effectively.

With bigger artists, there is often a business manager whose sole job is to manage just the finances of an artist.

For indie artists, usually, the manager is all these roles at once, including playing the role of an agent to book live shows when an artist is starting out.

So what about the deal? What's in it for the manager? Managers usually take a percentage of the artist's income. This typically ranges from 10 to 20% and is usually 15% for independent artists, in my experience.

A manager can sign an initial six-month honeymoon contract to see if things are working out. If things are going well for both sides, it can proceed to signing a full management agreement that will typically cover up to three years, after which it goes on a one-year rolling basis. That simply means, if no party cancels the contact in writing, the same terms apply for another year.

I will detail management contracts and cover off sunset clauses and percentage breakdowns in part four of this book.

Beware that there are many people that claim to be managers, with zero experience and understanding of how the industry works. Check credentials and speak to other artists they have worked with. And once you master the music copyright section of this book, ask a potential manager a few copyright questions. Any manager worth their salt should be able to explain to you how the different royalty streams work.

RECORD LABELS

In a nutshell, record labels manage the business side of an artist's recorded music by taking care of the distribution, marketing, PR, and collecting royalties for a release. And these business elements are essential to both the music and the artist's success.

This is why as a music artist you either need to sign to a record label, you need to have your own record label, or at a minimum, run your career within a record label framework.

MAJOR LABELS

In the last 30 years of the music industry, there have been various mergers, acquisitions, and rebranding between the major record labels, and today there are 'The Big Three'. Universal Music Group, Sony Music Entertainment, and Warner Music Group.

If you aim to be a pop star and are under the age of 21, signing to a major record label is still your best bet if you want super stardom. If it doesn't work out, you can go indie, but if it goes right, you'll be a superstar riding round in limos, private jets and headlining Coachella Festival.

INDIE LABELS

Any labels not under the control of 'The Big Three' are considered independent record labels, even if they are large multinational music companies. Indie record labels tend to be more artist-friendly, often originally founded by music artists, and usually release non-mainstream music focused around a particular genre or music scene. They often also nurture, develop and steer the creative side of projects. Which can be extremely important and pivotal to artists development and marketing campaigns.

There are too many indie labels to list here; however, notable examples are XL Recordings, Warp, Domino, 4AD, Dischord Records, and Mushroom.

ARTIST LABELS

Artist labels are record labels set up and run by artists and their teams. The significant difference between the more established indie labels mentioned earlier is that artist labels are typically newer and have less output. Worth bearing in mind that the artist/owner will invariably be the priority releasing artist in this structure. There are thousands of these labels, and if they become established enough, they will eventually become regarded as a typical indie label.

UPSTREAM DEALS

Some artists and indie labels will have upstream deals with major record labels. They still operate independently, but they have an agreement in place with a major label that if an artist they sign looks to cross over into the pop scene, they upstream the music to the major who then invests in a mainstream campaign to push the music and artist into the top 40.

An example of this is an artist called Wilkinson in the UK. Wilkinson was signed to indie label RAM Records and got an upstream deal to Virgin Records, owned by Universal. This gave them more options to invest in bigger budget music videos and national radio campaigns, helping propel singles into the top 40 mainstream charts.

You could think of an artist's recorded music output path as follows; first releasing on an artist label, signing to an indie record label, and eventually signing or upstreaming to a major record label.

But whatever stage of an artist's career you or someone you manage might be at, you need to ensure you have the business side of your music career organised efficiently. The administration, the distribution, the marketing and sales. Essentially, this is the role of a record label.

This is why starting your own label, or at a minimum, understanding, thinking, and acting like a record label, is vital to your success in the music industry.

From my experience, successful artists don't wait to get a manager or wait to be signed but simply get on with it. They create the music, start their own label, distribution, marketing, and grow a fan base quickly to drive their own success.

By doing this, they attract good managers, agents and, eventually, offers from larger labels or music companies to help them grow further and succeed.

DISTRIBUTORS

What is a distributor?

In a nutshell, music distribution is taking your final mastered song and artwork files and ingesting them into a system that distributes them to all the music stores: Spotify, Apple Music, Amazon, Google, Deezer, etc.

Distributors then collect the music royalties from these stores, create sales reports and send these to you every month. There is an approximate delay of about three months between an actual sale or stream of music and when you receive the sales reports and royalty money.

As each store requires slightly different content delivery formats and various software for reporting sales, distributors have often developed their own software systems to automate the process.

It's important to note that a distributor is not a record label and does not own your music or copyrights. They may offer 'label services', but that does not mean it's a record label deal.

They provide a service and take a fee or percentage from your revenue for providing services.

How do they make money?

Every record label has a distributor of some sort they work with, as you can't simply upload your music directly to Spotify, Amazon, Apple Music, and Beatport.

Some distributors offer deals where they manufacture physical products and distribute these to the physical music stores (that still exist!). Triple V in the Netherlands is a good example of this. If they believe a track has enough of a buzz, they will press up physical copies of vinyl and distribute them to music stores worldwide. The margins are so low that the manufacturing cost pretty much covers the profits on smaller runs, but you may make a profit if you press over 1500 units or have a vinyl hit. Plus, it is nice to have your music pressed on vinyl – and it looks cool hanging on your wall.

But let's concentrate on digital distribution, as that's where most of your revenue will come from. Once established, you can always look at working with someone to manufacture and distribute your vinyl, or you can do it yourself – more on that in part four of the book.

Let's look at the different types of distribution companies available.

AGGREGATORS

An aggregator amasses hundreds of digital platforms under one roof and takes catalogue music and distributes it. The Orchard is a good example of an aggregator company. They often have direct links to the major online music stores databases and back-end systems like Apple Music, Amazon and Spotify and provide quality control.

Often smaller distributors will plug into these bigger aggregators and use them for their back-end to handle the digital distribution of their content. As an independent artist or record label, you probably won't have a big enough catalogue to work with these types of distributors, but it's good to know they exist.

SERVICED DISTRIBUTORS

These distributors can offer what they call 'label services' or 'label management' where, for a higher commission, they can do all the heavy lifting involved in label administration for you. They provide email services for promotion, built-in accounting, and the good ones will have an account manager available to answer your questions when you're confused, or there is an issue with a release in a store.

Examples of these are Believe Digital, Ingrooves, and AWAL. They all have worldwide offices in the UK and the US and marketing teams inside the company that can help promote your bigger releases or albums. They often work with very established and older artists that previously had major record deals and now want to release their own music with a team around them.

These distributors also have an application process, so you will need a business plan when speaking to a label management company. When you apply, you will give them your business plan and your first three releases, the label's long-term goals, and how you will run your promotion and marketing. Often after you have achieved some success as a self-distributed label, these companies will reach out to you, as they will recognise the value in your music catalogue.

Suppose you are going to be predominantly an electronic record label. In that case, there are specialist distribution companies that focus on electronic music that also have a good relationship with Beatport and can help you get a label account there. The major players to consider are FUGA, Label Engine, Label-Worx, and Symphonic.

All service distributors take a percentage of your sales, and typically this will be anything from 15 to 30%. Usually, it's toward the higher end if you're starting out, and once your music royalties grow higher, they usually lower the percentage. Another bonus is they don't charge upfront fees.

Because they take a percentage, this means it is in their interest for your music to do well, as the more music royalties you make, the more money they make. Contrast this with self-distribution platforms that charge an upfront fee but have no financial interest in your music selling well.

SELF-DISTRIBUTION

These distributors offer simple, no-frills distribution. They provide no marketing support or extra accounting or promotion services. They usually charge just a flat fee to distribute your music. They sometimes operate as aggregators as well. There are no ongoing costs or a tiny percentage, but they will charge an upfront fee. Companies such as DistroKid, CD Baby, and Tunecore are examples.

These are great options when starting out because of the low cost of distribution. While they offer limited support, this won't be an issue if you understand the distribution process by following what you learn in this book.

These companies focus on individual artists that want to sell their own music directly without a major record label. Technically, that means the artists are the record label, so even if you choose to sell only your own music, you still need to build an organised structure around you. The structure you make is essentially what a record label is.

THE LABEL MACHINE DISTRIBUTION

Since 2023, we have our own in-house distribution platform available for our members. While we don't have offices all over the world (yet!), we would class ourselves as a Serviced Distributor as we don't have ongoing fees, and opt to take a small % in the back-end.

We also provide a full suite of marketing services for promotion, built-in artist royalty accounting, and we have a direct line 24/7 to answer any questions when you're confused, or there is an issue with a release in a store.

MANAGEMENT COMPANIES

Management Companies are typically a collection of music managers that work together with a roster of artists. Examples of these companies are UAA, Red Light Management, Q prime, ATC, and C3.

The biggest ones are often part of a larger talent agency that works with actors, sports stars, and celebrities, such as the United Talent Agency, Creative Artists Agency (CAA) and William Morris Endeavor (WME).

If you start a record label and sign new talent, you may find yourself managing the younger and less experienced artists when releasing their music. This is natural, as a label can be a powerful force when launching and supporting an artist's career. At Never Say Die Records, we started NSDMT Management for this reason.

We found that in putting together a release for an artist and presenting them professionally, we would have to write their bio, arrange their logos and press photos, register their music with the PRS, and introduce them to agents. Essentially doing what a manager does.

If you find yourself in this position, consider formalising the management activities and creating a management arm for your music label.

Some people argue that having your management and label team as the same people under one roof is a conflict of interests. When speaking about major label deals, I would agree, but it can be advantageous for indie labels.

You can make decisions and move forward quickly on opportunities, as there is no back and forth on emails with everyone stirring the pot and adding their opinions on what should or shouldn't be done. AKA – having too many cooks in the kitchen.

If you start managing artists, just don't double-dip. In a typical management agreement, a manager takes, for example, 20% of all revenue an artist makes, which would include record sales. However, if you own the label and already take a cut of record sales, you don't take a further 20% from this. Otherwise, you're double-dipping. It might seem obvious, but still worth noting.

If you want to sign artists to a management contract, you can use a typical management contract in part four that explains each clause and what you do or don't need.

PUBLISHERS

A publisher's role is to ensure songwriters and composers receive payment when their compositions are used commercially. As an artist, if you sign to a publisher, they will own the rights to collect on the music copyrights, and it is in their interests to exploit the music. This is different from the master rights – which is what the record label exploits.

It is worth pointing out that record labels don't have publishers. They work alongside them. An artist has a publisher, not a record label. This is because publishers represent the composers' music copyright, and a record label is not a composer.

If this already sounds confusing – you are not alone. This is why there is an entire section of the book dedicated to this in Part Two – Music Copyright.

For the time being, it's important to remember that there are two sets of music copyright in recorded music:

- The actual recording.
- The underlying composition (what the publisher represents).

Publishers exploit the music to create as many revenue streams as possible. These are:

- Getting radio plays.
- Getting the music onto a popular artist's album.
- Facilitating co-writes with other artists
- Getting sync deals. This is further divided into music on TV shows, music in advertisements, music in video games and music in films.

Publishers also derive income from collecting the royalties generated by the music's public performances, such as radio and TV plays of the song, which copyright holders are entitled to receive by law.

And publishers derive income from collecting the copyright through mechanical licences, which are needed by record labels to reproduce a song. This is set at a statutory rate of 12.4 cents per reproduction cents per reproduction in the US and collected by mechanical royalty societies such as the Mechanical-Copyright Protection Society (The MCPS) in the UK or The Mechanical Licensing Collective (The MLC) in the US.

Hang on a second! Did I just say record labels need a licence to release music? Yes, you do. However, many distributors will have an option to pass the mechanical licence to a mechanical royalty society, automatically saving the hassle of independent record labels accounting to them directly.

Just remember that the music publisher or publishing company is responsible for ensuring the songwriters and composers they represent receive payment when their underlying compositions are used commercially.

PERFORMANCE RIGHTS ORGANISATIONS

Performing Right Organisations, or PRO's for short, provide intermediary services between copyright holders and those who use and 'perform' copyrighted works. PROs collect royalties for rights holders when their music is performed publicly. A public performance can mean anything from being performed live at a gig to being played on radio, TV & streaming services, shops, bars, & movies.

The PRO essentially collects public performance royalties and distributes them. They also ensure that all locations playing music have a licence to do so.

Members can be composers, songwriters, publishers, recording artists, or other copyright owners. If you're any one of the above and want to get royalties for your music being played publicly, you need to sign up to a PRO that handles the composition royalties.

Record labels need to register with PROs that handle the sound recording royalties. We go into more detail on this in later chapters.

When your artists earn money from the exploitation of their records (whether from their songs being played on radio/TV or in clubs/shops), those royalties are collected on behalf of the artist.

Companies exist in which to do that on the artist's behalf.

Key royalty collection societies in the US are:

ASCAP. (The American Society of Composers, Authors, and Publishers). ASCAP is the oldest working PRO, having launched in 1914. It's also the second-largest in the US, boasting about 20 million works from approximately 990,000 members.

BMI. (Broadcast Music Inc). As the largest PRO in the US, BMI represents about 12 million musical works and more than 750,000 musicians.

SESAC. (Originally stood for Society of European Stage Authors and Composers). Among these PROs in SESAC is the smallest and the only one that's a for-profit organisation. It caters for over 1.5 million musical works from more than 30,000 affiliated writers.

The MLC. (The Mechanical Licensing Collective). Launched in 2019 to administer blanket mechanical licences for eligible streaming services in the US, The MLC collects and pays royalties to songwriters, composers, lyricists, and music publishers.

SoundExchange. They administer royalties for the broadcast of music over a digital transmission for master right owners and performing artists.

Key royalty collection societies in the UK are:

PRS. (Performing Rights Society). PRS pays royalties to members when their work is performed, broadcast, streamed, downloaded, reproduced, played in public or used in film and TV. They work closely alongside MCPS (Mechanical-Copyright Protection Society) which collect the mechanical licence royalties.

PPL. (Phonographic Performance Limited). PPL gives licences to radio stations, TV broadcasters and digital media services to play recorded music in the UK as part of their programming. They also give licences to music suppliers to copy recorded music for in-store music systems, jukeboxes, compilations for exercise classes or in-flight entertainment systems.

If you are outside the US and UK, you can find who your countries PRO is by visiting en.wikipedia.org/wiki/Performance_rights_organisation

We will talk in more detail about Performance Rights Organisations' role in Part Two – Music Copyright.

DJS

The DJ, aka Disc Jockey, comes in all shapes and sizes. There are club DJs, producing DJs, radio DJs, wedding DJs, bedroom DJs and virtual DJs.

DJs are the original influencers in the music industry, selecting the music they feel is best and playing to their audiences, either on the radio, in a recorded mix, or at a club or festival.

DJ culture plays a vital role in the electronic, hip hop, and trap genres of music. Developing relationships with other DJs in these genres will be critical to your success as an artist and label. Having a good network will enable you to more easily get remixes done, create music collaborations, and have other DJs support your music.

If you are an artist producing this type of music, you'll most likely be a DJ yourself, and if not, you need to learn, as when your music becomes more popular, DJing is an easy way to monetise your income through playing live shows.

For all other music genres, the DJ plays a vital role in promoting your music, especially radio promotion. A national radio DJ can break an artist if they love the music and want to support it. You can also get producing DJs to remix your song to open it up to a new audience or create a remix version of your indie rock song that can be played at clubs and dance music festivals.

DJ PROMOTION

If you're just starting out, you will want to hire a specialist DJ plugger who will be someone that will send your music out as a promo on your behalf to their contacts. As you gain support for your music, you also want to build up your own network of contacts so you can eventually email DJs directly with your record labels music.

Typically, most independent record labels will usually combine sending out personal emails to DJs and music curators they've created a relationship with and using a DJ plugger company for regional or international DJs.

We will go into more detail about how you set this up in part three of the book.

FANS

Without music fans, none of the music industry would really be possible. They are probably the most important part of the industry. Ever notice how successful artists always thank the fans, saying without them it wouldn't be possible? Because it's true.

From a business point of view, fans are the customers, and you have to have happy customers to have a healthy business. Artists and labels that can connect with fans meaningfully will always carve out a successful career.

Most of the marketing we talk about in this book is about connecting with fans and growing a fan base. Once the music is uploaded to the distributor, a key role of a record label is to connect the music to fans through marketing and PR.

When I did a survey on 182 independent record labels, asking what they wanted help with the most, the top request was to help grow their fan base. We all know this is important.

For electronic, hip hop, trap, and club music, there are two types of fans. The usual traditional fans listen to your music on Spotify, Apple Music, the radio. Then some fans play your music as part of the profession, either professional or hobby DJs that buy your music to use in their sets, both online and in club and festival sets. You need to cater to both sets of fans if you are running a record label in these genres.

Successful labels and artists need to build up a large base of fans. Not only to listen to your music but also to buy your artists and label merchandise and come to your live shows. Building up a meaningful connection with fans through your marketing is the most critical factor that determines your success, and it's why we deep dive into this subject in part three of this book.

MARKETING

Marketing is a large topic and covers the marketing of your label, your music and your artists.

And there is an almost unlimited amount of information out there about how to market your music. It's the industry's most common area, and there is endless advice and services offered online. And for a good reason.

Marketing is an essential part of having a successful music career. In fact, it's an important part of any successful career in almost any creative industry. It's essential to start a new music business as you'll need a good marketing strategy to reach new fans and grow your network.

Now I'm sure you know what marketing is, but for the sake of clarity, here is a definition of marketing for the music industry:

"The action or business of promoting and selling music, including market research and advertising."

There are many areas of marketing and marketing strategies you can use depending on how the music is being enjoyed and via what medium. For example, a live event, streaming on your phone or buying a vinyl pressing of an album.

In this chapter I'll discuss the overall theory of *what* music marketing is, and in part three of the book, I'll show you *how* to market your music.

Here is an overview of music marketing as a taster.

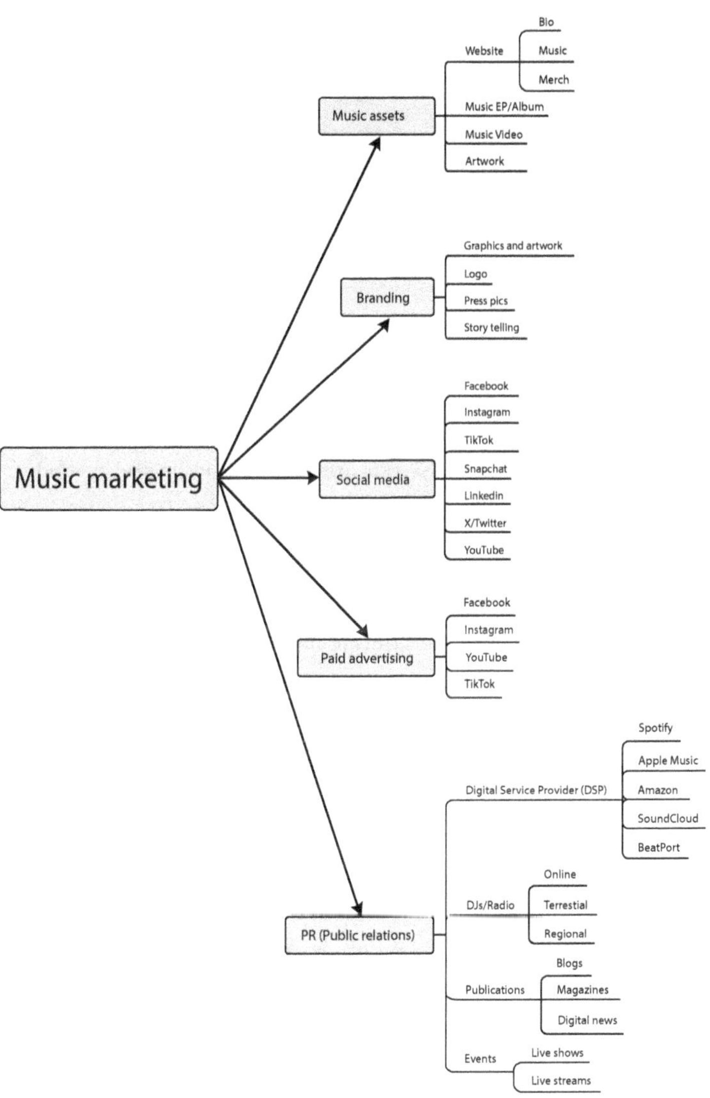
Music marketing
Music assets
Website
Bio
Music
Merch
Music EP/Album
Music Video
Artwork
Branding
Graphics and artwork
Logo
Press pics
Story telling
Social media
Facebook
Instagram
TikTok
Snapchat
Linkedin
X/Twitter
YouTube
Paid advertising
Facebook
Instagram
YouTube
TikTok
PR (Public relations)
Digital Service Provider (DSP)
Spotify
Apple Music
Amazon
SoundCloud
BeatPort
DJs/Radio
Online
Terrestial
Regional
Publications
Blogs
Magazines
Digital news
Events
Live shows
Live streams

You use your music assets to create your branding, which tells a story organically through your social media and inorganically through paid advertising and PR. Your marketing strategy is the plan that lays out the roadmap and details of this structure.

Marketing is something I especially enjoy. If you read my online bio, it says, 'I love nothing more than finding and working with true creative talent and sharing what they create with the big wide world.'

Which basically means I love marketing creative products.

I believe good marketing is telling an interesting story about what you offer in a way that connects with people emotionally.

Therefore, artists that have a great honest story about who they are, where they came from and where they are going, do well. This is especially true when looking at the long-term marketing efforts of artists using social media.

The artists that are always online daily posting what they are doing, what they feel, their opinions about the world connect so well with fans and create a good following.

Sometimes, this storytelling is a natural extension of someone; by simply being themselves, having a good time, parting, playing shows, and taking pictures of what they are doing, they tell a story.

For others, it is something that needs to be worked on and planned. There is no right or wrong way, but it needs to be focused in today's modern music industry. Some artists use anti-marketing; they post almost nothing, which can work well if the music is unique enough. The artist Burial famously did this exceptionally well.

MUSIC ASSETS

Marketing also includes creating all the marketing material. As they say, 'Content is King' and the more good content you have, the more eyeballs and ears you'll be able to get on your music.

This is where having a designer on your team can be an enormous benefit and money saver. Being able to knock up an Instagram post about a new development on a music release, or needing to quickly edit a tour poster due to additional dates being added is essential when you're busy handling several releases and artists simultaneously.

Conversely, spend some time learning to use the free content creation tools available to help create videos, pictures, and posts that anyone can access and use easily. Some examples are Canva.com, and Adobe Express, which you can use directly on your mobile phone. We will go into more detail on these in part three.

BRANDING

When it comes to working on storytelling and branding in music, the full embodiment of this is when an artist does a 'concept album'.

David Bowie was one of the first artists to do this successfully time and time again. He would invent himself as a new character and create a whole backstory, an album of music, and a stage show and take this to his fans. His album "The Rise and Fall of Ziggy Stardust and the Spiders from Mars" is an excellent example of this.

When we worked on The Prototypes' 'City of Gold' album, the artists had created a concept album. The theme was around finding a long lost city of gold, and the album followed a theme that started with an epic introduction to the world they created. The album artwork reflected this, and we worked with a live visual artist to create live visuals themed around an ancient city of gold that The Prototypes took on tour.

And just like an artist's story, the story about you as a record label then dictates everything that follows. The artwork, the tone, the press pics, the assets you create.

For record labels, the artwork is often the basis for your marketing. What is the tone? Fun and energetic? Dark and moody? Techie or organic? Focused on abstract images or people?

A great example of using simple pictures to create a theme is the YouTube channel 'Majestic Casual'. The creator used pictures of people chilling on sun-drenched beaches to promote interesting chill-out electronic music. All the music was already released on other record labels, the channel simply curated them under one style and tone, and now it has over 4.2 million subscribers.

SOCIAL MEDIA

It wouldn't be an understatement to say that social media, along with digital distribution, has transformed the music marketing landscape over the past 20 years, playing a crucial role in both organic and inorganic reach.

And from a label's point of view promoting the music, the more you can create and share, the more you say to the world,

'We believe in the project, the music, and in this artist'. People pick up on this and subconsciously think, 'I've got to pay attention!'

The funny thing I have noticed with great social media marketing is that often other industry folks will say, 'Oh, I see your new EP is doing well' when they haven't even listened to it. They have just seen all the marketing noise and figured it must be good music and doing well as typically an indie record label would not be investing in awful music.

The creation and consumption of vertical videos have become integral for effective music promotion and marketing. This format caters perfectly to mobile users, capturing attention quickly and enhancing engagement, which is vital as mobile consumption continues to surge.

As social media marketing sits at the top of the marketing funnel, it's often one of the first places a new fan will discover an artist. A great way of getting a potential fan to move through the funnel is getting their email address, and one of the most popular ways of doing this is with a download-for-email tool.

From a marketing perspective, social media is often the starting point of the marketing funnel, making it a critical discovery zone for new fans. An effective method to engage these potential fans further down the funnel is by capturing their email addresses, often through a download-for-email exchange. At Never Say Die Records, we often released tracks as gated downloads in return for an email, using platforms like Topspin, which seamlessly integrated this feature with email management.

Interestingly, the tracks offered for "free" in these exchanges frequently ended up being the bestsellers of the EP, suggesting that word-of-mouth and direct engagement through strategic content sharing, including vertical videos, significantly boost music sales. For instance, a fan might play a downloaded track at a party, sparking interest and subsequent purchases by other attendees.

These days, where streaming is becoming the more relevant currency of music, we often gate music in return for a follow on Spotify or Soundcloud or both. We will go into more detail about how to do this in later chapters.

PAID ADVERTISING

Paid advertising is any form of advertising that you have to pay to get your music or brand in front of an audience. This can mean paying for advertising in magazines or handing out flyers at gigs, or the most commonly used today, digital advertising through paid ads on the various social media platforms such as Facebook, Instagram and TikTok.

Paid advertising on social media platforms has become essential after Facebook decided that music brands and artists had to pay to reach their followers on social media.

The two most common forms are boosting posts to existing fans or sponsored posts to a targeted audience. The modern-day reality is that you have to put money aside for paid advertising to promote your music and when launching a new act or label.

However, by understanding and mastering the 'fan funnel', it's possible to get better value for money to reach an audience than you would spend on a music video, PR, or radio plugging.

We will go into deeper theoretical and practical examples for fan funnels in part three.

A side mention here is the practice of paying for views or streams, which is a grey area in paid advertising. There are dubious offers to increase your Spotify or Soundcloud streams available online, and it's always mixed results and ultimately a false economy. More and more frequently, Spotify is auditing and deleting thousands of songs that they are discovering have gained streaming numbers from bots, mostly likely from the paid streaming services. Buyer beware.

However, there are legit services to increase play count on platforms such as TrueView for YouTube or sponsoring video views on Facebook, Instagram, and TikTok. These services work and are effective in growing your audience if you have great video content. They can help social proofing, which is the practice of getting streamer view counts high enough to get the ball rolling that views start happening organically as more fans view the content.

PR (PUBLIC RELATIONS)

PR in music is when you reach out to build relationships with magazines, blogs, DJs and DSPs by sending them news as a press release announcing your label's new music.

As you can see from the diagram, it covers many areas, so the next chapter goes into more detail.

Finally, remember, like most things creative – marketing is 1% inspiration, 99% perspiration. It's all about consistent execution and taking action every day.

PR

In music, PR, aka public relations, is reaching out to the extended areas of the music industry such as magazines, blogs, DJs, and the DSPs to promote your artists' music on their channels.

In the world of music PR, you have different areas:

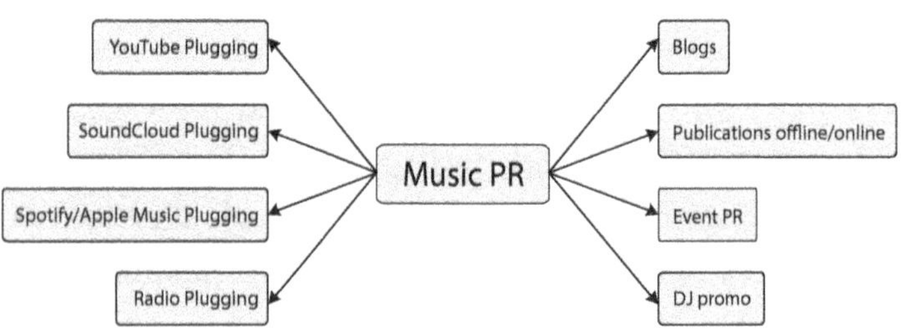

Each of these areas takes up time and money, so depending on your music style and release, e.g. single, EP, album, you will want to focus on some or all of these areas.

PR is like the sister of marketing, and in smaller teams, you'll often have one person covering both sides under the activity' PR and Marketing'. This is called servicing your PR in-house, and with good systems in place, it can be very effective.

At Never Say Die, we started doing our own PR in-house, hiring interns to implement our systems and templates. This then became its own PR company, 6th Degree, which eventually broke off to become its own company Second Nature PR, which is still running with the original team.

You can also serve out your PR to specialist music PR companies for a paid fee. This can be a one-off fee for a campaign, but if you are regularly releasing music, you would typically have a PR company on a monthly retainer, and they will cover all PR activities.

The advantage of working with a PR company is that they will already have a relationship with the editors and contributors of these sites. It may be easier to get published as the editors' trust the PR company's taste in clients.

How much should you budget for a PR company? You can pay anything from £500/$625 – £2400/$3000 for an indie music campaign. This would cover pitching to blogs, publications and YouTube channels for music premiers & interviews, with the price on the top end to include radio and Spotify plugging.

Plugging is when someone pitches your music to music channels to convince them to include it on their channel. Traditionally, plugging focused on radio only, where labels would pitch to radio producers saying 'this is the next big hit'. The radio plays the music, and if it got a positive reaction, they would keep playing it, and the song would move up the charts, creating success for the artist.

Today, plugging also refers to pitching music to YouTube and SoundCloud channels and Spotify and Apple Music playlists.

Getting your music onto a niche indie channel with a large subscription base can help break a record, meaning that it gets enough plays that it takes off and starts getting the attention of radio stations.

With Spotify plugging, you pitch your music to Spotify playlists' curators, and the in-house Spotify curated playlists via Spotify for Artists. If you get on a popular playlist, you can rack up hundreds of thousands of plays quickly, which gets your music heard by thousands of fans and generates royalties.

YouTube plugging is pitching your music to popular YouTube channels, such as UKF, The Sound You Need, Trap Nation, and Indie Air. Likewise, for SoundCloud channels, many niche channels cover almost every music genre, and getting them to repost your track can lead to thousands of plays.

The most common way to incentivise a music channel to add your music to their channel is to offer them a 'premier', giving them the exclusive rights to play the track first. The art of plugging is trying to get a premier on the channel with the largest subscriber base, increasing your chances of the most amount of people hearing your music.

PR covers getting your music featured on blogs and publications (both online and offline) alongside plugging.

When reaching out to blogs and publication PR, we don't say blog plugging; instead, it's referred to as 'pitching'. A music pitch aims to get them to publish the release and a story or interview about the artist alongside it.

Examples of blogs are Pitchfork, Consequence of Sound, StereoGum. Publication examples would be traditional magazines such as NME, Rolling Stone, and Mixmag.

These traditional and bigger publications will also have their online versions, so pitching to these, you're aiming to get featured both online and offline.

It's worth pointing out that while everyone wants to be in print, the reality is all eyeballs are online. Rolling Stone in March 2024 had 110K magazines in print circulation and their online readership is 19 million a month. So aim to get your music published on the online edition. It's nice to be in print, but it doesn't mean more eyeballs.

While getting on blogs and publications isn't as much of a focus in PR these days, it is still an essential part of the overall marketing. It gives the record label and artists credibility and extra reach to their readership base. All blogs and publications have their social reach across their X, Facebook, Instagram. They will often post links to their articles across these channels, further expanding our music when they feature you.

If you or the artists aspire to become international touring artists, you need to apply for visas to tour various countries. The most difficult country to get visas for is the US, and you need to provide evidence you are a legitimately successful artist to get a visa to tour. One of the key areas of proof is showing them evidence of your music being featured in publications, so focusing on PR may be essential to artists careers.

With bigger projects such as albums, you will often organise something around the release, such as an album launch party. If this is the case, you must involve event PR, which is more specialised regional and city-based PR.

Now you have a good understanding of PR, you might think, do I use an external company or do it in-house? The answer is both.

If you are in this for the long game, you will want to do it in-house as it will allow more control over the music releases and be invaluable in building relationships with key people in the industry.

And when you have the bigger album projects with tours, bring in external PR companies to help spread the music.

LIVE SHOWS AND TOURING

For many music artists, especially bands who play live instruments, playing their music live to an adoring audience is the ultimate high. Playing out live also gives a massive dimension to an artist's career, allowing genuine connections and interactions with fans while creating dynamic content to help connect with your audience worldwide.

And the income generated from live shows can be the largest revenue stream for artists, especially for DJs or solo acts, as the costs for touring are low, and there are fewer people to split the profits with.

Playing live is also a great way to promote music releases, especially at the start of the artist's career.

Sometimes bands will arrange a regional tour that does not make them money and supplement the tour expenses with their own money or a label advance if signed to a mini/major record label.

Or the manager gets the band a support slot with a more successful touring artist, allowing them to build up a new audience of fans. And for established artists, the album tour provides a promotion platform for the fans to experience the album tracks live.

As you can see, live shows can be a big part of an artist's success, which is why the COVID epidemic was devastating to the music industry, with touring artists having their live shows dry up overnight. Since then, with the virus better managed, live events have made a comeback. The enduring demand for live music among fans and artists alike ensures that live performances remain a vibrant and vital aspect of the industry.

The key players for live shows and touring are the artist, the manager, the booking agent and the event promoters.

The artist's primary job for tours is to rehearse as a band or practice as a DJ to provide an entertaining show. Early in an artist's career, if they have no management, it's also usually their job to find early gigs at local bars and pubs that are willing to book them for a show.

For artists with a manager, the manager will be the point of contact for the other key players, work with the booking agent to negotiate performance fees and tour dates and with the event promoters to arrange travel itineraries and logistics on show nights.

The booking agent's role is to secure a show or a tour for the artist. They represent the artist when dealing with the event promoters, brokering the deal and securing shows. You can't hire a booking agent; they will reach out to the artist or manager when there is sufficient demand for shows to generate a profit.

The event promoter or talent buyer (as they are known in the US) role is to arrange the actual live show. They have to book the venue and sell tickets to fans and, hopefully, sell out the venue. They make a profit after deducting the expenses of the show from the ticket sales. There are in-house venue promoters, regional promoters, and national promoters to handle different artists and shows.

We will go into more detail on these roles in the next chapters, and you can read more about the show booking process and how in part four of this book.

From an artist's point of view, if you're a singer-songwriter who plays an instrument, you should start playing live, form a band and do gigs. If you make electronic music and don't play out live as a DJ, then start now.

Unless you have a phobia of clubs and gigs, this really is essential. While music revenues from your record sales can keep your head above water in your career, the money you make from playing live shows will allow you to create a really successful career.

BOOKING AGENTS

The booking agent's job is to handle the live performances of an artist. This covers arranging and securing show bookings, negotiating the best deal, collecting the performance fees, pitching the artist to festivals, securing hospitality (riders, hotels, local travel), logistics (travel and flights) and approving billing (where the artist name appears on a line-up of promotional material).

They work on a percentage of the artist's revenue, much like a manager. For DJs, typically, their fees will be 15% to handle everything above as an all-in service and 10% if they only book the show but do not arrange the advancing of the show. For bands, typically, their fees will be 10% across the board. The term 'advancing' refers to arranging the travel routes, hotel bookings and hospitality in advance of the show for a performance.

Some more experienced artists prefer to do advancing themselves so they can save 5% on agent fees. And some agents do not offer advancing (it can get messy, dealing with cancelled flights, less than favourable hotel rooms, etc.).

If you have a manager, it often makes sense for your manager to do your advancing if you are regularly playing. They are in contact with an artist more frequently and can respond to any last-minute changes or approvals that can happen with travel arrangements.

If you're at the start of your career, your manager will also act as your agent. It's usually best to wait for an agent to approach you rather than trying to get yourself an agent. If an agent comes to you, they see your potential and are more likely to work hard getting you gigs and growing your live show income.

An agent usually represents a particular territory in the world. The main territories are Europe, North America, South America, Asia, Australia and New Zealand. Often Asia, Australia and New Zealand are combined into one territory. Likewise, North America and South America are sometimes combined.

China, South Africa and India are independent, and your main agent will usually have contacts in those regions.

Typically, you have a primary agent in your home country who works with agents in other territories. So if you are based in LA, you will have your main agent in the US, and they will work with the agents around the world when booking shows. If you sign to a big agency like Creative Artists Agency, United Talent Agency or William Morris Endeavor, they have strategically placed offices in key global markets, but their reach extends beyond physical office locations through partnerships and networks, allowing them to arrange international tours more efficiently.

Your agent will organise tours around big releases such as an album. A world tour will typically encompass North America, Europe and the UK, Australia / New Zealand and, more recently, China.

When an artist has new music coming out, the first person you want to let know is your agent, as the best way to get more bookings is to put good music out consistently. There is a direct correlation between the number of live bookings an artist gets and the consistency of releasing music. And if you're an independent artist and get a radio hit, your bookings can go crazy.

EVENT PROMOTERS

Event promoters, or concert promoters, are the individuals or companies responsible for running music events such as concerts or festivals. In the US, they are known as talent buyers. They work closely with an artist's booking agency to secure the gig, make payments, and work with the artist's manager advancing (arranging travel and accommodation).

Some promoters run regular nights and events throughout the year; other promoters work for individual clubs covering all nights of the week and year. In contrast, others run bookings under the bigger agencies for the larger festivals such as Coachella, EDC, Parklife and TomorrowLand.

The major promoters worldwide are Live Nation, Eventim Live, AEG Presents, SJM Concerts, Feld Entertainment and DF Concerts.

Event promoters will sometimes work with particular agents and book multiple artists from one promoter. When this relationship is in place, they will usually book the same acts year-on-year, so developing a good relationship with event promoters can be hugely beneficial to your career.

Promoters are increasingly using data analytics to inform their booking decisions, pricing strategies, and marketing efforts. The role of social media in promotion and artist discovery has continued to grow, affecting how promoters identify and book talent as well. This is why it's essential for an artist to have a well maintained social media presence and solid monthly streaming numbers.

If the event promoter is a fan of the band, you're more likely to get booked year on year. This is particularly true in the DJ booking world, where the line-up of artists can largely remain the same.

When it comes to artist fees for performing, there are two main structures to be aware of.

In Europe and the UK, your performance fee is typically your fee to play a show for 60-90 minutes, and the promoter covers your travel, hotel costs, and rider (dinner and drinks for the event). Australia, New Zealand and Asia also follow the same deal structure.

US and Canada are typically an 'all-in' deal. This is where an artist's fee covers the performance fee, travel and hotel costs as once sum. However, the artist's fees will be higher to reflect this. The advantage of this arrangement gives artists more flexibility for booking flights and hotels.

This can be beneficial for artists that frequently travel, as it allows them to build up their own frequent flyer points to get better discounts for travel on other gigs and shows.

LAWYERS AND ACCOUNTANTS

Music entertainment lawyers and accountants are specialist professionals for dealing with the legal requirements around contract negotiations, financing, copyrights and tax requirements for the music industry. Their clients include artists, managers, record labels, and publishers.

LAWYERS AKA ATTORNEYS

Generally speaking, the term attorney is used in the US, and the term lawyer is used in most countries outside the US. A music lawyer is a specialised legal professional trained to deal with legal issues such as copyright claims, band disputes, and contract negotiations.

From an artist point of view, music lawyers act in the artist's best interests, ensure they get fair label and publishing deals, represent them in court, and act as managers for their artists, shopping them around to get a major record label deal.

Your requirement for needing a lawyer will depend on where you are in your career. As an artist or band starting out, you might not need a lawyer, but it can help start a relationship with one. Most lawyers will give you a free consultation to understand where you are, your aspirations and offer some advice on what to consider and when they will be required.

From a record label's point of view, the music lawyer will help protect the label from liabilities, handling business-to-business deals such as catalogue licensing deals and maximise label earnings when signing artists.

As an independent label dealing with simple recording contacts and licensing deals, you might not need a lawyer for every recording agreement you sign if you have a good grasp and understanding of your contracts. Having a good understanding will enable you to answer questions artists have when they sign and allow you to make minor changes to your contracts for individual deals.

However, if you find anything confusing or need to negotiate a larger deal outside your label's normal business scope, then get an experienced music lawyer.

Music lawyers charge by the hour or a fixed fee in the UK to prepare and advise on a particular contract. This is the same in the US; however, some US attorneys may agree to be paid a percentage of any deals they negotiate (such as an advance on a record deal), and this is typically around 5%. In the UK, lawyers are not allowed to work based on commissions of future earnings, in contrast to the US, where attorneys can.

There are legal professionals working in other areas of law, that will offer a confident pitch for music contract negotiations, with little or zero experience. This can be counter-productive. Always ensure a lawyer has proven music industry legal experience.

ACCOUNTANTS

Music accountants help artists, record labels, and music companies arrange and file tax returns, advise on financial business plans, and issue invoices on behalf of their clients.

If you are a working musician, you are considered 'self-employed' when filing your taxes, and you can complete your own tax returns.

Likewise, if your music label is uncomplicated and you are comfortable dealing with your monthly accounts and tax returns, there are many software options available (Quickbooks and Xero being two of the most popular).

Bear in mind as a label owner you will also have to do your royalty accounting for your artists, which is typically done using specialist software such as Label Engine, Infinite Catalog, and Curve Royalty Systems. These tools can help ensure that you accurately track and distribute royalties, manage contracts, and generate detailed financial reports.

In more complex scenarios or as your business grows, you may find it beneficial to hire a professional accountant who specializes in the music industry. They can provide valuable insights into financial planning, help you navigate the intricacies of music royalties, and ensure compliance with tax regulations.

SUCCESS

What does it mean to be a success in the music industry?

- Is it having your music available to buy and stream?
- Getting playlisted on Spotify's Today's Top Hits?
- Achieving a number one on the Beatport charts?
- Making money from your music?
- Signing a major record deal?
- Completing a sell-out summer tour?

The cliched version of success includes Billboard number ones, sold-out concerts, and being on the cover of Rolling Stone magazine. In reality, such heights are reached by approximately 0.001% of music artists.

A more realistic definition of success is:

- Releasing music regularly.
- Building a fan base large enough to support live shows.
- Making enough money to sustain your career without incurring losses.

It's crucial to recognise that not making all your money from music doesn't mean you're not successful. Many long-term music artists are multi-hyphenates, earning a living through multiple professions or skills, with music being one of them.

If one of your 'day' jobs or revenue streams is in the music industry, you can benefit from both worlds, participating as both an artist and a music professional. For example:

- Working as a graphic designer creating artwork and ads for other artists while producing and releasing your own music
- Running a record label to release your and other artists' music.

No matter how you define your success, one essential goal remains: giving it your best shot. Strive to achieve your goals with determination and effort. You may not control how fans and critics respond, but you can ensure your music has the best chance to reach top Spotify playlists, sell-out tours, and financial success.

Now we know how to define our own success, we can learn the practical ways to achieve it. But before we do that, we need to learn about music copyrights.

PART TWO

MUSIC COPYRIGHT

OVERVIEW

As far as the business side of music goes, music copyright is probably the most boring, complicated and difficult to understand.

It was the most challenging part of the book to write, as there are so many moving parts that can make it seem confusing. It is this confusion that allowed big labels and publishers in the past to take advantage of artists and sign them to unfair deals.

And if you are serious about creating a successful music career as an artist or label owner, then knowing how to navigate and collect your royalties due from music copyright is essential.

The good news is, at the end of this chapter, you'll understand more about the industry than half of the music industry executives I've worked with.

First, I'll explain the different types of copyrights in music. Then I'll explain with illustrations how all music copyrights flow within the industry. Finally, I'll explain how to register and collect all your copyright royalties as both a record label and as an artist.

WHY THE CONFUSION?

Publishing and master copyrights can be a difficult concept to get your head around when you are new to music.

The traditional set up for recorded music at major labels is that there are separate individuals for each role in writing and recording music, such as musicians, recording artists, performing artists, producers, mix engineers, etc. Each role has certain copyrights attached to it, which affects publishing and master recording ownership.

In contrast, many modern-day independent artists typically make music on a home computer set-up as a single person (or maybe a duo) who composes, plays, records, mixes and produces the music (i.e. performs each of the separate roles as one person).

And because the indie artist is doing many roles and has many overlapping copyrights, it can get confusing when we talk about publishing and master recording rights for modern music artists.

THE FUNDAMENTALS OF COPYRIGHT

Understanding the difference between a 'Composition' and a 'Sound Recording' is fundamental to understanding how music copyright works.

Another fundamental fact to understand is that copyright law works differently in the UK, EU and US. Not hugely different, but as most modern music is released internationally, you need to understand the differences between the major territories. I'll explain how it works in the UK and the US, as well as a few other important territories.

Finally, if you are an artist with a record label, you'll sometimes be looking at copyright from the perspective of an artist and sometimes from the perspective of your record label. For each copyright section, I have described it from each perspective so you can understand how it works from both sides.

Let's start with putting on your artist's hat and understanding copyright…

HOW COPYRIGHT WORKS

As a musical artist, you create. And every time you make something, whether that be writing down a lyric, recording a guitar solo to your computer, or bouncing a beat out as a WAV file, your work becomes automatically copyrighted.

Copyright falls under intellectual property. If you are the original creator, then you own that intellectual property. If it was a group that created the work, it is automatically split equally unless the group previously agreed to a different percentage of splits.

The term of this copyright is generally 70 years after the death of the last surviving creator.

You can assign the copyright to other people or companies, in which case you'll give them the copyright ownership. The copyright can be transferred to other people and other entities or by licensing copyrights to other companies to generate revenue.

There are many ways revenue is generated from copyrighted works, the most lucrative being when you (or someone else):

- Perform or play the work in public.
- Broadcast the work to the public.
- Sell recordings digitally/online as permanent downloads.

When you hear a song, there are always two musical copyrights that make up the song.

There is the composition side of the copyright and the sound recording copyright. Sound recording is also known as master recording, and the terms are used interchangeably.

While traditionally, there were many individuals for each role in making a finished piece of record music, many modern-day independent artists perform each of the separate roles as one entity.

An indie artist will be the one who composes, plays, records, mixes and produces the music.

Because the artist does so many roles and has many overlapping copyrights, it gets confusing when we walk about composition and sound recording rights.

So let's break down in more detail how these two sides of music copyright work…

COMPOSITION VS SOUND RECORDING

Understanding the difference between composition and sound recording is fundamental to understanding how music copyright works. After reading this section, you'll know exactly what music industry royalties will be owed to you, and you won't miss out on collecting them.

When you hear a song, there are always two musical copyrights that make up the song. If you are a solo producer, you automatically own both sides of the copyrights, the composition and the sound recording.

WHAT IS A COMPOSITION?

When an artist composes a musical melody with or without lyrics, they have created a musical composition.

As soon as that composition is written down, e.g. in musical notation, or recorded on tape or digitally, the composition is automatically copyrighted. You might also find compositions being referred to as musical "works."

Depending on what country you are in will define what copyright laws affect you and what you can do to protect your rights. It's different for the US and the UK. To prevent confusion, especially if you are releasing music internationally, the vital thing to remember is: what country does the songwriter pay taxes to? That is the country that the copyright laws apply to.

WHAT IS A SOUND RECORDING?

When someone creates a finished recording of a composition's performance, then you have a sound recording. When the mix engineer completes the final mix of sound recording tracks, this is known as a master recording, and it's why sometimes the sound recording copyright is referred to as the masters.

The master is the final recording that will be pressed to vinyl, CDs and uploaded via a distributor to Spotify, Apple Music, Amazon, etc.

Just like compositions, when a sound recording is created, it is automatically copyrighted. Again, the country the master was recorded in affects the copyright laws.

DIFFERENCE BETWEEN COMPOSITION AND SOUND RECORDING COPYRIGHTS

It's important to know that many different sound recording copyrights can exist for a single composition. When an artist creates a sound recording of another artist's composition, it is sometimes called a cover.

For example, The Beatles' 'Yesterday' has been covered in sound recordings over 3000 times by artists such as Marvin Gaye, Elvis, Frank Sinatra, Liberace, Marianne Faithful, and Joan Baez. In fact, the track holds the Guinness World Record for most covers of a song.

If you cover 'Yesterday', then The Beatles own the composition part of the copyright, and you would own the master sound recording part of the copyright.

In the mainstream music industry, four main parties are stakeholders in a song – two for each part of the copyright.

The composition is divided between the writer/composer and the publisher. If you are an independent artist without a publisher, then you are both the writer and publisher. If you do have a publisher, your deal usually means they will own the rights to composition copyright, unless you have a publishing admin only deal, in which case you still retain the composition copyrights, and the publisher takes a service fee for registering and collecting royalties only.

The sound recording is divided between the performing artist and the record label. Again, if you are an indie artist releasing music on your own label, you are the performing artist and the record label. If you do sign to a record label, the label will usually own or license the copyright for a set time.

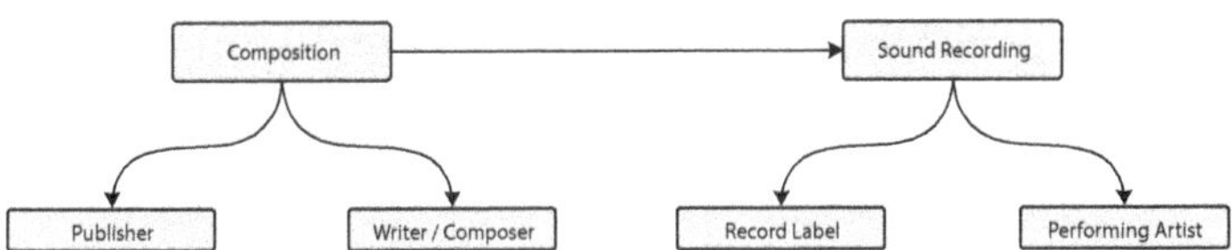

If you are an indie artist with no publishing deal, releasing music on your own record label, you could think of yourself as all four parties: writer, publisher, performing artist and record label.

As your team grows and you start signing deals with business partners (such as record labels and publishers), you start dividing up your copyrights to each of these parties.

If there is more than one writer for a song (in a band, for instance), then the writer copyright is divided. You may also agree a percentage of the writing credits go to a producer.

If you sign your compositions to a publisher, they then own a share of the composition that pays a percentage of royalties to you as defined in the publishing agreement.

Suppose you sign your music to a separate record label. In that case, the Sound Recording rights are divided between the Performing Artist and the Record Label. The Record Label will control the rights and pay the artist a percentage of royalties to you as defined in the recording contract.

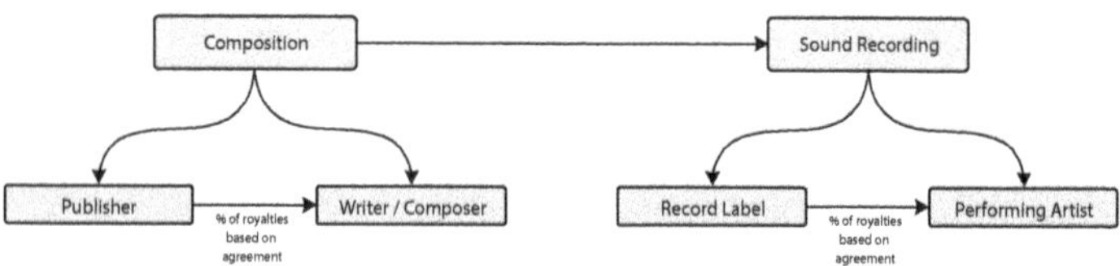

It's essential to think of music as being divided into these four main parties, even if you are some or all of the parties yourself, as each party is treated separately in the music industry. If you can remember this, you are on your way to mastering copyright in the music industry.

Let's have a look at some real-world examples.

Say I write the song '176 Nights in Dalston' with fellow artist Robbie B and split the composition 50/50. In return for a producer helping us produce the song in his upmarket LA studio, we give the studio producer 20% of the publishing.

The producer owns 20% of the composition, and Robbie B and I split the rest 50/50.

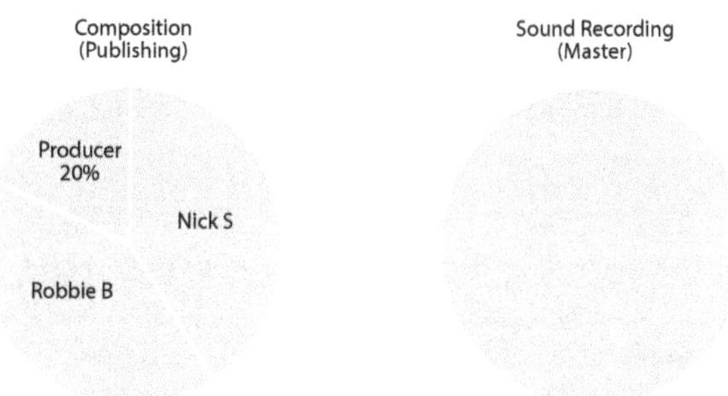

I make a sound recording in a studio, creating the master. I take the master to a record label and I sign a recording agreement that gives them 50% of the master's copyright in return for the costs of recording the song. My friend Molly records the vocals, and I give her 10% of the masters for performing on the track, and I give 5% to a mixing engineer for mixing it down.

So the masters look like this.

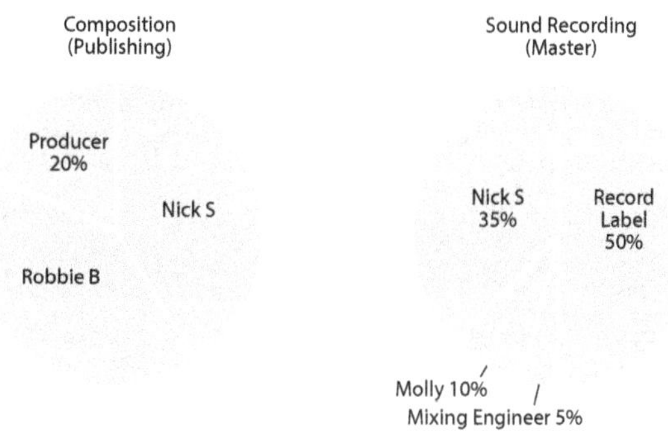

Then, after the label releases the track and it does really well, I have publishers reach out to me and offer me a publishing deal. I agree to the deal and sign a publishing agreement with them for 50% of my publishing, including this song and any songs I write in the next three years.

So now the share of the publishing on this track would look like this.

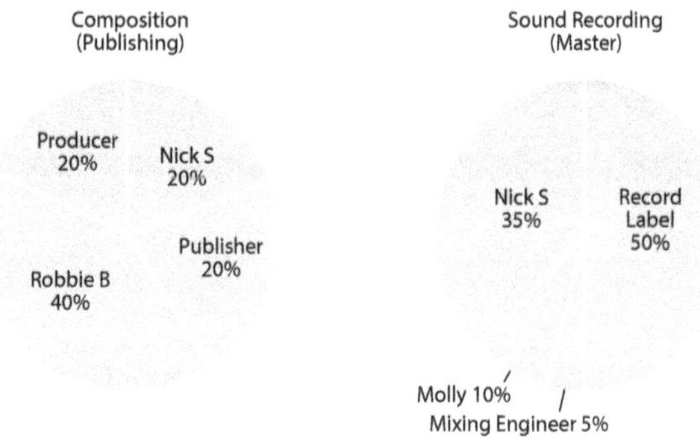

This shows you why it is essential to understand that you have separate masters and publishing. Once I have written '176 Nights in Dalston', many people can record covers of it. They can split the masters up however they like, and I don't get a say in that, but I still get the publishing, the underlying composition of the song.

The way royalties are split up changes depending on how a song is consumed, and there are different splits for a song sale and other splits if the track is licensed for a movie or TV show which we will look at in more detail in the following chapters.

MASTER LICENCE AND MASTER OWNERSHIP

It's worth mentioning that when we talk about signing over the copyrights to a record label, there are two ways these copyrights can be signed. An artist can sign a master license deal, which means they sign over the masters for a set period, for example, a term of five to seven years. Or they can sign a master ownership deal in which there is no term, and they have signed the rights in perpetuity, aka forever.

For more information on different record label deals, refer to the Record Label Deals chapter in part three.

In summary:

The composition is created by the writers of the track and is typically represented by a publisher.

The sound recording, aka masters, are created by the performing artists and producers and are typically represented by a record label.

If you are an artist with your own record label, then you will wear two different hats. As an artist, you need to be concerned with both the composition and the sound recording side of music. But when you have your record label hat on, you are mainly concerned with the sound recording royalties of copyright.

So now you have a good idea of the difference between the two sides on music copyright. If you're still perplexed, email nick@thelabelmachine.com with "confused with publishing" in the subject line, and I'll send some more videos breaking it down.

UK VS US COPYRIGHT

There is a lot of confusion on copyright as many books either describe copyright in terms of US or UK law. As these countries' music copyright differs, different laws apply on copyright.

The critical thing to remember is where the record label or writer is based. Where do they pay tax? This defines which copyright laws apply to your music and what steps you can take to protect it should you wish to.

COMPOSITION COPYRIGHT

If you are based in the US, you have to register with the US copyright office. The fee for registering up to 10 unpublished works (including songs) using the "Group of Unpublished Works" application is $85. However, you don't need to submit the composition to the US copyright office to get basic copywriter protection. Is it worth doing for every track you write when starting out? Probably not, but get into a habit of doing it at the start of every year. If you do have a massive hit at some point and you want to have undeniable proof you wrote it first.

Note: If you are bulk registering tracks with the copyright office, the writers need to be the same on all the songs; you can't have different combinations of writers for different songs.

If you are based in the UK, there is no official method for copyrighting work. However, electronic emailing or saving the work can create evidence of creation and ownership, providing a time-stamped copy. You can also mail or save a physical copy of the work; for example, send the work to yourself by recorded delivery or store it with your bank. The work must be time stamped and remain sealed for this to provide any legal proof.

If you are based elsewhere globally, you can find and contact your copyright office to find out how to copyright your music should you wish to at wipo.int/directory/en/urls.jsp.

SOUND RECORDING COPYRIGHT

If you are in the US, you can register a sound recording's copyright with the US copyright office, and you can copyright both composition and sound recording with one form. Again, you don't have to do this as a legal requirement, as you will be covered by basic rights when you record your master sound recording.

In the UK, similar to a composition, there is no official way to copyright work. However, evidence of creation and ownership can be created by an email or saving of the work or sending a sealed physical recording of the work to yourself.

HOW LONG DOES THE COPYRIGHT LAST?

Composition copyright in most countries lasts for 70 years from the end of the calendar year in which the author dies.

The copyright for sound recordings lasts for 70 years from when it is first published.

If the music originates from outside the European Economic Area (EEA), the copyright lasts for as long as the music is protected by copyright in its country of origin, provided that this does not exceed 70 years.

DO I ACTUALLY NEED TO DO THIS?

In reality, if you are starting out as an indie artist, none of this is really necessary. None of the artists I have worked with have sent themselves copies of music in the post, and no one has ever been contested in court. However, if you are worried someone is out to copy your music, then as I mentioned, you can bulk register songs in one go for peace of mind if you are in the US.

The important thing is ensuring the work is registered with the organisations that track royalties for your copyrights (PROs) which we will discuss in the next chapters.

ROYALTIES

Now we know how music copyright ownership is split between composition and sound recordings, we will look at how music is exploited or monetised through the business of music.

When we say exploited, we mean making money from the value of both the compositions and sound recordings. The payments that the copyright owners receive for this exploitation are called royalties.

There are two main ways royalties are generated from music. One is from music sales, and the other is for the public performance of songs.

MUSIC SALES

When most people think of music royalties, they imagine a fan buying a record at a shop for $5, who sends the money to the record label who pays the artist their share.

Or with streaming, someone listens to a song on Spotify, and Spotify sends between $0.003 and $0.005 to the record label who pays the artist their share. Yes, when streaming, it's a very tiny share.

Those are two examples of the many types of royalties generated from music sales of which we will cover in more detail.

PUBLIC PERFORMANCE OF SONGS

Other royalty streams can be earned for a song's performance in public, online, in films, on radio, or streamed. These royalties change for different countries and change if the song is being sold physically, downloaded, or streamed. These types of royalties are generated from the Public Performance of Songs.

Now you understand the two types of copyright (sound recordings and compositions), and the two main ways they generate royalties (sales and performance), we can go into more detail on how they all work together and how to make sure you collect all your royalties for you as a label and for your artists' music.

To keep things simple, just remember there are four main areas of music royalties:

- Sound recording royalties from music sales.
- Sound recording royalties from public performance of songs.
- Composition royalties from music sales.
- Composition royalties from public performance of songs.

RESPONSIBILITY AS A RECORD LABEL

As a general rule of thumb, sound recording royalties from music sales are tracked and collected by record labels. The remaining three royalty areas are tracked and collected by various Performance Rights Organisations (PROS) and distributed to publishers, labels and artists.

Thus, as a record label, you are primarily focused on the royalties for sound recordings. It is not the job of a record label to sign or collect the royalties for compositions. That's what publishers do. So if you are an unpublished artist or artist manager, you will be responsible for ensuring you register and collect these other three areas of royalties related to compositions. And if you are a published artist, your publisher will be responsible for registering and collecting these royalties.

OK, let's start with Sound Recording Royalties from music sales.

SOUND RECORDING ROYALTIES FROM MUSIC SALES

Sound recording royalties from music sales are the record label's responsibility to manage.

As a record label, the sound recording sales will be the bread and butter of your revenue. These are royalties generated from the sale of music downloads, CDs, or vinyl to a music consumer or, more commonly now, the streaming of a song on Spotify, Apple Music, Tidal, and Amazon Music.

To legally sell the sound recordings, a record label needs to have the rights to do so. You need these rights from the performing artists, the band, and/or producer and thus must sign the rights in a recording contract. This is where the term 'signed' a record deal comes from.

The recording contract will state what sound recordings you have the right to, how the royalty income will be divided between the label and artists, and when they will be paid.

As a label, you pay the royalties directly to the performing artists. Sometimes you may pay the producer separately, but it is often the artist's responsibility to pay the producer from their share.

Typically, a label accounts for artist royalties at least twice a year, every six months. However, some labels account every three months and others every month. When a label processes royalty accounts, they issue royalty statements to the artists (via accounting software). The artist invoices the label for the royalty amount, and the label pays the artist via bank transfer or PayPal.

A recording contract can be for the life of copyright of masters or for a set amount of time, such as 15 years. Either way, it gives the label the right to sell the music and collect music royalties.

Remember, sound recording royalties from music sales is the record label's responsibility to manage.

SOUND RECORDING ROYALTIES FROM PUBLIC PERFORMANCE OF SONGS

Sound recording royalties from public performance of songs is the responsibility of both the record label and the artist (or artist's manager/publisher) to manage.

Public performance refers to the performing or playing of copyrighted work publicly, for example, during live concerts or live performances in a public setting. When this occurs, there are public performance royalties generated for the copyright owners which is why if you play live it's important to register where, when and what songs you played for every gig (more on this later).

Likewise, royalties are generated for playing recorded copyrighted work publicly, such as music streaming, satellite radio, music videos, FM radio, or a TV show. The live venue, broadcaster, network or service that benefits from playing music have to pay the royalty.

NEIGHBOURING RIGHTS

In most countries around the world, when there is a public performance of a song, there are laws and systems to pay the master right owners and performing artists for their work's public performance. They are enforced by the Neighbouring Rights Laws and are typically referred to as 'neighbouring rights' for short.

Neighbouring rights are collected by performance royalties societies in countries that enforce them and, at last count, it was just over 80 countries.

In the UK, the society that collects these royalties is Phonographic Performance Limited, better known simply as PPL. PPL licenses the use of recorded music when played in public, broadcast on radio or TV or used on the internet on behalf of record companies and performers.

The good news is that you can be from anywhere in the world and still use PPL to collect your neighbouring rights; you don't have to be based in the UK.

However, what is important is that the country you are based in does enforce neighbouring rights laws. This is why some artists choose to record music in countries that enforce these laws to collect these royalties.

The one country that doesn't pay is the US due to previous heavy lobbying by the US broadcasters, as it would require them to pay out millions in licenses.

However, in 1995 the Digital Performance Right in Sound Recordings Act of 1995 (DPRA) was a US law introduced that gave them an exclusive right "to perform the copyrighted work publicly by means of a digital audio transmission."

This means the master right owners and performing artists get a royalty paid only for the broadcast of music over a digital transmission, for instance, Pandora and satellite radio services such as Sirius. But not for any other public performance or public playing.

The largest company in the US that collects and administers these royalties is SoundExchange. They pay 50% of the revenue directly to the master copyright owner (you, the label), 45% directly to the featured performing artist, and the remaining 5% to the AFM / SAG-AFTRA funds for non-featured artists. If you self release, you would collect both the copyright owner and featured artists revenue share.

They pay out monthly, and I have had substantial royalty payments for labels' music being played across the digital radio networks.

Suppose you are based outside the US, and your country has laws for Neighbouring Rights. In that case, you can register with PPL in the UK, which will have an agreement with SoundExchange to collect royalties on your behalf and any other international public performance royalties.

Remember, sound recording royalties from public performance of songs are the responsibility of both the record label and the artist (or artist's manager/publisher) to manage.

COMPOSITION ROYALTIES FROM MUSIC SALES (AKA MECHANICALS)

Composition royalties from music sales are the responsibility of both the record label and the artist (or artist's manager/publisher) to manage.

LABEL'S PERSPECTIVE

Let's look at this from the perspective of the record label first. Every time the company wants to reproduce or distribute a song that they did not write, they need to get permission from the composition copyright owner.

This is issued in the form of a mechanical licence, which generates mechanical royalties for the composition rights owner. A label or recording artist can request these directly from the composition copyright holder (or their publisher) or via a mechanical royalty society, usually the HFA (Harry Fox Agency) in the US and MCPS (Mechanical-Copyright Protection Society) in the UK.

As a record label, you are responsible for paying mechanical royalties for physical sales and digital download sales, but not streaming sales. Streaming platforms pay the mechanical royalty directly to the composition copyright owner.

The mechanical licences have a fixed royalty rate that has been determined by the law and has to be paid by something called the statutory rate.

In the US the statutory mechanical royalty rate for physical recordings (CDs, vinyl, tapes) and digital downloads is 12.4 cents per song for tracks up to five minutes in length, and 2.38 cents per minute (or fraction thereof) for songs over five minutes.

In Europe, the mechanical royalty is based on the percentage of what is known as 'PPD' or published price to the dealer, which is the sales price to retailers. The effective rate currently is 8.712% of PPD.

When issuing mechanical licenses via a mechanical right society, the label accounts monthly, which is obviously a lot of work. This is fine for large major record labels, but what about smaller indie record labels?

The good news is, most distributors will have an option for digital download mechanical royalties to be automatically paid to the publishers or copywriter owners (artists) through the mechanical royalty society such as HFA or MCPS. This saves indie labels from a lot of administrative overhead. You should do this if your artists are published (or expect to be published in the future) so the distributor can take care of mechanicals. You can set this option for each music release separately too.

If your distributor does not have this option, or your artist is not published, then you can pay the mechanical royalties directly to the artist in your artist statements.

ARTIST PERSPECTIVE

Now let's look at this from an artist's perspective. As mentioned above, most distributors have an option to pay mechanical royalties directly to the publisher or copywriter owner, which means you also have the option to not pay those mechanical royalties and have them pass directly to the label.

If you release your own music on your own label and are not published, make sure the mechanicals go straight to you. Likewise, make sure your distributor has this option before signing to them.

For any music you release on other record labels you don't have control over, you will need to check if the label has been collecting your mechanicals directly to you, and if not, then you need to collect them yourself.

If you don't, you will not receive the mechanical royalties owed to you. It is important to realise that these mechanical royalties are paid to publishers, not Performing Rights Organisations (PROs). PROs such as ASCAP, BMI or SOCAM do not collect your mechanicals.

If you are in the US, you will need a publisher, admin publishing company or royalty collections company to collect these for you. We will explain the options available on how to collect mechanicals in more detail in the collecting royalties chapter.

In the UK, you can register with MCPS (Mechanical-Copyright Protection Society) who collect and administer mechanicals for artists. They also send this information to PRS, so you can collect both your mechanical and performance income from one place.

Remember, composition royalties from music sales are the responsibility of both the record label and the artist (or artist's manager/publisher) to manage.

COMPOSITION ROYALTIES FROM PUBLIC PERFORMANCE OF SONGS

Composition royalties from public performance of songs are the artist's responsibility (or artist's manager/publisher) to manage.

Like a sound recording, when a composition is broadcast or used in public performance, the composition owner is owed a royalty.

To recap, public performance examples are music performed during live concerts or live performances in a public setting or publicly playing copyrighted work through music streaming, satellite radio, music videos, FM radio, or a TV show.

The live venue, broadcaster, network or service that benefits from the playing of the music have to pay the royalty.

For example, a bar playing music to entertain its patrons needs to pay for that right. They need a public performance license to publicly perform a musical composition.

As you can imagine, this is quite a big task, and it is the job of performing rights organisations (PROs) to administrate and issue licenses for the public usage of music signed to them.

There are PROs in almost all countries. In the UK, there is only one society, which is called PRS (Performing Rights Society. In the US, there are three major companies: ASCAP, BMI, SESAC, and in Canada, there is SOCAN.

PROs generally do an excellent job of administering and collecting performance rights for music. However, they are not perfect, and that is one of the reasons why established music artists will have a publisher who will help make sure their music is being registered and collected properly.

A PRO works by offering users (any venue playing music, cafes, restaurant, live venues) a blanket license for all music for a fee. They then perform sound surveys on venues on which music is being played to determine how the collected money is divided between music copyright owners.

On this point, there is some controversy and indie musicians and labels have often complained they are not fairly represented compared to major record label artists. This is especially true in electronic dance music, with the large majority of music played in clubs not being represented fairly.

There have been some efforts to find a solution with Pioneer creating KUVO, which detects which music is being played through an external box plugged into the club mixers, but it has had mixed results so far.

As a live performing artist, the best way you can get around this is to register your sets after every gig. In the UK, PRS makes this very easy, and if you play most of your own music in your set, your public performance cheques can be quite healthy.

Streaming services such as Spotify also pay out for public performance licenses as well as TV, cable, and radio. All major networks have to submit cue sheets from all screened TV shows and films.

Public performance income can be significant if you get radio play. An A-list rotation track on the BBC in the UK for a month will pay out about £15,000 – £20,000K (US$20,000-$38,000). A-list rotation tracks are usually top 40 hits, but you get an idea of how valuable these royalties can be.

When it comes to payment, the legal requirement for PROs is to pay out separately to the artist and publisher (if you have signed with one) at a 50/50 split. This is to prevent publishers from having too much power over the royalties.

If you don't have a publisher in the UK, you need to tell PRS to give you 100% as the writer. In the US, if you want to access your publisher's share, you will need to register yourself as a publishing company. However, you can easily do this with ASCAP with just your mailing address, email address, and US tax ID number.

All the major collection agencies worldwide talk to each other and transfer the money to the organisation you are registered with. If you have performance money collected by PRS in the UK, they will send it to ASCAP, and if you are registered with ASCAP in the US, they will work with PRS in the UK.

It can take up to two years to collect all foreign royalties after a publication.

Remember, composition royalties from public performance of songs are the artist's responsibility (or artist's manager/publisher) to manage.

SYNCHRONISATIONS

Music synchronisations, more commonly known as 'syncs', is the process of combining songs with moving pictures, such as film, TV shows, and video games.

They can be very lucrative when you get your music synced, but if you're writing original music as an artist, they come along very infrequently.

You can build relationships with sync agencies, and if you have access to great music and have the time to build relationships with the decision-makers at the agencies, it can be lucrative.

But you have to put the hours into building those relationships to get the jobs. There are also ad agencies that get music written on 'spec' or specification. You have to find and build relationships with the key decision-makers to get these jobs too.

Large publishers have dedicated team members and departments that solely focus on securing sync deals. This is usually a big drawcard for prolific artists with a solid output of material looking to sign to a publisher and a record label putting out a lot of material.

In my experience, the biggest and best syncs have simply come about because the music was great and the director of the film, or creative director of the advert (in the case of TV ads) or trailer editor, liked the music they had discovered independently. We got an email out of the blue requesting to use it and negotiated a sync deal.

It's not to say they should be ignored as an income source, but often artists believe this is the holy grail of money in the music industry (especially when they hear of a relatively unknown artist getting a $20,000 sync deal for placement in a TV advert). What I'm saying is, unless you dedicate your career to being a sync producing musician, don't count on this for an income stream. It's more a cherry on the top when it comes along.

Furthermore, the proliferation of affordable AI-generated music is likely to reduce the demand for custom sync music from music supervisors, leading to a gradual decline in revenue streams over time.

However, as a record label owner developing your music catalogue, investing time in making your tracks available for synchronization opportunities can still be highly beneficial.

The primary sources of syncs are TV shows, film trailers, video games and brand ads via advertising agencies (for online or TV or both). Electronic music has lots of opportunities with video games and movie trailers, especially if your music genre is in flavour. For instance, 2010 – 2015 were great years for dubstep as almost all action films wanted some sort of dubstep track in the trailer.

If you sign a publishing deal, syncs will also come under the agreement, which means you depend on your publisher to get the syncs. Most publishers will agree to have a clause in the agreements that states that they take a smaller separate percentage for any syncs secured by the artist directly. This means you get a larger share of any deals you or your manager secure via your own contacts.

With so much music out there, music supervisors like to work with music that is easily cleared on both the masters and publishing side. For this reason, as a record label owner working with underground artists who have not signed their publishing, it helps to have a clause in the recording contract that gives you non-exclusive rights to clear the publishing side of the track for syncs only.

As a record label, this allows you to quickly maximise your catalogue as you'll have both the masters and the publishing cleared, which makes you easier to deal with for sync teams or sign the music to a non-exclusive sync publisher.

Tip: Most syncs used are instrumentals, and it makes good practice as a label to request instrumental versions of all tracks you sign. If a lucrative sync comes in, but they need an instrumental and the artist has lost the project file, it can be very frustrating. I've had artists recreate an entire track to get a sync – stress that could have been avoided if the instrumental had been bounced out as a mix initially.

SYNC INCOME SOURCES

Let's look at the different areas you can use your catalogue for sync income.

ONLINE LIBRARIES

There are catalogue publishers that have large online libraries that showcase the repertoire they represent. They have online searchable databases that arrange the music and catalogue it into musical style, mood and themes.

These services are suited to people looking for quick and relatively cheap access to music beds and background music.

Examples are Jingle Punks, The Music Supervisors, and Music Vine, and Envato Elements.

They usually offer very low fees for syncs but can be a good place to put your older catalogue music. If you sign up with one of these companies, the services are usually non-exclusive. They usually offer a 50% split on all syncs that are placed, and you have to submit your catalogue of music and for review before being accepted.

There's an increased focus on AI-generated music, which is changing the landscape of production music, so there will be more competition and lower fees in the coming years.

Tip: Check with any deals with catalogue publishers that they don't re-label tracks for registration with PROs. If they do this, it will mean they will also collect on the public performance side of the deal as well, which they don't have rights to. It's a slightly shady thing companies have been known to do, so always check.

SYNC AGENTS

Sync agents specialise in finding music for mostly TV shows, advertisements, and occasionally film trailers. They are typically non-exclusive sync agents, but some may ask to be excluded from your catalogue for a particular territory, for example, North America or Europe.

With a non-exclusive agent, you sign an agreement that pre-clears them to secure tracks for an agreed fee of anything from 10-30%. Almost all sync deals I have done via this set-up came from non-exclusive agents that reached out to me, and they typically took 10-15% of the total fee for arranging the sync licence.

CUSTOM MUSIC SYNCHRONIZATIONS

When a composer creates a specific piece of music to specification or spec, it's called a custom music sync. This is very common in the advertising world, and often the turnarounds are tight, for example, a 24-48 hour turnaround.

Typically, composers who work in this world have agents representing them and source these spec jobs for them. You need to be available to quickly communicate for these jobs, as there are changes to the music right up to the deadline. This can be pretty stressful, and composers need to act in a very professional manner.

An old writing partner of mine, Bruce Gainsford, has built a career doing this, but I know it took him years to get to a stage where it was a good money earner, and he had a head start from his existing contacts in the industry from his days as a guitarist in a touring rock band.

Tip: If you choose to pursue sync music as an income source for film, TV or advertising, you need to develop relationships with the agents and music supervisors that make the creative music decisions. You need to be in regular contact and let them be aware of the music you are releasing.

Usually, there is a music brief, and the director or producer is looking for a very particular sound. You want to make sure that when the style of music you have is being required, you're at the top of the list that they think of.

Build relationships with these agencies and email them often with what your music releases. They are always passionate music fans, and they love to hear about new music and being kept in the know.

SYNC FEES AND ROYALTIES

How much can you expect for sync? The number of times I have been at industry sync panels and a music supervisor is asked this question, and they NEVER give a straight answer. And to be honest, as the range of fees is so large there isn't really a correct answer.

However, I understand this frustration, so I'll give some hard numbers of tracks I have had synced.

My first sync was one of my own productions: 'Break It ft. Afrika Bambaataa' was featured in a FIFA Street 4 game, and I got US$4,000 all-in. We had a Zomboy track synced for the 'Hansel and Gretel' feature film trailer for US$38,000. The Prototypes made a track on spec for a Honda TV ad in Japan for US$5,000. Eptic had a track in a McDonald's TV ad for just three seconds for US$8,000. Memtrix got a sync for the Wipeout Omega game for US$3,000.

The fees listed above are for 'all-in', so the total sync fee was split between the master licence, which goes to the label, and the synchronisation licence, which goes to the publisher (or directly to the composer/producer if unpublished).

These were also MFN – which is short for 'Most Favored Nation'. This means that the master rights owner and the publishing rights owner are paid equal fees. So the fees mentioned above were split 50% for each side.

Except for the Memtrix track, all the examples came about by someone reaching out to us as they had heard the track elsewhere. Regarding the Zomboy track, they wanted something from Skrillex but could not afford him, so they picked up a Zomboy track, which was more affordable.

SYNC ROYALTIES

Like all tracks, there is a composition side (publishing) and the sound recording (masters) to register and collect performance royalties on. This is separate from the one-off license fee paid for the synchronisation of music to moving images described in earlier examples.

In the UK, broadcasters use a blanket license to use any music registered with MCPS and PRS who collect and pay out royalties to their members.

In the US, broadcast royalties are paid by the broadcaster of a television show, film or advertisement to the PROs, such as ASCAP, BMI, and SESAC.

Typically, when you get a request, you will be offered a sync fee and asked who controls the publishing. For indie music, a sync agent will usually reach out to the record label first for the masters and then ask who the publisher is (as often with unpublished indie artists, the artist controls their own publishing).

MICRO SYNC INCOME

Micro-Sync is a revenue source derived from platforms such as YouTube and TikTok. It's the same concept as licensing for film/TV with the synchronisation of music to a moving image, but on a much larger scale. On YouTube, the mass use of music in User Generated Content creates thousands of these micro music syncs. Micro-sync revenue generates both mechanical and performance royalties.

LICENSING DEALS

A licensing deal is where another music label 'licenses' the use of music for a set time for an agreed fee or royalty share per release. The difference between this and a traditional record deal is there is no transfer of copyright between parties.

License deals are commonly used between different record labels and music rights companies. A common licensing deal is when a catalogue record label licenses music for a music compilation.

A music compilation is a collection of songs from different artists that a record label sells as one release album. Compilations can be a collection of music from only one label. Many labels release a 'Best Of' in December each year featuring their most popular tunes, especially electronic music labels. Imprints such as Ministry of Sound, Defected Records, and UKF have had successful series for years.

A compilation can be a collection of songs from a film as well. This is especially popular when the film background music or score heavily relies on using commercial songs as the soundtrack. Famous examples are 'Guardians Of The Galaxy', 'Pulp Fiction', 'Trainspotting', and 'Mama Mia!'.

Another typical compilation released by specialist labels is compilations set around a theme or an idea such as a music style or a club night. The most famous of these and arguably the best selling compilation of all time is the 'Now That's What I Call Music' series which has been running since 1983 and is a sub-label of the three majors: Virgin, EMI, and UMTV. Other more underground compilations of this type are 'Late Night Tales Presents..' and the 'FabricLive' series, which both feature curated tracks from influential music artists.

While I've only mentioned the more famous complications, many indie record labels release complications that fall under one of the styles above with huge financial success in their particular niche.

Another typical licensing deal is when a record label from a specific country wants to release your music in their territory. For example, if a track is doing well in the UK, a local German record label will reach out to license the exclusive right to promote and sell the music in Germany.

This can be beneficial for the music's rights holder. While they have to share the revenue with the sub-licensor, up to 50% sometimes, the local record company will sell far greater quantities of the music due to their expert local knowledge and distribution contacts.

Licensing can go both ways. As a record label, you may want to release a 'Sound of Summer' compilation that contains most of your label's catalogue and add a few other songs that are similar to your label but from other record labels. You would then license these tracks and account to the other labels the same way you would account to your artists.

Licensing is also a way to start a record label with no music signed exclusively to the label. How? You use a licensing agreement to license music non-exclusively that's already been released, either from other record labels or directly from music artists.

For a non-exclusive license with an individual artist, you have an agreement with an artist to sell their music on your record label, and you share in the profits 50/50. The artist still keeps 100% of the music rights. Similar to a recording deal, but it has a time limit and as it's non-exclusive so they can still put it on their SoundCloud channel or even on their own label if they have one.

If you license from another record label, again, you have a non-exclusive license agreement to sell the track on your record label, with your label getting royalties from sales that come through the sales on your distribution channels. Usually, you will share the profits 80/20 (in your label's favour) when licensing from other record labels. You may sometimes have to pay an advance upfront for the deal, such as $500-$2000.

That is why sometimes you see the same track appear twice with different artwork on music platforms as the track has been licensed out to different labels.

If you're starting out, this can be a key way to build up a catalogue of music. Then when established, you can start signing artists exclusively to the label. We cover this in more detail in the 'Music Compilations' chapter later in the book.

YOUTUBE MONETISATION

As all other music uses, when someone uses your music on YouTube, they need a sync license and master license from the owners. And, of course, there is a public performance royalty for all plays of your music, which is collected via a PRO.

Also, if a channel owner that uploads your music has any adverts running on their channel, they are earning advertising revenue, which as a copyright owner, you are entitled to.

55% of the ad revenue is accounted towards the copyright holders of the music.

That's the theory. However, in reality, lots of YouTube uploads don't end up asking for licenses from the correct party simply because they don't know they had to, and the administration side of this is cumbersome.

To get around this problem, YouTube created the Content ID system that rights holders use to easily identify and manage their content on YouTube.

Rightsholders submit their music to the Content ID System, and it is recorded in a large database. When a video is uploaded to YouTube by users (User Generated Content), it is scanned against this database of files, and when a match is found, the video gets a Content ID claim.

Many digital distribution companies have an option to collect your YouTube royalties via an opt-in checkbox. As a label, you can also sign up to YouTube and become a verified partner or use a third party specialising in YouTube monetisation such as Audiam and AdRev.

To maximise your income and ensure your copyrighted work is being matched correctly, we recommend working with a third party network or YouTube collection company. They can also negotiate better advertising revenue for you, as they typically represent a larger content library. Some distributors have this service built-in as well.

A third party will take a percentage of the royalty revenue – anything from 10% to 50%, depending on the services they offer.

The royalties you get from YouTube or TikTok are called micro-sync royalties.

Below is a diagram of who owns the different parts of a video on YouTube.

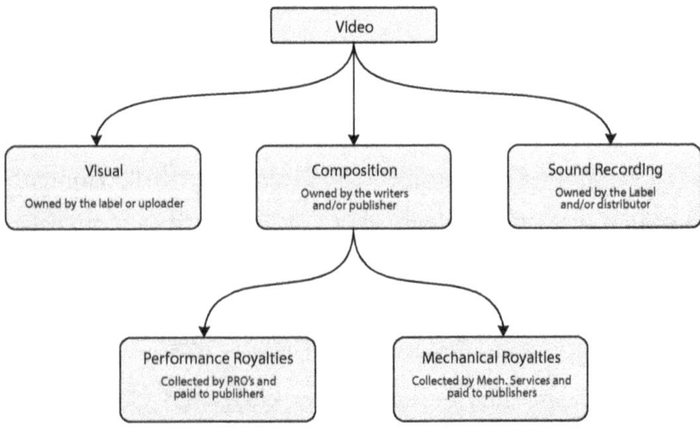

It's important to note that monetisation needs to be turned on for micro-sync royalties to be collected.

Some thresholds have to be reached for monetisation to activate. These thresholds are at the time of print are:

- A minimum of 500 subscribers and three public video uploads within 90 days
- And either 3,000 watch hours in the past year or 3 million YouTube Shorts views in the past 90 days

Videos on channels not eligible for monetisation with 10,000+ views are manually reviewed.

COVER SONGS

To explain music copyright with cover songs, let's work through an example cover song.

Say I write and record a song called 'Bright Lights' and put it online to download and stream through my own record label. I own the publishing for that song because I wrote that song, and I own masters because I recorded my performance and uploaded that song.

I own 100% of the royalties on that song for both the publishing and the master sound recording.

Let's say someone called JDubz makes a cover of that song and releases it online through a record label that takes 50%. So the song has the same melody and lyrics but a different master recording of that song.

I still own the publishing, but I have no claim to their masters as that's their version of my song. They own the masters of the song, but I still own the publishing like this.

RELEASING A COVER SONG

If you decide to record a cover song yourself or sign an artist who has a cover song to release officially and sell it on your record label, you must:

Obtain a mechanical license if you release music in a country that requires one.

Credit the original songwriters. You do this in the composers and publishers field when you upload to your distribution platform.

You can't mention the original artist's name in the track or release title.

MECHANICAL LICENSES FOR COVER SONGS

You need a mechanical license to pay the publisher/songwriter those mechanical royalties to distribute your cover songs in the USA (excluding steaming), Mexico, Canada, Japan, India and Pakistan. If you do not obtain a mechanical license, you cannot distribute your cover songs in these territories.

For all other territories, you don't need a license as it is dealt with at the point of sale, and stores pay the collection societies directly.

USA

In the USA, there is a crucial difference between releasing a cover song for streaming and for downloading. For streaming platforms (like Spotify, Apple Music), mechanical licenses and royalties are usually handled automatically by distributors through blanket agreements managed by the Mechanical Licensing Collective (MLC), meaning independent artists don't need to secure a separate license for streaming-only releases. However, when offering a cover song as a digital download, or selling physical copies, artists must obtain a mechanical license themselves because blanket coverage does not extend to downloads or physical formats. This can be done through either the Harry Fox Agency (HFA) via Songfile or Easy Song Licensing. Songfile allows you to search for a license for any song. Please note these services only supply a license for releasing the song in the US.

- songfile.com
- easysonglicensing.com

Mexico

In Mexico, the digital music rights society is called EMMACSACM, formed as a joint venture by two different PROS (EMMAC & SACM). Visit their website for a list of publishers collected by this society to obtain a license for a cover.

- emmacsacm.com.mx

Canada

Canada has two different PRO groups (CMRRA & SODRAC) that joined to form CSI. To release a cover in Canada, you must check if the song is represented in CSI's repertoire.

If it is, you are free to release the cover as the store will organise the correct mechanical royalty is paid to CSI at the point of sale. If not, you must contact the publisher or copyright holder for that song and apply for a mechanical license.

You can search either CMRRA's or SODRAC's repertoires to check if CSI represents the cover song license.

- cmrra.ca/music-users/need-a-license
- sodrac.ca/licences-audio

Japan

The PRO for Japan is JASRAC and has a repertoire which you can search for licenses. If you cannot find a song on the database, contact JASRAC via email to see if they represent that song.

- jasrac.or.jp/ejhp/users/index.html

India and Pakistan

To obtain a mechanical license to cover a song in India or Pakistan, you need to go directly to the rights holder for that song. Neither of these countries has their own PRO that also issues mechanical licenses. IPRS is a PRO in India but does not offer licenses.

HOW MUCH?

When obtaining a license, you need to estimate how many downloads you expect to sell and multiply that amount by 12.40 cents (the US government's mechanical royalty rate for songs five minutes or less).

If you expect to sell 1,000 records of a Foo Fighters cover song, then $124.00. You also pay a service fee to Songfile or Easy Song Licensing of approximately $15. The service passes this fee along to the publishers of Foo Fighters.

What if you sell more than 2,500? You will need to keep 12.40 cents aside for each track you sell and then contact the publisher directly to pay them the mechanical fee directly.

STREAMING

When you apply for a licence, you will be asked how many interactive streams you expect. Simply choose none. Spotify, Rdio and Deezer already pay mechanical fees to publishers, so you would be double paying.

YOUTUBE

While a sync license is technically required to release a cover on YouTube, in practice, publishers often choose to monetize the video with ads rather than remove it.

We Are The Hits has a database of popular songs that will give you a license to legally release on YouTube. They work with Sony/ATV, Universal, Kobalt, EMI and WB to ensure you have the correct licence. This is a good place to search if you want to cover a song as they have a database of around three million songs.

- wearethehits.com

SAMPLES

It is fairly common knowledge that hip hop, rap and electronic dance music artists sample other music heavily. In the case of drum samples, this has been going on ever since hip-hop days, and the Amen Break has been the staple diet of drum & bass producers for years.

Historically, you don't need to clear a drum beat. But what about recorded vocals and melodies?

First of all, let's look at what I call wholesale sampling and creative sampling.

Wholesale sampling is lifting a whole piece of very well known music and looping it up into a new song. An example of this would be 'I'll Be Missing You' by American rapper Puff Daddy and singer Faith Evans who sampled 'Every Breath You Take' by The Police.

Creative sampling takes a very small sample from a track and manipulates it with effects, and uses it in a new song. An example of this is The Prodigy's 'Voodoo People' that sampled the first two notes of Nirvana's 'Very Ape'.

With so much user-generated content, artists now sample clips of YouTube and TikTok. For example, on 'Scary Monsters and Nice Sprites', Skrillex sampled Rachael Nedrow (aka "speedstackinggirl"), shouting 'Oh my gosh' after a speedstack on YouTube.

An excellent website to find out if a song uses samples is Who Sampled: whosampled.com

So do you need to clear the samples? The hard-line is you need to clear them all by obtaining a license for, you guessed it, the composition and master recording.

In reality, with wholesale sampling, samples will be typically cleared, and it can be fairly straightforward if both the new track's artist and the sampled artist are on the same major record label.

But with creative sampling, this is rarely done in the real world, even though technically, you should clear a tiny sample. It's simply such an administrative burden for an indie artist that sampled a recording from a film or TV dialogue or an obscure older indie song to track down the copyright owner.

Likewise, the administration costs on a copyright owner chasing down the royalties on an underground indie track do not match the amount of money obtained, which is why many indie tracks that sample in this way get looked over.

The rule of thumb is that if you don't expect your track to be a hit on radio, especially top 40 radio, and you use creative sampling, you are pretty safe to release the music. Bear in mind that if you are chased down by the sample's copyright owner, you will have to negotiate a percentage of the total royalty earned by the track to the copyright owner. They can request 100% of the rights; however, you may still be able to negotiate something fair with the copyright owners.

Of course, should they decide to take 100% of the earnings from a track that blows up (which happened with Bauuer's 'Harlem Shake'), the trade-off is that the artist benefits from the increase in live gigs due to the popularity of the track.

If you want to use a recognisable sample that you cannot get copyright clearance for, a popular way to get around it is with a 'soundalike'.

Companies will recreate a sample to sound like the original music for a nominal fee, which could be a vocal, an instrumental piece, or even a whole track. They go in deep and research where the original track was recorded and what instruments and equipment were used. They then recreate that set-up and play the music, often bringing in pro musicians. And the results are very impressive, and as it's a new master recording, you have 100% rights to that master recording.

The best I can recommend for soundalikes is A-Mnemonic: a-mnemonic.com.

MUSIC ROYALTY FLOW

Now you have read about the different types of copyrights, let's look at how the music royalty flows for recorded music. The following flowcharts track how the various royalties flow for both the sound recording and the composition.

Note: As we are focused on recorded music, the flowchart doesn't include performance royalties from the live performance of music.

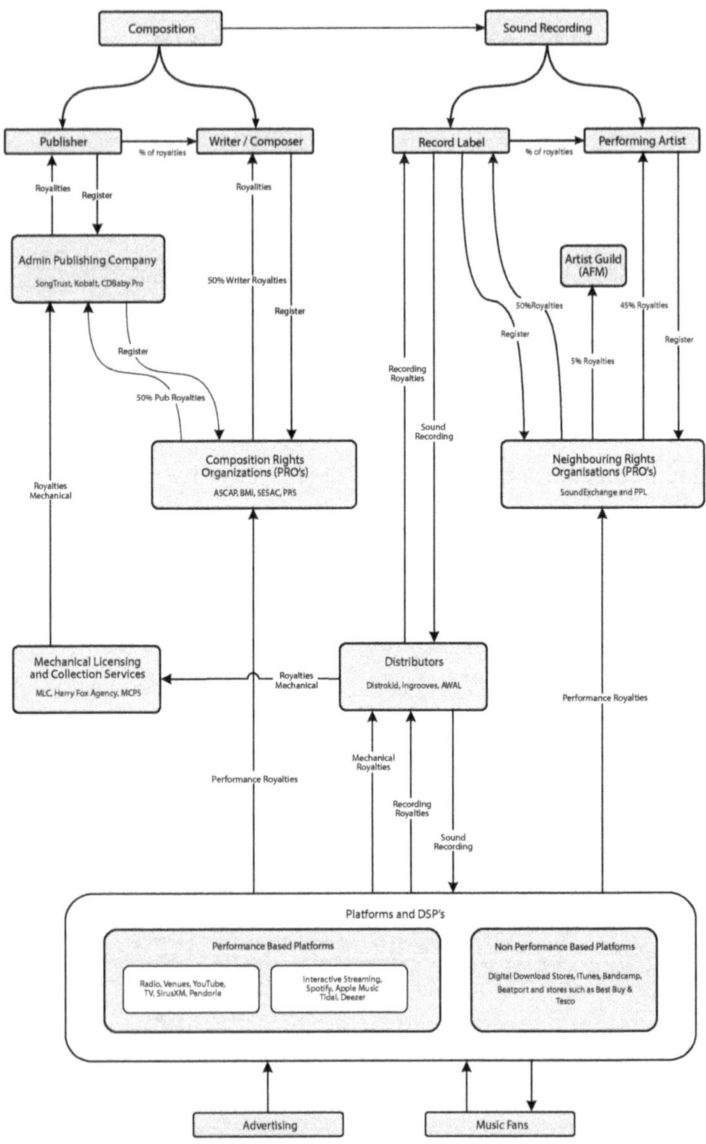
Composition
Sound Recording
Publisher
% of royalties
Writer / Composer
Record Label
% of royalties
Performing Artist
Royalties
Register
Royalties
Admin Publishing Company
SongTrust, Kobalt, CDBaby Pro
50% Writer Royalties
Register
Artist Guild (AFM)
50%Royalties
45% Royalties
Register
Register
Register
5% Royalties
Recording Royalties
50% Pub Royalties
Sound Recording
Composition Rights Organizations (PRO's)
ASCAP, BMI, SESAC, PRS
Neighbouring Rights Organisations (PRO's)
SoundExchange and PPL
Royalties Mechanical
Mechanical Licensing and Collection Services
MLC, Harry Fox Agency, MCPS
Royalties Mechanical
Distributors
Distrokid, Ingrooves, AWAL
Performance Royalties
Mechanical Royalties
Performance Royalties
Recording Royalties
Sound Recording
Platforms and DSP's
Performance Based Platforms
Radio, Venues, YouTube, TV, SirusXM, Pandoria
Interactive Streaming, Spotify, Apple Music Tidal, Deezer
Non Performance Based Platforms
Digital Download Stores, iTunes, Bandcamp, Beatport and stores such as Best Buy & Tesco
Advertising
Music Fans

RECORD LABELS AND DISTRIBUTORS

Because there are thousands of more record labels than music services, there needs to be a middleman who can facilitate music exchange between the record labels and services.

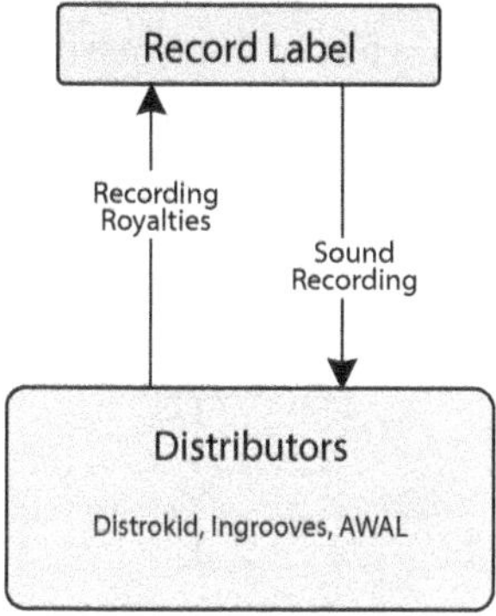

As a record label, you want to sign one agreement, upload your music to one place, and then distribute it to hundreds of music stores.

This middleman is the distributors and aggregators we talked about in earlier chapters. They will ensure your single, EP or album is correctly placed on all platforms and take a fee and/or percentage cut of the royalties for these services.

Sometimes distributors also work with other distributors to get the music to countries they don't have a contract in. Some distributors also sit under a larger global distributor such as The Orchard, and you might not even be aware of this as it all happens behind closed doors.

The critical thing to remember is that it's the distributors' job to get your music to as many platforms as possible around the world and collect the money from these platforms.

PLATFORMS AND DSPS

Music royalties come from the sale of recorded music through digital download platforms such as Apple Music, Beatport and the physical sales of music at stores such as Best Buy and Tesco. Music royalties also come from music streaming on DSPs (Digital Service Providers) services such as Spotify, Deezer, and Tidal.

The platforms and DSPs receive money from music fans buying and listening to music, monthly subscriptions, and advertising income.

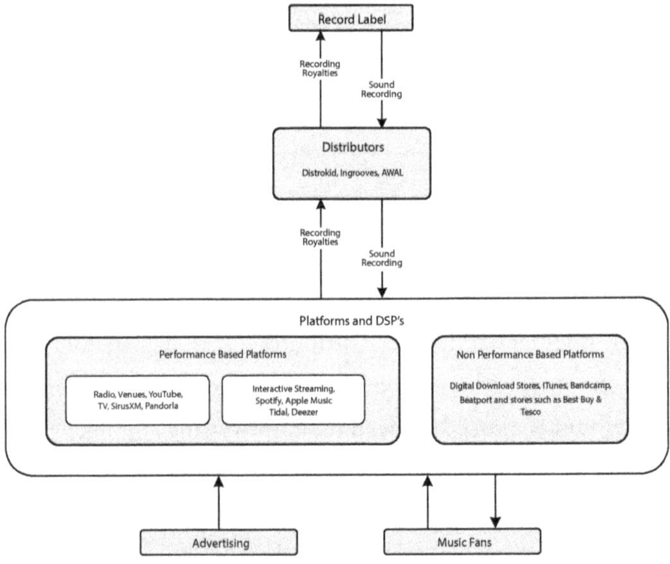

As you now know, there are four main areas of royalties:

- Sound recording royalties from music sales
- Sound recording royalties from the public performance of songs

- Composition royalties from music sales (aka mechanicals)
- Composition royalties from the public performance of songs

Each of the platforms and DSPs generate different types and combinations of these royalties. A simple way to think of this is that if the royalty involves a 'music sale', it's usually generated on a non-performance based platform. If the royalty involves a 'public performance', it's usually generated on a performance-based platform.

Performance-Based

Performance-based royalties are paid to the PROs on the sound recording side and composition side. These include royalties generated by on-demand interactive streaming such as Spotify, Apple Music, Tidal and Deezer. This includes non-interactive streaming from digital radio such as SiriusXM and Pandora and includes public performance on terrestrial radio, TV broadcasts, YouTube, and music played in venues such as bars and restaurants.

Non-Performance Based

Non-performance based royalties are paid to the label through the distributors. They include digital download stores such as Apple Music, Beatport, and physical sale of CDs and vinyl through Best Buy, Tesco, and Amazon.

As you can see, a record label's Recording Royalties are generated from both performance and non-performance based platforms. The rest of the chapter will show the flow of money for the various performance-based royalties.

NEIGHBOURING RIGHTS (PROS)

The public performance royalties generated from the sound recording played on the performance-based platforms and DSPs (Digital Service Providers) are collected by the Neighbouring Rights PROs.

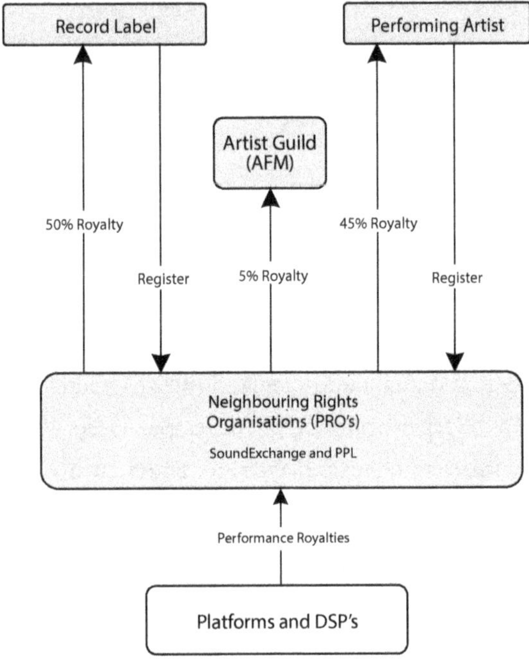

As you can see, it is the responsibility of both the record label and the artist (or artist's manager) to register these works, such as PPL and SoundExchange. When collected, the PROs distribute 50% to the record label, 45% to the featured performing artist, and the remaining 5% to the AFM / SAG-AFTRA funds for non-featured artists.

PUBLISHERS AND ADMINISTRATORS

Moving over to the composition side of the music flow, we have the Publisher and the Administration Publishing Companies to manage the flow of composition royalties.

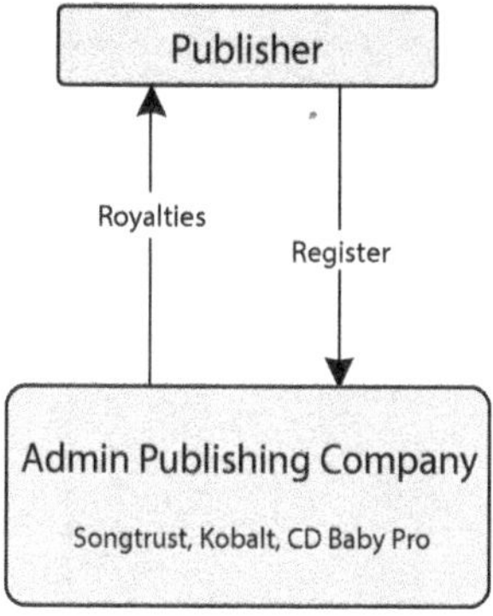

The publisher legally owns a percentage of the composition if the writer has signed a publishing deal. The Admin Publishing Company will then act on behalf of the publisher to register the compositions with PROs and mechanical license services. They will then collect the publishing performance royalties and give them to the publisher for a percentage fee for the work.

In the modern music industry, you find that some admin publishing companies are also a publisher and own composition rights, and some publishers offer the services of admin publishing companies as well.

COMPOSITION RIGHTS (PROS)

The public performance royalties generated from the composition played on the performance-based platforms and DSPs are collected by the Composition Rights Organisation PROs such as ASCAP, BMI, and PRS.

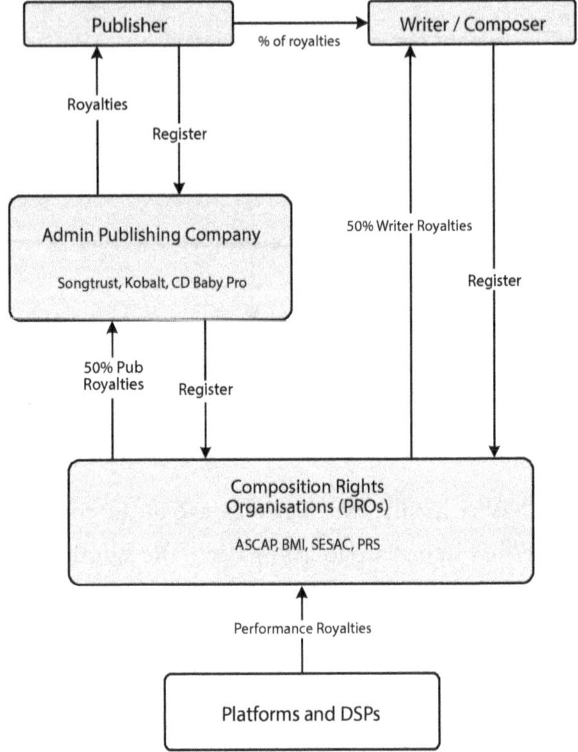

These are then distributed to the publisher via the admin publishing company and directly to the writers registered with the PROs.

If you are an artist signed to a publisher, then the publisher and/or the admin publishing company will register your songs for you. If you are not signed to a publisher, you will need to register your songs, but you will also collect all the performance royalties.

MECHANICALS

As of 2018, the mechanical royalties generated from the composition played on the non-performance based platforms and DSPs are managed by the newly established Mechanical Licensing Collective (MLC). The MLC, created under the Music Modernization Act (MMA) of 2018, is now responsible for administering blanket mechanical licenses for DSPs in the United States.

This organiztion collects and distributes mechanical royalties to songwriters and music publishers, streamlining the process that was previously managed by agencies like the Harry Fox Agency (HFA).

In the UK, mechanical royalties are managed by the Mechanical Copyright Protection Society (MCPS). MCPS is responsible for collecting and distributing mechanical royalties to music publishers, songwriters, and composers.

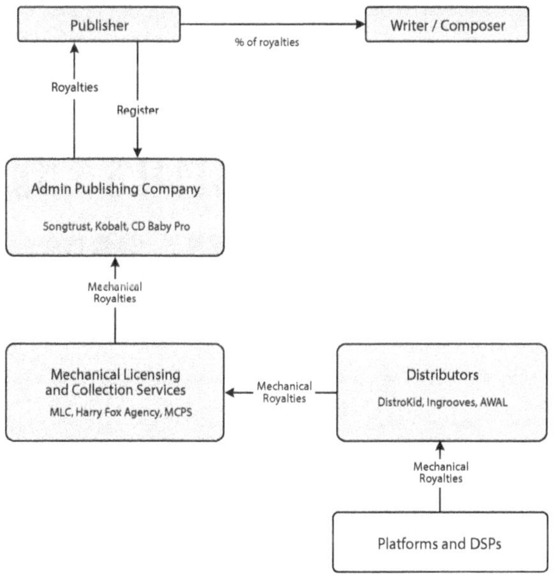

It is important to remember that in the US, these mechanical royalties are paid to publishers, not PROs and being a member of ASCAP, BMI, SOCAM will not enable you to collect your mechanicals. You will need to register yourself as a publisher with your PRO or sign up to an admin publishing company to receive these mechanical royalties.

If your label releases cover songs on a physical format such as CD's or as downloads , you need to obtain a mechanical licence, but this licence can be obtained through services like the Harry Fox Agency's Songfile, Easy Song Licensing, or directly from the copyright holder.

However, if you are releasing a cover song strictly on streaming platforms like Spotify or Apple Music, you do not need a separate mechanical licence. These platforms handle the licensing and royalty payments through The Mechanical Licensing Collective (MLC)

COLLECTING ROYALTIES AND REGISTERING WITH PROS

At this point, you should have a better understanding of how the different music copyrights and royalties work. To ensure you are collecting all your rights, you need to make sure you register your music with the royalty collection agencies as both a record label and as an artist, so they know where to send the royalty payments.

Sound Recordings

In summary, the main areas of revenue streams for Sound Recordings are:

- Sales Royalties generated from physical and digital downloads of records.
- Streaming Royalties generated from digital streams on Spotify, Apple Music, Amazon Music, Deezer, and all other music platforms in the world.
- Digital Performance Royalties generated through neighbouring rights organisations like SoundExchange and PPL when songs are performed publicly.
- Sync Royalties generated from TV, film, video games and ad commercials, paying for the rights to use master sound recordings.

Compositions

The main areas of revenue streams for compositions are:

- Performance Royalties generated through performance rights organisations like ASCAP, BMI, SESAC, and PRS when songs are performed publicly.
- Mechanical Royalties generated from labels licensing the rights to produce songs in physical and digital form, including cover songs.

- Sync Royalties generated from TV, film, video games and advertising companies paying for the rights to use the song's composition.

Updates

Once you have registered your details with each of the PROs, you need to ensure you update them every time you have new music officially released so they can track the royalties due to you and pay you. Bear in mind, you have to have music released officially for sale before registering with PROs, so if you are starting out, return to this section after your music is released.

So who registers what? Let's work through them from a record label's perspective and an artist's perspective.

RECORD LABEL REGISTRATIONS

Sales Royalties

As a label, you will collect the sound recording royalties from music sale downloads when you release music. These will be passed on to yourself if you are an artist or to your signed artists. These royalties are collected from your distributor.

Streaming Royalties

As a label, you collect these royalties when the sound recording is played in interactive streaming services such as Spotify, Apple Music, Deezer, Tidal. These royalties are collected from your distributor.

Digital Performance Royalties

These are generated from playing copyrighted work publicly, such as non-interactive music streaming, satellite radio, music videos, FM radio, or a TV show. These are called neighbouring rights. If you are based in the US, you need to register your record label and your releases with SoundExchange. Record labels based in Canada register releases with Re:Sound.

- soundexchange.com
- resound.ca

If you are in the UK, you register with PPL. PPL will also take registrations from any label worldwide, so if you are outside the US or UK, you can still use PPL to collect and pay your digital performance royalties.

- ppl.co.uk

Sync Royalties

These are generated when a TV show, film, ad commercial, trailer or video game requires the master licence. You get paid directly from the TV studio, advertising producers, film production company or games company. Typically, you will have a sync agent acting as an intermediary between you and the studio, who will handle the paperwork for a small fee and usually handle the sync (composition) licence.

YouTube Royalties

If you allow YouTube to monetise your music uploads and

run ads, you can earn revenue from these ads, which are split 45%/55% in your favour. Most distributors have an opt-in box to collect these for you. As a label, you can also sign up to YouTube and become a verified partner or use a third party that specialises in YouTube monetisation, such as Audiam and AdRev.

- audiam.com
- adrev.net

Compositions

As a label, you don't collect any composition royalties, as you are expected to pay royalties to the copyright owner in the form of mechanical royalties. Most distributors will have an option for digital download mechanical royalties to be paid directly to the publishers or copywriter owners, who then pay the artist. You should do this if your artists are published or expect them to be published in the future so the distributor can take care of mechanicals. You can set this option for each music release separately too.

ARTIST REGISTRATIONS

Sales Royalties

The music you have signed to a record label will pay your record sales royalties, determined by your record agreement. If you own your record label, the royalties will be going straight to you from the distributor.

Streaming Royalties

As above, the music you have signed to a record label will pay your streaming royalties, determined by your record agreement. If you own your record label, the streaming royalties will be going straight to you from the distributor.

Digital Performance Royalties US

To collect your digital performance royalties in the US, you need to register with SoundExchange. They pay out 45% to the featured performing artist and the remaining 5% to the AFM / SAG-AFTRA funds for non-featured artists. If you are a non-featured artist, you need to register with AFM / SAG-AFTRA.

- soundexchange.com
- afmsagaftrafund.org

Digital Performance Royalties UK

To collect your digital performance royalties in the UK, you need to register with PPL. They collect for non-featured and session artists too. They will also collect your SoundExchange royalties if your music is played in the US. If you are outside the UK and US, you can still register with PPL to collect your digital performance royalties.

- ppl.co.uk

Mechanical Royalties US

If you are in the US, you will need a publisher, admin publishing company or royalty collections company to collect your mechanical royalties for you. If you are published, your publisher will register your music and collect and pay for you.

For those without a publishing deal, you have two main options:

Sign up with an administrative publishing company to collect your mechanical royalties. Companies like Kobalt, Tune-Core Publishing, Sentric Music, and SongTrust offer this service. For example, SongTrust will manage your mechanical royalties for an administrative fee of 10-15%, while you retain ownership of your publishing rights.

The second option is to register yourself as a 'publishing company' with ASCAP if you're a U.S. resident. This option allows you to collect your mechanical royalties directly using just your mailing address, email address, and U.S. tax ID number.

- kobaltmusic.com
- tunecore.com
- sentricmusic.com
- songtrust.com

Mechanical Royalties UK

If you are based in the UK, you need to register with MCPS to collect your mechanical royalties. They work closely with PRS (below), and you can register at the PRS For Music. Alternatively, as like US music artists, you can register with an admin publishing company, such as Kobalt, Tunecore Publishing, Sentric Music, and SongTrust.

- prsformusic.com

Performance Royalties US

If you are based in the US, you need to register with one of the PROs, either ASCAP, BMI, or SESAC to collect your performance royalties. Which one depends on your preference, they all offer similar deals, the two most popular being ASCAP and BMI.

If you play live, you must register your live sets with your PRO to collect your performance royalties. This means uploading your tracklist to their system to track your public performance to collect your royalties generated. Even a support act on tour can make thousands of dollars.

- ascap.com
- bmi.com
- sesac.com

Performance Royalties UK

If you are based in the UK, you need to register with PRS to collect your performance royalties. As mentioned, they work closely with MCPS, and once you have registered with both companies, you can collect both your mechanicals and performance income from PRS.

Like the US, if you play your own music live, or you DJ and play your music in your sets, it is important to register your live sets with PRS. Once they have your live set in the database for the shows you played, you can collect your performance royalties generated.

- prsformusic.com

Performance Royalties Internationally

If you are outside the US, Canada, or the UK, and your country supports music copyright, you can find your PRO on the Wikipedia page.

- wikipedia.org/wiki/performance_rights_organisation

Sync Royalties

If your music is featured in a TV show, film, ad commercial, trailer or video game, they require a sync licence. You get paid directly from the TV studio, advertising producers, film production company, or games company. As with a master recording license, typically, you will have a sync agent acting as an intermediary between you and the studio who will handle the paperwork for a small fee. They will usually handle both the master and composition license fee, often as an 'all-in deal' with the fee being split evenly between the master and sync licence. They will also help negotiate other parts of the deal such as whether the song will be exclusive to the sync (higher fee) and what fees will be paid if they use it again after the original term of the deal ends.

PART THREE

THE PROCESS

OVERVIEW

Twenty years ago I read Michael Gerber's book 'The E-Myth'. The essence of this book is the revelation that just because you work as a technician in a particular industry doesn't mean you have the skills to run a business in that industry. A technician in this case meaning someone doing the actual work, e.g. doctor, musician, builder. Running a business is a skill, and the reason so many first time businesses fail is that the technician doesn't have the skills and resources to run a business in their industry despite working in that industry.

This adage also applies to the musician or music manager that decides to start a record label. They think, "I work in the music industry so I can run a record label". Wrong. A record label is a business, and you need to learn how to run a record label business.

My mission is to give artists and music entrepreneurs the resources and skills needed to run a successful record label business. I have been in your shoes, starting out knowing very little about building a record label business and had to learn the hard way, but you won't have to as I'm going to give you a detailed blueprint to follow! It's like a super organised business plan you will use to start and run your own label.

There are a multitude of questions to ask yourself as you start to run a label. Which distributor? Which logo designer?

Where to find fans? Where do I find this contract or that contract? You get the picture. I will walk you through the blueprint step by step, offering suggestions and recommendations from my industry experience.

And, of course, anything you want to find out more about, Google it! I have collated enough key information in this book to provide you with a tried and tested blueprint to get from point A of being disorganised and overwhelmed, to point B of being organised, streamlined and making money. But the internet is a fantastic resource for further learning, so don't be afraid to use it if you want to deep-dive into a particular area.

Some stuff can be really fun, like designing the logo and thinking about branding, and some of it not so much, like setting up company accounts! You'll be required to make some big decisions like how you want to split your profits and navigate the legal process of setting up a company. But I'll give you the tools and real-world examples to make these bits, if not fun, then at least a lot easier than if you were on your own.

I have divided part three of the book into four main processes.

The Set-Up. This is the process of setting up an official record label or music company.

Creating a Record Release. This is the process of releasing and distributing your music.

Marketing and Promoting the Music. This is the process of marketing and promoting the music release to fans.

360° Music System. This is the process of growing both the labels and artists fan base long term.

But first – all this information in your hands is useless unless you can take action with it. This is why I'm going to spend the first part of the process doing a deep dive into how to take this knowledge and turn it into results.

THE SET-UP

The first section of the process deals with setting up an official record label. These are all the essential parts you need to complete to have a record label business.

- The right mindset
- SMART goals
- A record label name
- Record label backbone
- A business plan
- Label branding
- Design tools
- Label logo
- Website
- Social media handles
- A distributor
- Understanding of budgets
- Emails and email marketing
- Company registration

MINDSET

The following three chapters cover having a good mindset, setting goals, and how to take action to achieve these goals.

You might be thinking, whoa, hang on a sec. I thought this book was about starting and running an indie music label? What's all this about motivation and goal setting?

Well, the truth is, the biggest factor in deciding if you'll actually manage to start and run a successful label is your ability to set goals and take action. To be honest, those abilities determine the success of most things you want to achieve in life.

Thus, if it is my goal to help you start and run a successful record label or music business, then this book wouldn't be complete without giving you the knowledge and tools to help you with these abilities.

Your ability to set goals and take action all starts with the right mindset.

MOTIVATION AND DISCIPLINE

Motivation and discipline are the backbones to success. Set your goals and stick to them every day, and you will definitely achieve success; and the more driven and efficient you are, the more success you will achieve.

And to stay motivated and disciplined, you need to have the right mindset: a growth mindset.

This chapter is about understanding and implementing a growth mindset to get anything done, and more specifically, starting and running a record label successfully.

Starting on any goal is difficult. Any new task or mission you decide to take on will get tough at some point.

You will ask yourself:

- Can I do it?
- Do I have the right tools?
- Am I good enough?

And the answer is YES if you have the right mindset!

Anything worth achieving is going to take some hard work. So you need to be mentally prepared and ensure your mind is in the best shape when taking on a new challenge or task, whether you are looking at the big picture of launching a record label or a smaller task such as writing a business plan.

It's the same as doing exercise, you get in the right clothes (tools), you go to the gym (resources), and you stretch before you begin (prepare).

Or starting a record label – you switch your computer on (tools), you follow The Label Machine (resources), and you set your goals and your mindset (prepare).

I've started many businesses, and even when it's something I've done before, such as a record label, I still need all the help I can get mentally to ensure I achieve my goals.

Understanding and implementing a growth mindset has been invaluable. And once you understand this, you can implement its theories over and over again.

WHAT IS A MINDSET?

The growth mindset is a mindset for success. It's based on the theories published in the book 'How to Develop a Growth Mindset' by Carol S. Dweck.

Dweck is one of the world's leading researchers in motivation and is a professor of psychology at Stanford University. She's endorsed by the mighty Bill Gates, so she knows a thing or two about achieving what you want with a growth mindset.

Mindset is a way to describe the way people think about ability and talent. It can be thought of as a scale with a fixed mindset on one side and growth mindset on the other.

A fixed mindset suggests your abilities are innate, set in stone and can't be changed. A growth mindset suggests your abilities are something you can improve through practice.

A growth mindset is the opposite of a fixed mindset.

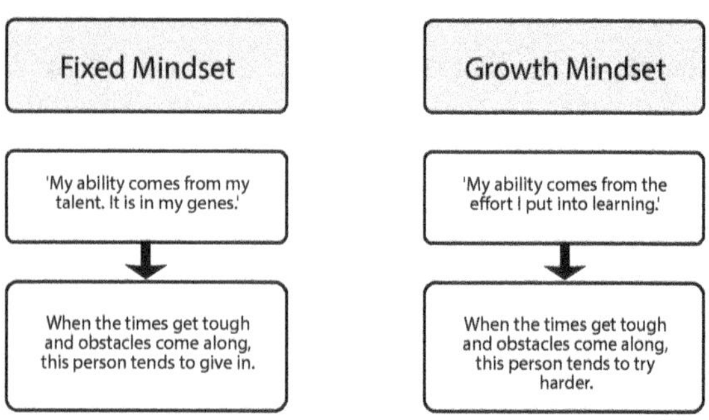

The important lesson here is to realise that your ability is not set in stone with intelligence or talent. It comes from the effort you put into learning.

To implement a growth mindset, you need to remember the four steps of a growth mindset:

1. Recognise your fixed mindset thoughts.
2. Recognise that you have a choice.
3. Respond to your fixed mindset thoughts with growth mindset thoughts.
4. Take the growth mindset action.

Breaking these down

1. Recognise your fixed mindset thoughts.

opportunityisnowhere

Do you see opportunity is nowhere? Or opportunity is now here?

What are fixed mindset thoughts? Let's take a look at some fixed mindset characteristics and how they compare to those of a growth mindset.

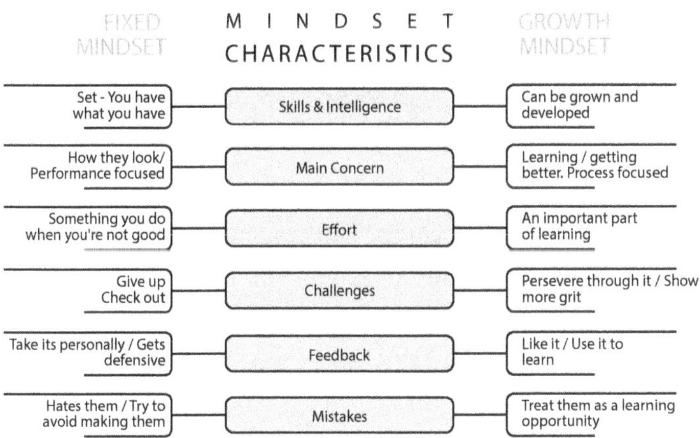

2. Recognise you have a choice.

Once you have a belief, it is hard to change, but it can change. You always have a choice.

You need to break the cycle if it is negative. If you have negative self-talk, recognise that 'it's my choice to have these thoughts'. If you have any negative behaviour, remember that it is your choice to continue with that negative behaviour or choose to stop or change it. And if you get negative results, don't blame yourself, but know that you are part of a self-fulfilling prophecy, and you have a choice to change.

You break the mindset by responding to your fixed mindset thoughts with growth mindset thoughts.

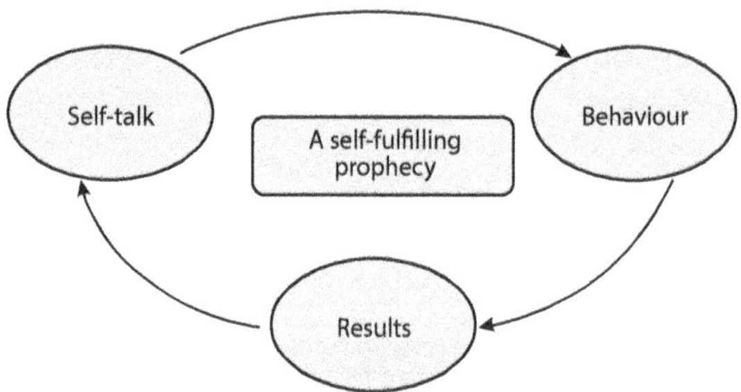

"Between a stimulus and response, there is a space. In that space is our power to choose our response. In our response lies our growth and our freedom. The last of human freedoms is to choose one's attitude in any given set of circumstances." – Viktor Frankl (Austrian psychiatrist, survivor of Auschwitz)

3. Respond to your fixed mindset thoughts with growth mindset thoughts.

Believe that intelligence and ability can grow.

These are not fixed in place by predetermined factors that are set in stone or set by your genes. They are malleable. You can actually practice for an IQ test and get better at it over time if you really want to. In fact, I had a friend Derek at my high school that sat the Mensa IQ test, and when his result came back, he got 142 points, just eight points short of being an official genius at 150 points. Mensa told him he could practice and come back and sit the test again! He never did, but the point is that even the people who give out IQ tests know you can improve your IQ with learning and practice.

Say, "If I try more, I will succeed".

Say things like, "I am not good at interacting with fans online yet. But I can learn".

Think that difficulties can be interesting.

Know that difficulties may be overcome by changing strategies. You can keep learning and trying new approaches until you find one that works.

When things go wrong, don't blame yourself or others.

Things will go wrong. 100%. And when they do, it is never one individual event that causes things to go wrong; it's a cluster of events that cause problems. Even if you genuinely make a mistake, it's usually never in isolation, or if you did make an error, it was because you were affected by external stress you had no control over. For example, the COVID pandemic or someone close to you being sick. There are things beyond your control that affect everybody. So when things go wrong, don't blame yourself or others.

Difficulties are inevitable, and a catalyst for you to find out more.

When things get difficult mentally, it means you have come across something you are not familiar with and might not understand. This is the time to learn more about it, how to approach this difficulty and find a strategy that will make it easier.

4. Take the growth mindset action.

With your thoughts, make a conscious effort to remember at all times:

- Intelligence is not fixed. This is scientifically proven. Education and mental exercise increases IQ. We all learn at different rates and in different ways.
- Many of the most successful and creative people were once judged to have low intelligence.
- What you can achieve, nobody knows.

With attitude, remember at all times:

- What you will achieve will be primarily down to your effort.

- To learn requires effort. Remind yourself, if the work is not hard, you are not learning.
- When you learn, connections in your brain are created that make it more efficient at learning more. You will become smarter.

With actions, remember at all times:

- Great learners learn by asking questions. They seek support when things go wrong.
- Reach out to your support network. If you don't feel like you have a support network, The Label Machine has a community of like-minded music entrepreneurs that you can approach for support and feedback.
- Great learners make mistakes. This is how we learn.
- Be careful what you tell yourself. You have a choice which thoughts absorb and which thoughts you discard.
- Be careful what other people tell you. Do they have a fixed mindset or growth mindset?

Taking growth mind actions is what motivational coaches like Jim Rohn, Zig Ziglar, and Tony Robbins teach and why so many people have unlimited success when they implement these thoughts, attitudes and actions in their life.

If you can start working on the growth mindset today, then the world is your oyster.

Not only will you be able to achieve your record label dreams, but you'll be able to achieve anything you want in life.

PRACTICAL ACTION

So how does this work in the real world? When you are about to start a task or don't know how to move forward, just remember the three steps.

1. Recognise – What is my mindset? Fixed or growth?
2. If it's fixed – tell yourself you have a choice on what to think, on what mindset to have.
3. Then make a conscious effort to respond to fixed mindset thoughts with growth mindset thoughts. e.g. 'Difficulties are inevitable and a catalyst for you to find out more.'

You can download a list of these, including the ones mentioned earlier, to your mobile note app for quick reference by visiting the Book Resources tab on The Label Machine website.

FINAL THOUGHTS

With access to a computer (tools), The Label Machine (resources) and growth mindset knowledge, you now have everything to guarantee record label success.

By setting simple goals and taking daily action, nothing is holding you back from starting, running and growing your own record label.

> "A year from now, you will wish you had started today." – Karen Lamb.

MORE READING

Here are some outstanding business and motivational books that inspired me and will help keep you motivated:

The E-Myth – Michael Gerber
This again is about creating processes, or operating manuals for your business, and was instrumental in creating the blueprints for my record labels that eventually led to the creation of The Label Machine. Essential reading – he is a great storyteller, and it's an easy read, if a little cheesy at times.

The Slight Edge – Jeff Olson
This is about creating simple disciplines you apply every day to achieve massive success. It was a game-changer for me, as it taught me about the power of working a little every day consistently to achieve your goals. Be disciplined and consistent.

Building a StoryBrand – Donald Miller
This book teaches businesses how to clarify their messaging by using storytelling techniques that position customers (fans) as heroes and the brand (record label) as a guiding force, ultimately enhancing their marketing effectiveness.

Mindset is something you have to work on every day. In the next section, we will use practical examples to create your goals and stay focused on your work.

GOALS, MISSIONS, AND SYSTEMS

When you set a mission statement or a goal, it's important that they are SMART.

SMART is an acronym for Specific, Measurable, Achievable, Relevant, and Time-Bound. This concept has been around for decades and remains a powerful tool for setting clear and actionable objectives.

However, while SMART goals are essential, it's equally important to focus on the systems that will drive you toward success. A goal is the outcome you want to achieve, but a system is the process you follow that leads to that outcome. In other words, goals set your direction, but systems are what keep you moving forward.

SMART GOALS

To write SMART goals, I find it helpful to break them down into specific, actionable steps. Here's how each element works:

Specific

- What do I want to accomplish?
- Why do I want to achieve this?
- What are the requirements?
- What are the constraints?

Example: I want to start a record label to produce my own music, so that I can get 100% of revenue and royalties for my music. I require a good business model and plan, and a networking strategy. I'm constrained because I am not good at social media/promotion, I don't know how copyright works, and I only have 4 months until festival season.

Measurable

- How will I measure my progress?
- How will I know when the goal is accomplished?

Example: I'll know I have reached my goal when I have an active website and my music is available on Spotify, Apple Music, and Amazon.

Achievable

- How can the goal be accomplished?
- What are the logical steps I should take?

Example: I will work on this by setting regular time aside each day, and I have The Label Machine as a resource.

Relevant

- Is this a worthwhile goal?
- Is this the right time?
- Do I have the necessary resources to accomplish this goal?
- Is this goal in line with my long-term objectives?

Example: I want to do this before the summer festival season. This will help me increase my royalty income for my music in the long term.

Time-bound

- How long will it take to accomplish this goal?
- When is the completion of this goal due?
- When am I going to work on this goal?

Example: I'll work five days a week by setting 25 minutes aside each day. This will take six months to complete and will be finished on March 3rd.

SYSTEMS: THE PATH TO SUSTAINABLE SUCCESS

While goals give you a clear endpoint, systems are the daily routines and habits that keep you progressing toward those goals. Think of goals as the destination and systems as the journey.

For example, if your goal is to start a record label, your system might involve setting aside 25 minutes each day to work on specific tasks like researching industry trends, developing your business model, or building your network. This consistent effort is what ultimately drives you to achieve your goal.

PUTTING IT ALL TOGETHER

Now, if you put each of these sections together, you have yourself a SMART goal:

Example: I want to start a record label to release my music and have control over the copyright royalties. I'll know I have reached my goal when I have an active website and my music is available on Spotify, Apple Music, and Amazon. I will work on this by setting regular time aside each day, and I have The Label Machine as a resource. I want to do this before the summer festival season, and it will help me increase my royalty income for my music in the long term. I'll work five days a week by setting 25 minutes aside a day. This will take six months to complete and will be finished on March 3rd.

And you can shorten it to a mission statement:

My mission is to work for 25 minutes every day to start a record label in six months, so my music is available on all music platforms, allowing me to grow my music income.

Remember, while setting SMART goals is crucial, the systems you build around those goals are what ensure consistent progress and long-term success. By focusing on both goals and systems, you increase your chances of achieving sustainable success.

FOCUSED WORK

How to get anything done.

> 'Lack of direction, not lack of time, is the problem. We all have twenty-four hour days.' – Zig Ziglar.

And it's very true; what you choose to direct your focus on within your 24 hours will make a huge difference in reaching your goals. And, if you want to reach any goals, you need to take action.

No action = no results.

And if you have a plan and you know what you need to do, then surely it's as simple as just taking action, right?

However, there is that ugly beast called procrastination. It affects everyone and stops us from taking action. So we need a solution to procrastination.

And there is one. And it works. And there is a way to supercharge it too!

When I was in my early 20s, I read a book called The Slight Edge by author Jeff Olson. The philosophy behind the slight edge is spending 15 minutes a day on something you want to get good at. These 15 minutes add up to reaching your ultimate goal.

While reading this book, I wanted to learn guitar, so I went out and bought a cheap one from a secondhand store in Spain where I was living at the time. And I decided each day I would pick up the guitar for 15 minutes and practise.

Some days I did more than 15 minutes, and sometimes I only picked it up for five minutes, but I did it every day. And then one year had passed, and I could play and sing my first full song, 'House of the Rising Sun' by The Animals, as well as playing the chorus and verse of many other songs.

Great, I thought, so the theory works!

POMODORO TECHNIQUE

Then a few years later, I heard about the Pomodoro Technique.

The Pomodoro Technique is a method of time management developed in the 1980s by Francesco Cirillo.

It works by breaking down your tasks into 25-minute intervals with short five or ten minute breaks in between.

Each interval is known as a pomodoro, from the Italian word for 'tomato', after the tomato-shaped kitchen timer that Francesco used as a university student.

You pick your task, set the 25-minute timer, and only work on that task for the next 25 minutes. When the timer goes off, then stop immediately and take a break. After the break, you can start again with another 25 minutes, and so on.

I use this technique every single day. In fact, I'm using it as I write this chapter you are reading.

Now, you don't need to buy a timer, there are free ones on the internet. And there is a great one at tomato-timer.com that beeps and tells you when to stop, which is important!

It's essential to STOP after 25 minutes. Unless you are just finishing a tricky part of work, stop, get up, stretch, look out the window, have a glass of water, and take a break.

It allows your brain to rest and reset, so after five minutes, you can come back and start another 25 minutes. If you don't rest and keep going past 25 minutes, you'll get fatigued and find it harder to keep motivated on your tasks.

If you use the Pomodoro Technique for something more creative, like writing music and you are in the flow, then certainly don't stop. But when you come to a natural stop of flow, then get up, take a rest, and come back after five minutes and start again.

This is super powerful, and I have shared this with so many friends and colleagues. Everyone has come back and said they are so much more productive and get more things done.

SUPERCHARGING THE POMODORO TECHNIQUE AND HOW TO FOCUS THE EASY WAY

Something I have discovered that helps you stay focused for a full 25 minutes is using Binaural Beats.

Binaural Beats therapy is an emerging form of sound-wave therapy in which the right and left ears listen to two slightly different frequency tones yet perceive the tone as one. The different patterns are:

Delta patterns: Binaural Beats in the delta pattern are set at a frequency between 0.1 and 4 Hz, associated with dreamless sleep.

Theta patterns: Binaural Beats in the theta pattern are set at a frequency between 4 and 8 Hz, associated with sleep in the rapid eye movement or REM phase, meditation, and creativity.

Alpha pattern: Binaural Beats in the alpha pattern are set at a frequency between 8 and 13 Hz, encouraging relaxation.

Beta pattern: Binaural Beats in the beta pattern are set at a frequency between 14 Hz and 100 Hz, promoting concentration and alertness.

We are looking to use beta patterns for when we want focused work.

You can search on YouTube for Binaural Beats Beta Pattern, and there are many videos lasting hours you can use.

You must use headphones; otherwise, this technique won't work. Binaural Beats work by sending different tones to each ear, so listening on speakers won't work as the sound gets mixed up before it hits your ears.

Over-the-ear headphones, noise-cancelling or in-ear headphones are best as they block out external sounds and distractions such as phone notifications.

Remember to save the Tomato Timer and a Binaural Beats YouTube video in your browser's bookmark tab so you can access them quickly.

If you apply the Pomodoro Technique to every task you do and keep focused using Binaural Beats, you will quickly complete any task you want and reach any goal you decide to set.

> "Success is the progressive realisation of a worthy goal or ideal." – Earl Nightingale

CHOOSING A RECORD LABEL NAME

How important is your record label's name? It's pretty essential, as you'll be saying it a lot! So it needs to be something you're comfortable saying out loud to a stranger, and that feels natural to say.

The next most important thing in choosing a name is finding out if it's already a record label name. The best way to check is to search on discogs.com. This website lists every record label in the world, so be sure to check here first.

If you are attached to a name already in use, see if the company is still active and if it's the same style of music. If not, you might be OK to keep your chosen name with slight adaptations.

For instance, when we were choosing a name for No Tomorrow, there was already a No Tomorrow Records in Spain, but it wasn't active, and it had only ever released Spanish music. We changed Records to Recordings, and boom, we had a label name: No Tomorrow Recordings.

Other options for using at the end of the record label name are:

- Records
- Recordings
- Music
- Entertainment
- Recording Company
- Nothing at all!

The second thing to check is the website and social media handles. If you can get something unique that can be used as names for a website, Facebook, X, Instagram and Snapchat, you have a sure winner.

There is a great online tool, called namechk.com which allows you to enter a name, and it instantly checks which handles are available across over 30 domains and 80 social media companies.

Now you have the tools, you have a few options for picking a name:

If it's an artist-led label – then you could use the artist's name as the label name:

- Use a doing word.
- Describe an experience or image.
- Take a word out of context.
- Make up a word.

This is where brainstorming can help.

There really is no shortcut to this; it's a process you have to go through.

A good tip: Look up different language translations of words that have meaning to you, for instance, Greek and Latin, as well as foreign words (Swahili is often a great choice); you might unearth a few good ideas.

And use thesaurus.com to get alternative ideas for your label name. Our 'Fake' record label we use for examples in our templates was found this way. 'Ersatz Records' literally means' fake records'.

Create a long list to choose from. Narrow it down. Once you have narrowed down your list of potential names, you need to test the best ones. Make sure the name:

- Sounds good over the phone.
- Won't be mispronounced or misspelt, which defeats the purpose.
- Conveys your style and brand.
- Is not taken (use discogs.com and namechk.com).
- Consider the acronym of the name. Action Syndicate Sounds becomes ASS.

When you think you have a name, sit on it for a couple of days and test it out with friends. Still comfortable with it? Lock it down.

There is no one place to register a record label name and claim it to be yours. Often people want to know what exactly makes you an 'official' record or music label. It's a combination of several elements all coming together that makes you an official record label.

- You have a public-facing brand, such as a website with the label's name.
- You have registered as a company trading under the label's name.
- You have commercially released music on major music platforms, e.g. Spotify, Apple Music, Amazon.

Releasing music is what Discogs uses as the basis to add you to its database.

You can register your label as a trademark that would give you further legal protection, but this isn't a priority when starting out. Focus on getting to your first ten record releases out first.

So, first things first, claim your public-facing brand by purchasing a website domain. You can use GoDaddy.com or 123-reg.co.uk or one.com and, at the time of writing, you can do this for just $1 on GoDaddy.

RECORD LABEL BACKBONE

The backbone of your record label business structure can be organised as a set of organised folders on your computer.

The best place to save all your folders and files is in the cloud. This way, they are all backed up automatically. Lose your computer? No problem.

The three main cloud drives are Dropbox, Google Drive or Microsoft OneDrive, and I recommend Dropbox.com as it gives the ability to easily share files with one click without having to set permissions, which makes it a winner. This is especially useful for sharing music files and artwork drafts with designers.

Dropbox gives 2GB of free data and 1TB on the annual plan. Google Drive gives you 15GB of free data and then has plans from 30GB and upwards.

You should always switch on two-factor authentication (2FA) for cloud drives, especially for sensitive folders. This adds an extra security layer, requiring both your password and a second verification step, like a code from your mobile device, to access your data.

Now you have a place to save, let's look at the key elements that make up a record label.

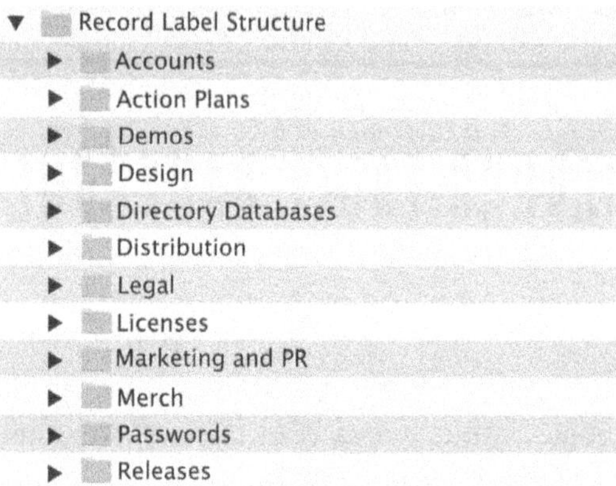

If, like many people, you struggle to stay organised online and end up with multiple folders that contain the same things, this will help keep everything organised.

Let's take a brief look at each folder.

Accounts: This is where you save invoices, receipts, and your royalty statements. Anything money related goes in here.

Action plans: Here is where you save your business plan, operating procedures, and job descriptions as you grow and hire people.

Content Media: For managing social media content, content calendars, and analytics reports for individual artists.

Demos: Keep music demos that your artists send to you in here, filed under each artist's name. As you grow, further subdivide this into the year of submission.

Design: This is where you keep essential design elements for the label, such as your fonts, icons, images, logos, and artwork release templates.

Directory Databases: In this folder, you store your database spreadsheets of contact information for important blogs, Spotify playlists, radio and DJ contacts, and music partners.

Distribution: Save your metadata, ISRC codes, and any specialist information you need to work with your chosen distributor here.

Legal: In this folder, organise your label's recording contracts, remix contracts, management contacts, GDPR policies and important company registration documents.

Licenses: In here, save any compilation requests and TV, film or game synchronisations you license your label's music too.

Marketing and PR: For each separate release, create a folder in here, e.g. RECORD001, to save all marketing-related assets such as press releases, social media banner artwork, and logos for each release. These folders are often shared with artists and agencies outside the label, so it's important to have them filed this way.

Merchandise: In here, save all your merchandise designs, customer information, and manufacturing details.

Passwords and Logins: Backup of your important passwords for social media accounts, website access, and distribution platform logins.

Releases: For each separate release, create a folder here, e.g. RECORD001, to save all in-house music information, such as the master WAV files, master artwork files, MP3s and press release drafts.

You might want to arrange your file structure slightly differently or add other folders relative to your record label, such as a live events folder, or management folder but this is an essential file structure for any indie record label to start with.

And if you want to save time, you can download a zip file with these folders already saved from the Book Resources tab on The Label Machine website.

BUSINESS PLAN

> "If you fail to plan, you are planning to fail" – Benjamin Franklin.

It's a cliché, but clichés exist for a reason, because they are true.

Running a successful record label is like running any other successful business, and first and foremost, you need a plan.

Every business I have started has begun with a plan. It doesn't need to be fifty pages worth of the minutiae of account details, but it is essential to write your goals for the first 12 months.

It's not just the final result of a finished business plan that is important; the process of creating a business plan is equally essential. It forces you to make realistic decisions on how you are going to move forward and make the label a success.

Once you have made these critical decisions and committed them to a document, any confusion or worry about what direction you need to go is removed. This will give you the confidence to move forward in a meaningful way, giving you the best possible chance of success.

Some distributors require a business plan before considering working with you. If you want to distribute your music with an established distributor such as Ingrooves, Believe Digital, or you want to put your music on a specialist music store such as Beatport, then you need to apply and get accepted by these distributors.

If you fail to show the distributor that you have a grasp on the business aspects of running a record label, you will get rejected, and you will fail at the first step.

In some countries, you need a business plan if you are opening a business bank account.

In short, writing a business plan is an essential step towards building a successful record label.

I would suggest before starting a label that you have at least three planned music releases you plan to release, with the first one ready to go.

By ready to go, I mean you have a finished single or EP of music that is fully mixed down, mastered and ready to go out to the public without any more changes. When you write your business plan, you will have these first three releases in mind.

Let's look at the main elements of a business plan and a brief description of each section.

TITLE PAGE

This includes your record label name, business address, email address and phone number.

SUMMARY

This is the section that will summarise the main objectives of your label. This section will actually be written last. After you have completed the rest of the document, you need to come back and summarise it into a short paragraph here.

Example 1:
Zonderling Records is an electronic record label based out of LA that aims to represent a genre of music heavily influenced by early rave, garage, jungle, and grime. We will produce limited edition runs of vinyl via vinylised.com, use interesting marketing ideas such as cassette mixtapes alongside traditional press and marketing channels.

Example 2:
420 Records is a new music record label focusing on building a brand that people can trust and turn to for the latest and greatest hip hop. Working to sell and distribute music and merchandise worldwide through stores such as Spotify, Apple Music, Amazon and Beatport.

Example 3:
Kudo Records is a new indie rock music record based in Seattle that is focused on signing the new wave of local live bands in the state. Our mission is to sell every band's music release with at least one merchandise t-shirt and support the live scene by running local stores at shows.

BUSINESS OVERVIEW

Introduction

Here you want to introduce the key people involved in the label and what experience, qualifications and training they might have, along with where you will be based and the future goals of the record label. For example:

Joe and Rich have been involved in dance music for a long time and have over four years of experience in music production and running music-related businesses. After releasing on various record labels in the past, the next logical step is to take their careers in the music business to the next level and start a record label. The label will be London based to begin with, but can be based out in LA within a few years of trading. Music will be the only product sold to begin with, but the record label will eventually be transformed into a brand big enough to sell clothing and other non-music related products.

Current position

This is a summary of where you are right now with your music plans. For example:

So far, Zonderling Records has the first release signed, a remix

EP of Joe and Rich's previous releases. Juke da Luke and Pressure Fresh have been singled out as potential first outside artist signings amongst other potentials such as Idle Kids and Origins of 90.

Growth plan

This is a summary explaining how you aim to grow your record label, and should include your financial goals. For example:

After releasing our first three EPs, we will expand into more releases from other artists, pulling remix favours to associate as many established acts to validate the label as possible. Using Joe and Rich's releases will help to attract an established audience to the label initially. After a year, we aim to be signing artists exclusively to the label and pulling in profit from the label's merchandise.

STRENGTHS, OPPORTUNITIES AND CORE VALUES

This is where you will list your strengths and opportunities as a record label. It allows you to create your unique selling point and critical success factors. If you have something unique that will ensure success, such as a link to a key industry contact, or opportunity, this is where you should list it. Your core values should answer questions such as:

- What is important to you as a label?
- Are you going to be pushing underground music, or working with more mainstream artists?
- Will you focus on signing original material or releasing cover songs?

Examples:

Strengths

- Understanding of the current music landscape via our DJing careers.
- Links to multiple artists with established fan bases.
- Advice and industry support via The Label Machine.

Opportunities

- Access to an industry database, press and music industry contacts.
- Access to other artists in the local area.

Core values

- Build a brand that people can trust and turn to for good quality music.
- Have the confidence to push new music as opposed to just following recent trends.
- Build on personal relationships within the music industry to create a successful brand that people want to be associated with.

BUSINESS STRATEGY

Outline your business strategy for the first five years. These are your tangible goals. How many releases do you aim to have? Do you want to sign new artists? When do you aim to break even on the revenue?

As a bare minimum, your goals should include releasing at

least three singles or EPs in your first year if you are a DJ or band releasing only your own music and six to eight records if your aim is signing outside artists. I would also aim to be breaking even from 18 months of your first release, so the label is supporting itself financially.

The three to five-year goals are what you will do if you achieve your one to two-years goals. These goals are more flexible and are likely to change but ensure you set goals of where you intend to go.

For example:

One to two years

- Have a steady flow of quality releases, building the label's reputation.
- Discover and sign at least two exclusive acts to the label.
- Break-even on all costs.

Three to five years

- Have a full roster of exclusive artists releasing under Zonderling Records.
- At least three Beatport number ones within their relative categories.
- Host small stages at festivals worldwide.
- Have office space in either London, Bristol or LA with three or more staff members.
- If streaming takes off in Asia, to capitalise on the next big territory boom.

DISTRIBUTION AND LABEL PRODUCTS

This section describes what your company sells, and how you will distribute your music.

Distribution channels

Who will you distribute your music through? Will you sell directly to fans at the start or later?

Example:

Distribute music to all major stores (Apple Music, Spotify, Apple Music, Deezer, Amazon and Google Play) via the DistroKid distribution platform.

You can also consider including the following Events and Merchandising sections if you are already established in your local area or in the music business as a whole. If not, you can move on to the next section.

Events (optional)

If you are doing events, who will run them, and how will they be promoted?

Example:

Label events will be arranged with our contact Zeal Promotions throughout North America, focusing on our home city Miami. Events will be promoted through local and national media coverage via 3rd Eye PR.

Merchandising (optional)

If you are doing merchandising, who will be responsible? Where will you sell and manufacture your merchandise? What prices will you use?

Example:

Abbie Street will organise and implement the merchandise for the label. It will be hosted on Shopify, and manufacturing will be carried out by a print-to-order manufacturer based in Miami.

LABEL MANAGEMENT AND OPERATIONS

This is where you list who will manage the label and any other team members you will have. You can also list any key partners you will use, such as The Label Machine, merchandise companies or management companies. For example:

Label Management Team

Joe Stone – Label Manager

- Responsible for A&R, signing and managing new artists.
- Managing the music distribution and royalties.
- Administrating and registering the catalogue.

Marlon Fever – Marketing Manager

- Responsible for online marketing and PR activities for releases.
- Overseeing the artwork and marketing asset creations.

Abbie Street – Merchandise Manager

- Organising and implementing label merchandise.
- Maintaining the Shopify website.
- Fulfilling the manufacturing and shipping.

MARKETING

What are your marketing goals, objectives, targets and promotional activities for the label? You will want to answer these questions in the sections below.

Goals and objectives

Describe your goals and objectives around the marketing: list the campaigns and plans you have in place and your future strategies.

Example:

- Research blogs and press publications that support our genre of music to create label brand recognition.
- Develop innovative marketing plans that utilise chatbots and other cutting edge technologies to build an audience.
- Increase sales through paid social media campaigns and PR strategies.
- Grow fanbase using Spotify playlist management.
- Increase direct-to-fan fanbase focusing on our email list growth.
- Increase awareness of artists and the label with third party revenue streams such as film, TV and game sync deals.

Target Market

Here is where you can clearly define your target market. It is crucial to put the music genre you will release, locations, and age group as a minimum.

Example:

We aim to sell to all audiences, but with an approach that focuses on appealing to the up-and-coming bass music markets such as the US and a core demographic of end users between the age of 14 and 30.

Advertising and promotion activities

Describe what advertising platforms you will use to promote the label and the releases. You might want to list creative ideas to get the brand out there, any PR companies you might use for your first release, and which social media platforms you will promote on.

Example:

- Using physical assets such as vinyl and cassette mixtapes, we will create a rich online experience based on real-life products, which we believe is missing from many digital labels today.
- We will use DJ promotion service The 6th Degree to garner maximum DJ support from the industry.
- We will run Instagram promoted stories and sponsored Facebook posts to create an awareness of new releases to fans of similar genres.

FINANCIAL BUDGETS AND FORECAST

This is the section where you can provide a financial budget and forecasts summary, such as:

- Startup label expenses
- Release expenses
- Optional expenses
- Cashflow forecast
- Optional revenue streams
- Profit and loss projection

You would create this in a spreadsheet and copy the summary into the business plan. For example:

Total Sales from Royalties	$11,940.00
Merch Sales	$930.00
Events Sales	$1,500.00
Gross Profit	$14,370.00

Total Expenses for Record Label Startup	$870.00
Total of Essential Costs for 1st Release	$949.00
Total of Essential Costs for 2nd Release	$699.00
Total of Essential Costs for 3rd Release	$699.00
Total of Essential Costs for 4th Release	$699.00
Total of Artists Royalties (50%)	$3,170.00
Total Expenses	$7,086.00

Net Profit	$7,284.00

WRITING YOUR OWN BUSINESS PLAN

It can be daunting writing your first business plan. But you have to remember that what you write is not set in stone forever. As your label progresses, your business plan will change too, and it should. It is meant as a reference document that you can use to show others that you have a plan and well-thought-out goals, and you should review it each year.

There are business plan templates with pre-filled examples to use, which you can access from the Book Resources tab on The Label Machine website.

LABEL BRANDING

All the successful labels I have worked with have had a strong brand identity. Stepping back and looking at any project, even outside the music industry, branding has a significant impact on its success. Well-marketed products, including music, films and books, can be pretty mediocre but will still sell well if the branding is on point.

Your brand will define you and your label; it will be how your audience will identify with you and recognise your label and determine how you communicate your core messages to the world in general.

Branding is a creative process, so be careful not to overthink it and end up with contrived ideas. If you have a natural knack for your own branding, and know who you want to connect with, then go with your gut instinct, even if this goes against any market research.

STARTING OUT

When you start out, it can be challenging to identify your brand or stand out and create a niche.

The good news is that you don't need to stand out! In fact, it helps to do the opposite. You want to find an existing niche or genre and fit in, so an existing fan base can connect with you.

Once established, you can start introducing your own style.

I'm not saying this is the only way; if you already have a clear, unique vision of your brand that you believe in, go with it, but if you don't, this is a sure-fire way of creating something that works.

And if you're worried about having a copycat brand, don't be. There are so many elements that come together to make up a label's brand, such as the name of your record label, the logo, images you use. Unless you carbon copy someone else's label – and by that, I mean using a similar logo, imagery and name – you'll always end up with a unique brand. It's tough to be an exact copy.

'Good artists copy, great artists steal'

Believe me, it's a great idea to use other people as an inspiration to create your brand. As you develop, your fan base grows, and your confidence increases, your own style will begin to grow into something unique. But when starting out, look at what already works and what fans connect with.

And some artists, whilst looking like they don't care about 'uncool' or 'corporate' marketing stuff, and look like they are living a crazy, edgy lifestyle, are actually super planning marketing artists who put a lot of thought into what they are doing.

Kurt Cobain from the 90s grunge band Nirvana was notorious for looking like he was wasted most of the time and having a don't-give-a-fuck-about-anything attitude.

However, after he died, his journals were discovered, revealing drawings, ideas and plans for the band's t-shirts, poster ideas, and notes to other similar bands.

The publisher Jim Barber said the writings constituted "a manual about how to be a rock star." He was essentially writing down the band's branding and marketing plans. Turns out Kurt Cobain did actually care and was very focused on Nirvana's brand identity.

ESTABLISHED ARTIST

If you're an artist with an established brand and tone of voice, this will be an excellent place to start the branding for your record label.

Many labels usually have a label head who is already a successful artist leading the label's brand. Steve Aoki has Dim Mak, Aftermath Entertainment has Dr Dre, Mad Decent has Diplo, Third Man Records has Jack White, mau5trap has deadmau5. The list goes on.

If this is the case with your record label, the branding can be an extension of what you already do.

BEYOND VISUAL IDENTITY

Whilst many artists focus solely on logos and colour schemes, effective branding extends far beyond visual elements. Branding forms the foundation of your music career and plays a crucial role in the 360° Music System which we'll explore in later chapters.

People don't fundamentally connect with brands, they connect with people. Across platforms like TikTok, YouTube Shorts and Instagram Reels, the most compelling content features human stories and authentic interactions. This human element makes content stick and branding stand out. It might be an artist discussing their creative process, a label founder sharing marketing approaches, or team members breaking down promotion strategies.

For real fan growth and genuine success, your brand must be personified. There needs to be a face representing it, whether that's you as the artist, or you as a label manager ensuring that your signed artists are visible, vocal and focused on storytelling.

THE THREE PILLARS OF MUSIC BRANDING

To develop a brand that resonates with audiences and supports your content strategy, focus on these three pillars:

1. Understand Who You Are

If a stranger in an elevator at a music conference asked what your label represents or who you are as an artist, could you reply with clarity? Most people stumble through vague descriptions, but clarity about your brand identity enables everything else.

Create a brand identity document by following these practical steps:

- Create a folder called "Brand Ideas" with a "Mood Board" document
- Identify 8-10 artists or labels similar to your style (limit major artists to just two)
- Research their social profiles, websites and artwork, taking screenshots of elements that resonate
- Search Instagram hashtags like #artists #artwork #logos for additional inspiration
- Look for patterns in what appeals to you: colours, styles, photography versus graphics

This mood board becomes invaluable when working with designers and helps establish your visual direction.

2. Understand How Your Brand Is Perceived

Consistency builds trust. Your brand needs to be cohesive across all platforms, from visual elements to communication style to release schedules. Think of it like a Netflix series: would you invest time in watching if only one episode existed with no schedule for future releases?

Your brand comprises three core components:

- **Identity**: Define yourself as a Leader, Adventurer, Educator/Reporter, or Reluctant Hero
- **Story**: Highlight what makes you unique, both within and outside music
- **Tone**: Decide how to convey messaging: professional, funny, entertaining, or factual

Setting up your brand correctly eliminates uncertainty around content creation and provides clear direction for style, pillars and tone. This clarity streamlines the creative process, making content creation both faster and more effective.

3. Understand Your Audience

Knowing who will connect with your music enables targeted promotion. Create an "Audience Profile" document answering:

Basic Demographics:

- Age range of typical listeners
- Top five countries where they're located
- Cities with existing fanbases (check Spotify for Artists if available)

Digital Behaviour:

- Which Spotify playlists they follow
- Instagram accounts they engage with
- YouTube channels they subscribe to
- TikTok creators they follow
- Primary social media platform they use

Deeper Insights:

- How they perceive themselves
- How they want others to perceive them
- Core beliefs and worldview
- Long-term ambitions and goals

Research Tools:

Google: Search for labels or artist names and look at the "People also search for" section on the right-hand side to discover related artists.

- Music-map.com: Input the name of an artist to find suggestions of similar musicians.
- Last.fm: Go to an artist's page and explore the "Similar Artists" section for further leads.
- Songkick or Bandsintown: These tools help track interest in live performances and see where your audience may attend concerts or events. It's also useful to understand which cities have active fanbases for live gigs.
- Chartmetric or Soundcharts: These platforms provide audience heatmaps, playlist adds, and deeper analytics about geographic trends. This data can help artists understand where their listeners are located and which platforms they are engaging with.
- Reddit: Use subreddits to explore communities centred around similar artists or genres. These can provide valuable insights into niche audience interests, behaviours, and trends.
- TikTok Creator Marketplace: This tool allows you to identify TikTok influencers who align with your brand, offering opportunities for collaboration and targeted fan engagement.
- Instagram Insights and Meta Ads Manager: These tools can give you detailed data about where your followers are based and what content they engage with most. Geo-targeted ads

can be especially useful for promoting live gigs or releases in specific locations.

This audience understanding directly informs your content strategy. When you know who you're speaking to and where they spend time online, you can create content pillars that genuinely resonate.

CONNECTING BRAND TO CONTENT

Your brand identity directly shapes your content pillars. Once you've established who you are, how you want to be perceived, and who your audience is, you can create consistent content themes that align with both your identity and your audience's interests.

For artists, these might include behind-the-scenes creative process videos, personal stories that reveal your journey, or content showcasing your non-musical interests that help fans connect with you as a person.

For labels, these might include artist development stories, marketing approaches, business insights, or thought leadership on industry trends.

The most successful music brands understand this critical truth: authenticity creates connection. When fans feel they know the people behind the music, loyalty develops naturally. This human-centred approach to branding creates the foundation for everything else in your music career, from content creation to monetisation strategies.

We will cover this in more detail in the forthcoming marketing chapters.

RETHINKING AUDIENCE BUILDING STRATEGY

In recent years, because streaming platforms allow labels and artists to distribute globally, it often creates new logistical and financial challenges. Early career artists may struggle to engage with fans spread across different regions, particularly when it comes to organizing live events, or shipping merchandise, both major revenue sources. That is why thinking about creating a local scene is crucial for long term growth.

By starting with a strong local base, it allows a label's artist to ensure steady attendance at live performances, whilst fostering deeper community ties through resonant local content. Artists can collaborate more effectively with nearby talent, venues and labels, and optimise marketing spend through geographically concentrated campaigns.

While global reach is advantageous, labels should also run in parallel a localized strategy in their hometown city that can offer more sustainable growth and stronger fan connections, ensuring a reliable base for live performances and community support.

DESIGN TOOLS AND ASSETS

When it comes to running a record label, you need to create a lot of artwork for the music and other digital assets to promote the music online.

You also need to create digital assets for the record label itself, such as a logo, website, and social media banners.

And once you have all these digital assets, you need to edit and change them to post them on the various social media profiles.

You can work with a designer (which I always recommend if you can afford it). However, even if you have a designer, sometimes they are not available, and they can get expensive when you just need to do some basic editing.

You might already have a good eye for what you want the label to look like and will create your artwork yourself.

Quickly creating graphics, a single cover, or editing photos is the second most valuable skill after making music. Loads of artists I know are visual artists, they kind of go hand in hand when it comes to creativity!

And, of course, two other big reasons are that you want to save time and money, so it's helpful to have your own arsenal of tools and assets at your disposal.

There are many good reasons to have your own design tools and resources for your record label.

WHAT WILL YOU BE CREATING?

Here is an essential list of the types of digital assets you'll be creating for your record label:

- Logo.
- Facebook banner & profile image
- Twitter/X banner & profile image
- Instagram profile image
- YouTube banner & profile image
- TikTok profile image
- SoundCloud banner & profile image
- LinkedIn banner & profile image
- Spotify Music header & profile image
- Apple Music header & profile image
- Email header /footer image.
- Website header & banner image
- Website Favicon
- Album/Song artwork templates

And then, there are the digital assets you need to create for each music release. You typically use the same artwork layout, but each platform needs to be edited in different sizes.

Release artwork for distribution in hi-resolution format 3000 x 3000 pixels at 72 dpi (dots per inch).

Facebook Artwork

- Release Date Banner: A banner announcing the release date, optimized for Facebook's banner size.
- Out Now Banner: To notify followers once the release is live.

Twitter/X Artwork

- Release Date Banner: Banner-sized for Twitter/X.
- Out Now Banner: Designed specifically for Twitter/X post dimensions.

YouTube Artwork

- Release Date Banner: Used for YouTube's cover art or as part of video content (e.g., thumbnails).
- Out Now Banner: Optimized for YouTube channel or video banners.

SoundCloud Artwork

- Release Date Banner: Specifically sized for SoundCloud banners.
- Out Now Banner: To notify followers about the new release on SoundCloud.

Instagram Artwork

- Release Date Square: Image format suitable for Instagram posts (1080 x 1080 pixels).
- Out Now Square: Optimized square image for Instagram posts and carousel format.

Instagram Stories

- Release Date Story: Vertical artwork for Instagram Stories (1080 x 1920 pixels).
- Out Now Story: Optimized for Instagram Story announcements.

Email Artwork

- Out Now Banner: Email header or banner image for your mailing list campaigns to announce the release.

Video Assets

With the growing popularity of video content, you also need to create the following video assets to maximize engagement across platforms:

Teaser Trailers

Short samples of the track (e.g., 15-30 seconds) featuring visuals. These trailers should be edited in different formats for each platform:

- Square: For Instagram and Facebook feeds (1080 x 1080 pixels).
- Banner: For YouTube and Facebook banners (2560 x 1440 pixels).
- Vertical: For mobile-first platforms like Instagram Stories and TikTok (1080 x 1920 pixels).

Full-Length Music Videos

- A complete music video for the release. This could be a traditional production or a visualizer, where abstract visuals are synced to the music. This video can be repurposed across platforms like YouTube, Facebook, and Instagram TV.

Lyric Videos

- A video featuring the song's lyrics as visual elements. These are relatively easy to produce but can significantly boost engagement on platforms like YouTube.

Behind-the-Scenes Videos

- Day in the Life: Showcase a behind-the-scenes look at the band's daily routine, music writing sessions, or rehearsals.
- Studio Footage: Clips of recording sessions, production work, and creative processes in the studio.

Live Performance Videos

- Bands or solo artists performing their music live. Consider creating separate videos for YouTube, Instagram TV, or even YouTube Shorts.

Production Tip Videos (for DJ/Producers)

- Screen Capture Videos: Using screen capture software, producers can create content where they share production techniques, breakdowns of tracks, or sound design tips. These are particularly effective for engaging with fans who are also musicians or aspiring producers.

Animated Artwork Videos

- Transforming your static album artwork into subtle animations or loops can add a dynamic element to video teasers, ideal for Spotify Canvas (looping visuals in Spotify).

Promotional Tools

- Countdown Timers: Use countdowns on platforms like Instagram Stories to create excitement for the release.
- Polls and Q&A Sessions: Utilize Instagram Stories to engage with your audience before and after the release. Questions about the track or polls on favourite songs can boost fan interaction.
- Pre-save Campaigns: Graphics for pre-save links to Spotify, Apple Music, or other platforms, which can be shared via all social media platforms and email.

How to Use the Above

You want to create a minimum marketing package for your music releases to ensure consistency with your fans, streamline your process for each release, and provide clear offerings for your artists. This approach makes it easier to hire freelance designers or multimedia creators to produce content, and allows you to utilize templates for quickly generating material. For bigger releases, you can build on the minimum package—such as adding special merchandise bundles—but at its core, this system creates a consistent brand that will be easily recognized.

As you can see, once you have some artwork designed, there can be a lot of editing of the artwork, and being able to quickly do this yourself is a valuable skill to learn.

TOOLS AND RESOURCES

There are two main things you need to create all these assets.

- Access to royalty-free images and designs that you use as your base elements to create your digital assets.

- Applications to edit your style's assets.

Royalty-Free Assets

When we say royalty-free, we mean you can use the designs and images for any project and don't have to pay the original artist who created them a royalty fee or credit them when you use the artwork.

We use a selection of the following platforms to access thousands of images royalty-free. There are two types of royalty-free image: those that are completely free to access and use, and those that are acquired by one-off payments or through a subscription service. The paid versions have a wider range of higher-quality images you can use.

Websites that offer free images:

PixaBay (pixabay.com) & Pexels (pexels.com)
Excellent for royalty-free photos and videos.

Mixkit (mixkit.co/vertical-videos)
Vertical videos that are really great quality.

Websites that offer images for a fee/subscription:

Shutterstock (shutterstock.com)
Shutterstock is good as you can pre-buy five quality professional images for $29 and use them any time. You can browse and save your favourite ones to come back and buy them when you need them.

Envato Elements (elements.envato.com)
Envato Elements is excellent as they have thousands of templates you can edit in Adobe and Microsoft's popular app formats. They cover images, videos, Instagram story templates so you can create super professional videos. You get unlimited downloads for $16.50 a month.

POND5 (pond5.com)
This has thousands of editorial assets, which are ideal for using in teaser trailer videos. The quality is great, and if you choose SD format, they are a fraction of the cost of other video stock websites.

APPS

Once you have all of these assets, you will need to use a design application to edit them for your own record label assets. For static images, Photoshop and Canva are the two of the most popular apps for creating artwork. For video editing, CapCut is beginner-friendly and free. Learning how to use these apps is super useful, and they are easy to master if you search for YouTube tutorials on the basics.

Canva (canva.com) A free, user-friendly platform offering numerous social media templates and sizes. Supports personal asset uploads, making it versatile for beginners and intermediate designers seeking efficiency.

Photoshop (adobe.com) The industry standard for professional design with comprehensive capabilities and built-in tutorials ($10/month). While requiring a steeper learning curve, it offers unparalleled creative control for serious designers.

Affinity (affinity.serif.com) A cost-effective Photoshop alternative offering advanced features beyond Canva but less complexity than Photoshop. Notable for its one-time purchase model rather than subscription.

Adobe Creative Cloud Free Tools (adobe.com) Adobe's ecosystem hosting professional applications including a free Starter version of Adobe Express for content creation and editing. Mobile users can access Adobe Fresco for drawing on iPhone at no cost.

CapCut (capcut.com) A powerful video editing application offering intuitive tools for content creators. Features include AI-powered editing, extensive effects library, and cross-platform functionality. Particularly valuable for social media content with its user-friendly interface and professional-grade output capabilities. Also runs on mobile devices.

AI Design Tools

AI-powered design tools have democratized the creation process, allowing anyone to generate high-quality visuals with simple text prompts or basic inputs. These tools can help you conceptualize ideas, create variations of designs, or even produce finished assets ready for your marketing campaigns.

Midjourney (midjourney.com)
Create stunning artwork and visuals through text prompts. Perfect for album covers, promotional materials, and unique brand aesthetics. Available through Discord with limited free options and subscription tiers.

Leonardo.AI (leonardo.ai)
Specialized in creating digital art and illustrations with extensive style controls. Excellent for developing consistent visual brand identities across multiple releases.

Runway (runwayml.com)
Goes beyond static images with video generation and editing capabilities. Perfect for creating short promotional clips and visual teasers without video editing experience.

TAKE ACTION

Open your browser and create a folder in your bookmarks section called Design Tools. Add the resource links listed here to this bookmark folder for easy access.

- Sign up for a Canva account.
- Sign up for a free Envato Elements account.
- Sign up for a free Adobe Creative Cloud account.
- Sign up for a free Open AI Account

Open your mobile device and find and download on the app store

- Adobe Express
- Chat GPT (for AI Images)
- Spark Video.

Once you have completed this, you'll have unlimited access to resources and tools to quickly create endless digital assets.

This makes creating designs super easy. Even if you hire someone else to create your artwork, these tools allow you to create mockups to show designers what you want and also to edit any assets a designer sends, should you need to.

The list of design tools and resources changes fast, so for the latest list and links, visit the Book Resources tab on The Label Machine website.

LOGO

When thinking about your logo's design, remember that you're usually looking for a name and symbol. Sometimes it's the same thing, but symbols can be good for avatars, social media profile pics and merchandise.

Begin with black-on-white designs to ensure versatility across artwork, merchandise, and digital platforms. This approach guarantees effective translation when colours are added later.

For final deliverables, secure multiple formats (.eps, .png, and .pdf) from your designer, typically provided in a compressed file upon completion.

Consider these four options for logo design, which also apply to single and album artwork:

OPTION 1: HIRE A PROFESSIONAL DESIGNER

Professional freelancers with experience designing for established artists and labels typically charge upwards of £700/$1000. Less established designers cost around £350/$500, but always verify their portfolio quality and have detailed discussions about your vision. Clear briefs lead to better outcomes and fewer revisions.

The typical process includes:

- Providing logos of brands you admire (your brief)
- Receiving a range of initial concepts
- Selecting one for refinement
- Getting 2-3 revisions
- Receiving final designs in standard formats

OPTION 2: POST YOUR DESIGN REQUEST ON A FREELANCE WEBSITE

Freelancing platforms allow you to receive multiple proposals and mockups:

- fiverr.com
- freelancer.com
- designcrowd.com
- 99designs.com

These sites let you post design requirements or run design competitions where multiple artists submit concepts. Many offer voting polls for feedback collection. The Label Machine logo was designed through DesignCrowd for approximately £120/$170.

OPTION 3: USE AN ONLINE LOGO MAKER

This budget-friendly option works well if you have a good design sense. Sophisticated platforms include:

- logojoy.com
- freelogodesign.org
- canva.com

Simply enter your label name, select preferred logo styles, and customize generated options. High-resolution downloads cost around £35/$50.

OPTION 4: LEVERAGE AI DESIGN TOOLS

AI-powered platforms have revolutionized the accessibility of professional-quality design. These tools offer a balance of customization, speed, and affordability:

- midjourney.com
- leonardo.ai
- runway.ml

The process typically involves:

- Crafting detailed text prompts describing your desired logo aesthetics
- Generating multiple variations based on your descriptions
- Refining prompts to achieve more precise results
- Downloading high-resolution versions for around £10-30/$15-40

While AI tools excel at creating unique visual concepts quickly, they sometimes require post-processing in design software to perfect typography or add finishing touches. Many independent artists have successfully created distinctive branding using AI tools as their starting point, especially for experimental or digital-first music projects.

Consider adding a logo animation for promotional videos (like YouTube intros). Quality animations cost approximately £175/$250, with skilled animators available on freelancer.com and fiverr.com.

WEBSITE

Your website can range from a simple logo page with social media links to a comprehensive platform featuring an integrated shop, chatbots and blog. Five main options exist when establishing your web presence.

OPTION 1: WEBSITE-IN-A-BOX

Services like Squarespace, Wix, Weebly, GoDaddy and our own Marketing Machine software offer point-and-click website building with minimal technical knowledge required. While customisation options are somewhat limited, this rarely poses problems for straightforward label sites.

These platforms conveniently bundle domain registration (e.g., recordlabel.com) with annual hosting services, streamlining the entire process.

OPTION 2: WORDPRESS

WordPress with a theme (like The Label Machine's Thrive Themes implementation) offers greater flexibility and dynamism through thousands of available plugins.

This option requires purchasing your domain separately and necessitates basic CSS and HTML knowledge for maintenance. Numerous YouTube tutorials can guide you through the process, or you can engage WordPress specialists from freelancer platforms when needed.

OPTION 3: AGENCY

Hiring an agency or freelancer to build a bespoke website represents the most expensive option, generally unnecessary for new labels given the alternatives available.

If pursuing this route when more established, insist on WordPress-based development to retain flexibility for changing developers or making basic edits yourself. Be cautious of proprietary code that could lock you into a specific designer.

OPTION 4: STORE WEBSITE

E-commerce-focused platforms like Shopify provide integrated selling solutions ideal for labels offering physical merchandise. Their all-in-one approach includes monthly subscriptions, domain registration, and numerous purchasable themes.

Alternatively, Bandcamp allows custom domains whilst handling backend delivery. This platform facilitates direct-to-fan music and merchandise sales, taking 15% commission.

OPTION 5: AI WEBSITE BUILDERS

The emergence of AI-powered website builders can generate complete websites from simple text prompts.

Platforms like like Lovable and Bolt employ sophisticated algorithms to create tailored websites based on your specific requirements. Simply describe your record label's aesthetic, functionality needs and content priorities, and these systems will generate a fully-formed website structure.

However, be mindful that AI-generated sites may require fine-tuning to fully capture your label's unique character. Consider these platforms as excellent starting points that provide professional foundations which you can subsequently personalise.

Real-World Examples:

Never Say Die initially used one.com with a built-in template before transitioning to a freelancer-built custom site years later.

Get Hype Records began with Squarespace before migrating to Shopify's versatile Supply Template when adding merchandise.

Which Option?

Solo entrepreneurs with limited technical inclination should choose website-in-a-box solutions. Those comfortable with technology or with budget for technical assistance will benefit from WordPress's flexibility.

For new labels, prioritise simplicity:

- Logo placement at top
- Music section (embedded SoundCloud/Spotify playlist)
- About section
- Social media links
- Artist page links
- Contact information

A custom domain enables professional email addresses like info@recordlabelname.com, hello@recordlabelname.com, or weare@recordlabelname.com, enhancing your professional image.

SOCIAL MEDIA HANDLES

Once you have a record label name, you need to register to each of the leading social media channels.

Essential

- Facebook
- Instagram
- Youtube
- TikTok
- X/Twitter
- Bluesky

- SoundCloud
- LinkedIn

Optional

- Snapchat
- Pinterest

It's worth registering the options; even if you don't post content, it's better to own them now. The primary aim is to get a social media handle that is the same across every platform. By that, I mean everything that follows the / for each platform is the same.

To do that, use namechk.com. This tool allows you to enter a name, and it automatically detects if it is being used already across 80 different media channels.

Ideally, you pick a handle that is available on all platforms. If your name is taken or is only available on some platforms, then try the following variations:

- Acronym of the label name.
- Label name missing out the vowels.
- Replacing letters with numbers, e.g. 5 for a S.
- Adding your country, e.g. UK/US/AU/FR.
- Adding RECS, INC, HQ, MEDIA, ENT at the end.
- Prefixing with WEARE, THISIS, REAL, THEREAL.

When registering each platform and claiming each name, it's helpful to use your generic record label contact email address, e.g. info@recordlabelname.com and not your personal email address, so you can share it with team members who may need to access it as you grow your record label.

Claiming each channel does not mean you are committing to posting on each channel every day, but you need to make sure your fans can find you on all media platforms and that there are instructions on where they can interact with you. For instance, you might not use Twitter as a channel, but claim the page, put your label details on the profile, and pin a tweet to the top, pointing towards where you post online regularly, such as Instagram.

DISTRIBUTION

There are three steps to setting up your distribution.

1. Decide what you need as an artist and/or record label.
2. Apply for an account with a distributor based on your needs.
3. Upload your first release to the platform.

Who to choose for distribution?

This makes up an essential part of your record label set-up, so it's important to review the different options available to you. There is no ultimate distributor as it depends on your label goals. You need to consider the following questions.

- What style and genre of music are you releasing?
- Are you releasing just your own music, or will you be signing multiple artists to your label?
- Will you be releasing cover songs?
- Will the artists you sign be mostly new artist projects, or are they artists with established careers?

Depending on your answers will help you decide on the best distributor for you. An excellent place to start is to use the distribution picker tool at thelabelmachine.com/distribution-picker. Just answer a few questions, and we will give you our recommendation.

The following chapter will give a detailed breakdown of the different distribution companies to get more of an idea of who will be suitable for you.

Once you have decided, you need to apply for an account that will be different for each company. If you are using a self-distribution platform, there is no application process; you just need a credit card and your music to upload.

If you apply to one of the companies listed as a serviced distributor in the next chapter, you will need to follow their application process. Ensure you have a solid business plan and at least three music releases already lined up before applying to these distributors. They can take a few weeks to get back to you, so make sure you give it plenty of time and not apply two weeks before you want to release your music.

If you have an industry contact at one of these distributors, ask for an introduction, as a personal recommendation will increase your chances of a successful application.

Once you have an account with your distributor, you'll need to follow the instructions for submitting your music. Each platform is different, but most of them have tutorials walking through the necessary steps.

CHANGING DISTRIBUTORS

Ideally, most labels will want to work with one of the serviced distributors. However, as these distributors are looking to work with established artists or managers with a track record, if you are starting out, it can be challenging to have a successful application to work with them straight away.

A great strategy is to go for self-distribution via a platform such as Distrokid, and then after you have put out three or four releases, approach one of the serviced distributors and show them you have a track record. Backed with a solid business plan and evidence of successfully releasing music, you will have an easier time getting a successful application and changing your distributor.

This is the strategy that many Label Machine members have used to work with serviced distributors.

REAL-WORLD EXAMPLES

Never Say Die Records

When we started Never Say Die, we had a solid first release and secured a Beatport Label account directly through music industry connections. Beatport was essential for our electronic music releases, but we still needed distribution to other platforms like Apple Music, Spotify and Amazon.

After researching available options, we chose Tunecore at £50 per year for each release (with discounts for multi-year purchases), allowing us to keep 100% of royalties. While £50 annually per release might seem costly at scale (£1,000+ for 20+ releases), consider our perspective:

We had several tracks generating approximately £80,000 annually at their peak. Had we used a traditional distributor taking 15%, that would have cost us £12,000. The £1,000 yearly investment suddenly seemed quite reasonable!

As our reputation grew, distribution companies approached us, but none could match our effective 2% rate with Tunecore compared to their minimum 15% fee. We maintained our Tunecore arrangement alongside our direct Beatport deal.

After four years, we migrated to Label Engine. Why? Our spreadsheet-based royalty accounting became unwieldy beyond our tenth release, particularly with electronic music's complex remix splits on EPs. DJ Lazy Rich's Label Engine platform specialised in record label accounting, simplifying the process through templates that managed release sales division between label, artists and remixers, calculating biannual payment obligations.

Years later, Label Engine introduced direct distribution capabilities. After negotiating favourable terms, we consolidated all our distribution through their platform.

No Tomorrow Recordings / Disciple Recordings

For No Tomorrow Recordings and Disciple Recordings, we opted for larger traditional indie distributors: Ingrooves and Believe Digital, respectively. We wanted to evaluate whether their 15% commission delivered meaningful service advantages.

These distributors assign a dedicated representative to oversee your label, answering questions and resolving distribution issues. They offer additional services like marketing support and YouTube monetisation, valuable resources for new labels.

Your representative typically works with an internal team communicating directly with major platforms (like Beatport). They submit your press releases, potentially increasing your chances for playlist features and genre banner placements.

We discovered that regular communication with our distributor representatives, sharing upcoming releases and artist signings, significantly increased the value and support we received. However, if you merely upload music and collect royalties without utilising these additional services, the difference between these distributors and self-release options diminishes considerably.

Get Hype Records

For Get Hype Records, we partnered with Triple V in the Netherlands. They offered a favourable distribution percentage and a P&D (pressing and distribution) deal for vinyl, advancing manufacturing costs. As Triple V distributes numerous top drum & bass labels, and Get Hype Records focuses primarily on drum & bass, this partnership made strategic sense.

Deathstar Cult

Deathstar Cult initially used Distrokid as they were a young label with early-career artists. However, they sought a service-oriented distributor with strong networks in India and China for long-term growth. After successfully releasing their fourth project through Distrokid, they applied to Horus Music distribution. Upon acceptance, they began distributing through Horus, benefiting from enhanced marketing support and specialised contacts in Indian and Chinese territories.

DISTRIBUTOR COMPANIES

Below is a list of the most popular music distributors. This is not an exhaustive list of every distributor, just a few options to get you started including our own distribution platform; we keep an updated list on the Book Resources tab on The Label Machine Website, so please check for the latest listings. The percentage and fees listed are correct at the time of writing.

SELF DISTRIBUTION COMPANIES

Amuse

A new and interesting distribution start-up that is using data analysis to find winning artists. There are zero fees or commissions as they use the data as a type of A&R to select artists doing well to offer a label deal.

- App-only (no desktop/web version).
- 0% commission of royalties.
- No distribution fees or $60 for 'Pro'

- Investment backed – beware of long term viability.
- Will offer a 50/50 upstream label deal on artists doing well.
- No admin publishing to collect songwriter royalties.
- No distribution to China.

CD Baby

Very established and was the first self-distribution company that allowed anyone to distribute to iTunes. They are leading the way in covering all royalty channels for artists. I have used them myself for music compilations as they have a very streamlined service.

- Artist focused.
- 9% commission of royalties.
- $5-$20 one-time distribution fees for UPC codes.
- Physical distribution.
- Publishing partner with Songtrust to collect songwriter royalties.
- Excellent sales/streaming reports.

DistroKid

A tech-driven, forward-thinking, slick, no-frills company. I use them for most digital releases, and you use just one page to distribute your album or single. In the last five years, DistroKid has gone one to be in the top 20 distributors of the world. They also offer payment splitting. However, each artist or remixer needs to sign-up for a $19/year account. They are (at time of writing) Spotify's officially preferred distributor for artists too.

- Artist and label focused.
- 0% commission of royalties.
- A yearly fee for unlimited songs.
- Option for automatic payment splitting between artists.
- No admin publishing to collect songwriter royalties.
- Option for Beatport distribution by application.

Ditto Music

UK based company that as well as offering distribution, has a range of upsell services such as radio pitching for your releases. They have popular inhouse owned music playlists to feature your music if it fits.

- Artist and label focused.
- 0% commission of royalties.
- Distribution fees that increase with the number of artists. (10 artists $119 /year)
- No payment splitting between artists.
- No in-house admin publishing to collect songwriter royalties.

Fresh Tunes

An international company with offices in Moscow, Dubai and London. They offer extra services like mastering and marketing, which is how they make their money. They offer language support for Spanish, Portuguese and Russian.

- Artist focused.
- 0% commission of royalties.
- No distribution fees.

- Can have music distributed in 24 hours.
- Investment backed – long term beware.

Horus Music

I had the pleasure of being on a UK music trade mission to India with the CEO of Horus music a few years ago as they wanted to expand into Asia and China. And the trip has clearly paid off, as they have got significant penetration in these growing markets. They also offer in-house marketing and PR services to label accounts.

- Label and artist focused.
- 20% commission of royalties or 0% for a fee.
- Distributes to China.
- Option for automatic payment splitting between artists.
- In-house playlist pluggers available (for a fee).
- Admin publishing to collect songwriter royalties.

LANDR

These guys were first known as an auto mastering service that actually delivered excellent results. We used them on a couple of EDM tunes, and they turned out great. They now offer distribution to the top digital stores and handle the licensing admin for cover songs.

- Artist focused.
- 0-15% commission of royalties.
- Yearly or Monthly distribution fee OR
- No fees with mastering membership.

- In-house playlist pluggers available (for a fee).
- No admin publishing to collect songwriter royalties.

OneRPM

This distributor is based in the US and has the largest market share for indie labels in Latin America. They are one of YouTube's fastest-growing multi-channel networks (MCNs), with over three billion plays per month.

- Label focused.
- Most dominant distributor in Latin America.
- 15% commission of royalties.
- Payment splitting.
- No admin publishing to collect songwriter royalties.
- Option for advances for artists showing traction.
- Excellent sales/streaming reports.

RouteNote

While not the biggest of the distributors here, they have focused on the Asian markets and claim to cover 95% of the world's music market, over 193 countries.

- Artist focused.
- 15% commission with no distribution fees OR
- 0% commission with distribution fees.
- Strong market presence in China and the rest of Asia.
- In-house playlist pluggers.
- No admin publishing to collect songwriter royalties.

Songtradr

This company originally started out as a sync licensing company with a music library searching system. They are the newest to the distribution game, but offer most of the benefits established distributors have.

- Artist focused.
- 0% commission with subscription.
- 10% commission with no subscription.
- No distribution fees.
- Inhouse sync pitch service.
- Payment splitting.
- No admin publishing to collect songwriter royalties.

Soundrop

This company is focused on cover artists, YouTube creators and video game music composers and has a limited number of platforms. They are great at splitting royalties between creators of a project and offering one of the best independent mechanical licensing services, which is great if you plan to release many covers.

- Label and artist focused.
- 15% commission of royalties.
- No distribution fees.
- Payment splitting.
- No admin publishing to collect songwriter royalties.

Tunecore

These guys have been around as long as CD Baby and were the original distribution company I used for Never Say Die. I haven't used them in the last five years, and since then they have been bought by Believe Digital. They have great reporting and offer Tunecore Publishing, tracking down songwriter royalties too.

- Label and artist focused.
- 0% commission of royalties.
- Yearly distribution fees.
- Admin publishing to collect songwriter royalties.
- Excellent sales/streaming reports.

SERVICED DISTRIBUTION COMPANIES

AWAL

These guys are owned by Kobalt Publishing, a very transparent, forward-thinking, tech-focused publisher that doesn't own an artist's publishing. AWAL is also very transparent and offers some of the best analytics and data reporting in the industry. Thus, they can see if an artist is getting traction in the industry and can provide playlist and physical distribution possibilities.

- Artist focused.
- 15% commission of royalties.
- No distribution fees.
- Sync and playlist possibilities for artists that get traction.
- Strict application only.

- Customer support can be slow without a representative.
- Excellent sales/streaming reports.

Believe Digital

We used Believe Digital after being courted by them at ADE (Amsterdam Dance Event) and had a great experience with them. They are one of the biggest independent distributors and have a great marketing strategy team and YouTube monetisation services. They also have robust sync licensing teams and can broker partnership deals with brands.

- Label and artist focused.
- 15 to 30% commission of royalties.
- No distribution fees.
- Sync and playlist possibilities for artists that get traction.
- Strict application only.
- Excellent marketing services.

InGrooves

They are a full artist and label service company on par with Believe Digital. We have used InGrooves for the last few years as a label distributor, and they have been great for placing banners on specialist music stores such as Beatport. They also offer publishing rights management.

- Label and artist focused.
- 10% to 30% commission of royalties.
- No distribution fees.
- Strict application only.

- Admin publishing to collect songwriter royalties.
- Excellent sales/streaming reports.

Stem Music

Originally started to help YouTube creators claim payments and even splits between collaborators, they have evolved into a full-blown music distributor. Their strong point is their payment splitting, which is probably the best among independent distributors. In fact, you have to provide agreed artist splits with everyone on the record before they will distribute you. They count Frank Ocean and DJ Jazzy Jeff as clients.

- Label and artist focused.
- 5% commission of royalties.
- No distribution fees.
- Investment backed – long term beware.
- Strict application only.
- No admin publishing to collect songwriter royalties.
- Excellent sales/streaming reports.

The Label Machine Distribution

Born out of a comprehensive music business ecosystem, our Label Machine Distribution combines artist and label services with advanced education and systemized growth strategies, positioning it as a hybrid between a distributor, marketing agency, and mentorship platform. Our service includes not just distribution but automated fan acquisition workflows, access to a dedicated mentor, and tools for managing CRM, funnels, contracts, and eCommerce. Ideal for those ready to run their label like a modern business.

- Label and artist focused.
- Beatport and Traxsource label account creation
- 10% commission of royalties.
- No distribution fees.
- Includes access to Marketing Machine CRM and growth automation tools.
- Built in royalty accounting for automatic artist payment splitting
- Excellent sales/streaming reports.

UnitedMasters

This distribution company focuses on hip hop and rap music. They have a strong sync division, and deals with big brands such as NBA 2K20. They are an investor backed distribution company and can offer advances to artists.

- Artist focused.
- 10% commission of royalties.
- Yearly distribution fee.
- Strong sync division for Hip hop music.
- No admin publishing.
- No Payment splitting.

ELECTRONIC MUSIC SPECIALIST DISTRIBUTOR COMPANIES

These labels will distribute your music to electronic music specialist platforms such as Beatport, Traxsource and Juno. Due to these companies' specialist nature, you need to apply to each of them for distribution. The Label Machine Distribution will also distribute your music to electronic music specialist platforms.

FUGA

FUGA is the world's biggest electronic dance distributor. Founded in 2006, they have expanded into the US and look to become one of the largest independent distributors, connected to over 260 digital platforms. They have many label service tools aimed at electronic labels, such as DJ promo and royalty management.

- Electronic music focused.
- Label and artist focused.
- 15-40% commission of royalties.
- No distribution fees.
- Strict application only.
- In-house PR and marketing.
- Excellent sales/streaming reports.

Label Engine

Label Engine was initially focused on helping electronic record labels easily import sales data from distributors and calculate complicated splits across tracks with multiple collaborators and remix fees. We have used Label Engine for our royalty accounting for many years, and since we joined, they have grown into a full-service digital distributor. They offer DJ promo tools and auto video creation and uploading to YouTube of your tracks.

- Electronic music focused.
- 15% commission of royalties.
- Distributes to Beatport.
- Has fee paid models with royalty percentage combinations.

- Offers royalty management tools.
- Offers DJ Promo tools.

Label Worx

Launched in 2006, Label Worx offers a Label Management System (LMS) that covers the various aspects for distributing your music to electronic platforms. They offer DJ promo tools, mastering services and a demo submission solution called Promo Worx. They also have a royalty accounting software solution that is designed to work for specialist electronic labels.

- Electronic music focused.
- 10%-30% commission of royalties depending on your sales history.
- Fees for extra services such as royalty accounting.
- Strict application only.
- Distributes to Beatport.
- Offers royalty management tools.
- Offers DJ promo tools.

Symphonic

The company was founded in 2006 and has grown to be one of the big indie distributors that offer PR marketing, plugging, music video distribution and advances for artists that gain traction. Besides a straight 15% commission, artists and labels can also negotiate a tailored deal as a dedicated partnership.

- Electronic music focused.
- Label and artist focused.

- 15% commission of royalties.
- No distribution fees.
- In-house playlist pluggers.
- Strict application only.
- Physical distribution.

Triple V

Triple V is one of the leading independent distributors in Europe that specialise in bass-heavy electronic music such as drum & bass. They have an extensive vinyl distribution network and can offer P&D deals for labels that get good traction.

- Electronic music focused.
- 5-15% commission of royalties.
- Offers vinyl manufacturing and distribution.
- Distributes to Beatport.
- Strict application only.
- Has mastering solutions in-house.

To get the most up to date list of distributors with website links, visit the Book Resources tab on The Label Machine website.

BUDGETS

How much will it cost to start and run a record label? There are unavoidable costs, plus optional investments, primarily marketing expenses like paid advertising, music videos, or external PR.

For reference, we started Never Say Die with approximately £5,000/$7,000. Our first seven releases were on vinyl, requiring steep physical manufacturing costs. Digital releases are much cheaper!

Your biggest investment is setting up your label's first release and infrastructure. When revenue returns, you can reinvest it into operational costs.

Many artist-based labels fund releases incrementally, using income from live shows, merchandise, or day jobs. Regardless of your approach, you must control and understand the label's finances and have a clear investment plan.

To determine your investment needs, understand the different expenses: start-up costs, label expenses, and release expenses.

For this chapter, all prices are in $US. If you're in another country, use xe.com to convert to your local currency.

LABEL EXPENSES AND RELEASE EXPENSES

Label expenses are the essentials to set up and run your record label. These are non-recoupable expenses paid out of the label's profit share.

What is the difference between recoupable and non-recoupable expenses?

A recoupable expense directly relates to releasing a song, artwork, PR, remix fees. These are release expenses.

A non-recoupable expense is not directly related to releasing songs, company formation fees, office rent, website hosting, employee wages. These are label expenses.

LABEL ACCOUNTING BASICS

When signing an artist, you agree to a Royalty Income split (specified in the contract), typically a 50/50 Net Profit deal for independent labels.

Before deducting recoupable expenses, this is called Gross Royalty Income. After deductions, it's Net Royalty Income.

> Gross Royalty Income – Release Expenses = Net Royalty Income

You then split the Net Royalty Income between artist and label as agreed, for example, 50%/50%.

> $100 Net Royalty Income = $50 Artist Royalty Income + $50 Label Royalty Income.

You send the artist their share, and the Label Royalty Income is yours.

To calculate label profit, add any other sales income (like merchandise) and deduct non-recoupable Label Expenses.

Label Royalty Income + Other Label Sales – Label Expenses = Net Label Profit.

Here is an example as illustrated by a record label's profit and loss summary.

Gross Royalty Income	11,940.00
Release Expenses	-5,600.00
Net Royalty Income	6,340.00

Artist Royalty Income (50%)	3,170.00
Label Royalty Income (50%)	3,170.00

Label Sales	2,430.00
Label Expenses	-1,252.00

Net Label Profit	4,348.00

LABEL EXPENSES

Let's break down some common label expenses for the first year of operation.

Record Label Budget	Essential Exp	Optional Exp
Label Expenses		
Logo Design	150.00	
Website Design + Hosting	310.00	
Email Platform	299.00	
Distribution Account	79.00	
Gmail Business Account	62.00	
Company Formation Fee (Delaware)	89.00	
CupCut/Canva Pro		119.00
Total Expenses	989.00	119.00

Logo Design

This price varies depending on what you choose in the Designing the Logo section. For the budget, we will use the budget amount for a freelance designer of $150.

Website Design and Hosting

Like the logo design, this will depend on what you decide to use in the Choosing a Website section; for the budget, we will use the budget amount for the annual fee of $310 for a website-in-a-box option.

Email Platform

This is the annual fee for a professional email provider to manage your email subscribers. We have chosen to use the Marketing Machine platform, which as a member has a $299 annual fee and includes access to all other marketing tools too.

Distribution Account

This is the annual fee for setting up a label account with Distrokid, but if you get distribution with a platform that works on percentages, such as The Label Machine's distribution, this can be omitted as it will be deducted from your label's gross income before it reaches you.

Google Workspace

I recommend using Google Workspace for your business. It gives you access to a suite of business applications for document and spreadsheet processing and the ability for Gmail to host your business email address securely.

Company Formation Fee

This is the service fee to incorporate your record label as an official business. This will depend on which country and state you are based in, and I have used the fee expense for forming a company in Delaware, USA.

Canva

Useful for editing images and formatting for social media. Many tutorials are available on YouTube for both Canva and other tools.

CapCut

CapCut is a user-friendly video editing app ideal for record labels to quickly create engaging, music-driven promotional content optimized for social media.

Both Canva and CapCut are an optional expense, however, so we have placed it in the optional costs section.

Other Business Expenses

Other non-recoupable business expenses worth considering are office space rental, travel, employee wages, and business rates. These aren't included in the budget template as they vary by location and are often unnecessary until you're established. Since COVID-19, many labels operate without offices. Add these under Label Expenses if needed.

If you intend to have these expenses from day one, insert them under the Label Expenses tab.

RELEASE EXPENSES

These expenses directly relate to releasing singles, EPs, or albums. This list covers essential and optional expenses but isn't exhaustive. If you have any other costs, insert a new line into your budget and add to the expenses.

Release 1 (Jan 20XX)		
Artwork	120.00	
Digital Release Fee	49.00	
DJ Plugging / PR	300.00	
Asset Creation	200.00	
Optional Expenses		
Sponsored Posts	300.00	
Spotify Playlisting	100.00	
Remix Fee		*450.00*
Radio Plugging		*1,500.00*
Music Video		*4,500.00*
Vinyl		*2,500.00*
Total of Essential Costs for 1st Release	1,069.00	
Total of Optional Costs for 1st Release		*8,950.00*

Artwork

The second most important creative asset after the music. If there's one place to spend more, it's here. Budget example: $120 via designcrowd.com or Fiverr. Alternatively, AI-powered design tools can create artwork at lower costs.

If you use a designer for multiple releases, negotiate a bundle deal, five pieces for $100 each provides artwork continuity for $500.

Digital Release Fee

If you use a self-distribution model, which will be likely if you're just starting, then most platforms will charge a fee to upload or have the music available on all platforms for eternity.

If you have completed the Choosing a Distributor section, enter the digital release cost here. For the purpose of the template, I will use the Distrokid 'Leave a legacy' fee as we have chosen them as the distributor in the label expenses sections.

DJ Plugging/PR

This expense can vary depending on your approach and the type of music you are releasing. In-house PR (by which I mean you or a member of your team will do the PR) costs less than agencies but still requires services like Submit Hub or Groover.

For electronic club music, specialist companies with DJ databases can distribute your music and collect feedback. These services start at $250-$500, but they review your music first and may decline if it's not suitable.

For our first release, we'll budget $300 for an independent PR agency to help reach radio and tastemakers.

Digital Asset Creation

This expense refers to creating marketing assets like teasers, lyric videos, or promo interviews. Budget example: $200 for a lyric video from a fiverr.com freelancer.

Promoted Posts

Essential for reaching fans on social platforms, even with large followings, so make sure you have included a budget for this. For this example, we will use $300 to create Facebook and Instagram promoted posts.

OPTIONAL RELEASE EXPENSES

These are expenses that will vary depending on each single, EP, or album you release. The general rule of thumb is that the bigger the track and artist, the more you will spend here. If the track has a commercial pop edge and the artist is a rising star, you may want to get an established radio plugger onboard to promote to radio stations. Or, if you have a track that's been picked up by a big YouTube channel, you may want to make a music video to help drive views.

Spotify Playlisting Service

A reputable Spotify playlisting service can give valuable momentum during the crucial initial release period, helping new artists get their streaming numbers above 1000. It's arguably the most essential optional expense, one that many labels choose to include in their budget.

A single placement on a prominent playlist can rapidly exceed one million plays, translating into earnings of approximately $4,000 to $5,000 (Spotify's current average payout per stream ranges between $0.004 and $0.005).

There is a handy tool called Streaming Royalty Calculator that is fairly accurate if you want to calculate streaming royalties: streamingroyaltycalculator.com

Investing in an experienced Spotify playlisting service can thus prove financially rewarding; for example, a $2,000 plugging fee might quickly pay off if the promoted track gains significant traction on playlists. At the $100 tier, expect approximately 2,000-3,000 plays, whilst the $300 tier delivers 7,000-10,000 plays.

TRUSTED PLAYLIST PROMOTION COMPANIES

Here's a list of reliable Spotify playlist promotion companies, with personal insights to help gauge what might work best for your goals.

Indie Music Academy

Led by Ryan Waczek, an impressive choice who genuinely delivers results. I've met Ryan personally and can vouch for his effectiveness.

- Excels at finding playlists ranking well in search results
- Identifies playlists with authentic engagement, ensuring no bots
- Offers educational resources for artists to boost playlisting chances independently

Playlist Push

One of the original playlist promotion companies, maintaining a solid reputation.

- Works with 900+ independent playlist creators, reaching over 25 million listeners
- Reasonably priced with campaigns starting around £200, average spend about £450
- Extensive curator network ideal for artists seeking broad audience reach

YouGrow Promo

Consistent performer with excellent Spotify campaigns. Their

CEO runs a tight ship with excellent customer service and responsiveness.

- Campaigns start at just £79, offering excellent value
- Feedback shows genuine, non-bot engagement
- Provides refunds or campaign transfers if placements aren't achieved

Playlist Promotion

Focuses solely on playlisting, recently expanding into YouTube promotion.

- Unique application process ensures artist-curator fit
- Approach indicates quality-focused rather than solely profit-driven

Daily Playlists

A must-use service as it's free! Met their team at ADE Music Conference and they are fantastic to work with.

- Paid option allows genre-specific submissions and back-catalogue uploads
- Artists report significant stream increases, with successful use across all genres.

You can get a list of reputable playlisting services in the Book Resources tab on The Label Machine website.

Remix fees

If you plan to have remix tracks on a release, you must add

this to the budget. If you are an electronic record label, once you are more established, you can have fellow label artists remix each other as favours, so this might not always need to be factored in as an expense. But if you want producers beyond your contact list to remix your work, then you'll have to pay a remix fee. Fees will be anything from $400 for new rising talent to $5000 for an established, well-known producer.

Radio Plugging

Radio plugging involves promoting a track to radio stations with the primary goal of securing airplay, ideally achieving B-list rotation and eventually progressing to A-list rotation.

Successfully entering these rotations significantly boosts exposure and can propel the track toward chart positions, such as the Top 40.

Radio pluggers usually charge a flat fee for their service, usually starting around $1500, supplemented by bonuses triggered if the track reaches certain milestones, like securing B-list rotation, moving onto A-list rotation, or achieving prime-time drive-show plays.

Music Video

Great for making a statement and providing additional content like behind-the-scenes material. Professional videos still start around $4,000 but consider leveraging user-generated content platforms like TikTok to reduce costs while boosting viral potential.

Vinyl costs

For physical releases, work with a manufacturer near your location to minimize shipping costs. Rising material costs may slightly increase manufacturing expenses, budget example: $2,500 for 500 vinyl records via discmanufacturingservices.com.

Professional mastering is required for vinyl pressings alongside digital versions, budget example: $150.

Recording, Mixing, and Mastering Expenses

As I'm focusing on the business side of running an indie record label, I have not included music production costs such as studio recording costs or mixing engineer expenses.

These days a lot of indie music is produced in home studios or smaller studios where the artists have taken care of the mixing, mastering and production costs themselves. This is also true for electronic music, and almost all electronic artists mix and master their own tracks.

Suppose the recording agreement with your artist includes covering the recording, mixing and mastering costs as part of the release. In that case, you will need to insert extra lines in the releases section of expenses, as these are costs that are recoupable from music royalties.

For this example, as I'm pressing vinyl, I'll have the release mastered by a professional engineer to get both a vinyl and digital master of the track for $150.

Note: If you're already engaged in the music industry or in your local music scene, I highly recommend that when starting a label you use all the contacts at your disposal and pull in favours where possible to keep costs down. Somewhere along the line, you'll be able to return the favour in kind.

And always look to incorporate AI-driven tools across areas such as mastering (LANDR), and design (Canva) to keep costs down when you can.

CASH FLOW

As you make sales, you can start tracking your cash flow. When you are starting out, you will have to forecast the royalties of the label. The following table is an example of a cash flow example for the first year of a record label, starting with the first release in January. It included four release and merch sales from September, as well as the revenue from an event in December.

Cashflow Forecast

	Royalties (001)	Royalties (002)	Royalties (003)	Royalties (004)	Merch	Events
JAN	340.00					
FEB	340.00					
MAR	340.00	372.00				
APR	340.00	372.00				
MAY	340.00	372.00				
JUN	340.00	372.00	400.00			
JUL	340.00	372.00	400.00		155.00	
AUG	340.00	372.00	400.00		155.00	
SEP	340.00	372.00	400.00	360.00	155.00	
OCT	340.00	372.00	400.00	360.00	155.00	
NOV	340.00	372.00	400.00	360.00	155.00	
DEC	240.00	372.00	400.00	360.00	155.00	1,500.00
Sub Total	3,980.00	3,720.00	2,800.00	1,440.00	930.00	1,500.00

Total Gross Royalties	$11,940.00
Total Sales	$2,430.00

This really is a guide for your first year, and I've used an average of the last few labels I have set up. It's to give an idea of what you can expect. As you make sales, you'll need to update this to get a better picture to forecast your finances. Check your finances after one month and revise your yearly projection accordingly. Do so again after the first quarter, and again after 6 months. I have been very conservative with the cash flow and these numbers as it's better to budget with realistic expectations.

For simplicity, I have based this budget on four releases a year, which is a good start if you are entirely new to running a label. However, once established after the first year, many labels will put out 15-20 releases a year, which is when you can expect to start making a good income.

BUDGET TEMPLATE

I have created a budget template in a 12-month calendar cycle and included tabs to estimate your cash flow and calculate your profit and loss. The whole budget is dynamic, and changing expenses and cash flow will automatically update your profit and loss and summary tables.

You can download a copy of the budget from the Book Resources tab on The Label Machine website.

While these budget examples should only act as a guide for your own label's set-up, they should still provide you with a clearer understanding of the costs involved in setting up your own label and budgeting for your first release.

EMAILS AND EMAIL MARKETING

Building your email list is one of the most important assets for your record label. All record labels I've worked with have established robust email lists containing hundreds of thousands of fan contacts.

Email lists give you direct control over fan engagement. You can direct fans to stream particular singles to boost their visibility in Spotify algorithms, support artists' live streams, or increase YouTube views for a new artist's first music video, all without paying Facebook boost fees to ensure your message reaches fans.

For bulk messaging, you must utilise email platforms such as Mailchimp, Brevo (formerly SendinBlue), Drip.com or The Label Machine's own email platform Marketing Machine.

These tools let you manage extensive email lists, send mass communications like release newsletters, and create automated email sequences for new fans, brilliant for establishing initial relationships.

There are four easy steps to follow to set up your own record label's email marketing platform so you can start building your list and communicating with your fans.

1. Create an account with an email marketing platform.
2. Create your email marketing sequence.

3. Incentivise new fans to join the list.
4. Schedule a regular time throughout the year to send newsletters to update fans on label activities.

STEP ONE – CREATE AN ACCOUNT WITH AN EMAIL MARKETING PLATFORM

Sign up to a platform. The Label Machine recommends Mailchimp (mailchimp.com), Brevo (formerly SendinBlue) (brevo.com), or our own Marketing Machine platform.

Mailchimp bases pricing on list size, becoming more expensive once you exceed 2000 subscribers, with automation features requiring a £15/month subscription.

Brevo offers unlimited contacts but charges based on email volume, ideal for large lists with monthly communications. Their free tier includes email automation sequences.

The Label Machine's Marketing Machine provides up to 10,000 emails monthly and unlimited subscribers as part of your membership, offering comprehensive communication capabilities without additional costs.

STEP TWO – CREATE YOUR EMAIL MARKETING SEQUENCE

Create an email sequence as follows:

> Welcome email --> Share with Friends --> Connect on Socials --> Latest Release

1. Welcome email

Subject line ideas:

- Welcome to the [record label family, community, club]
- We're [glad/stoked/humbled] you're here
- Here's your welcome [gift/track/song]

Be authentic—write as if emailing a friend. This may be a new fan unfamiliar with your label or artists, so properly introduce your label's vision, featured artists, and location.

Set clear expectations about email frequency and content. By referring to your list as a 'family' or 'community' rather than an 'email list', you create an inclusive atmosphere—an exclusive group offering more than social media.

Include {first name} personalisation to enhance personal connection and improve deliverability. Add social media links and sign off as a real person with your title (e.g., Sam Pull – XYZ Label Manager/Founder).

TEMPLATE:

Hi [first_name],

I want to personally welcome you to our [XYZ Record Label] community.

We're thrilled that you've joined us; here are two exclusive [remix/acoustic version/unreleased tracks] to say thank you. Just click and it's yours to download.

We are an electronic record label that aims to represent a genre of music heavily influenced by early rave, garage, jungle, and grime. Joe and Rich, who have been involved in the dance music scene for the last ten years, started the label after successful artist careers.

We are based in Denver and we throw parties during the summer; we look forward to meeting you in person at one of them!

[name]
[XYZ Record Label] Manager

2. Share with friends

Subject line ideas:

- We love your music taste
- Spread the [folk/techno/trap/genre] vibes
- Friends with benefits

Personal recommendations are the most reliable growth method for your email list and fan base. Position subscribers as music tastemakers. Make sharing simple—provide clear forwarding options and link to your opt-in page to drive more signups.

TEMPLATE:

Hi [first_name],

If you like our music style and have any recommendations, then send them this way or link us on [@XZYInstagram]

If you have any friends who are into our record label's style, then forward this email to them or share and we will send two free tracks.

All they have to do is click here [link to opt-in page]
[Your name]
[XYZ Record Label] Manager

3. Connect on socials email

Subject line ideas:

- Let's connect
- Want to peek behind the scenes?
- Let's hook up online

This email simply requests social connections and Spotify playlist subscriptions. Having followers on YouTube and SoundCloud is vital for reposting artists' releases.

Focus on your strongest platform. If you curate a genre-specific Spotify playlist, include that link.

Hi [first_name],

While you'll be the first to hear of releases here in the community, we also post teasers on Facebook and behind-the-scenes content/ photos and videos in the studio with our artists on Instagram. We would love to get to know you, so follow us on our socials and let us know about you!

Instagram link
Facebook link
Youtube link
Soundcloud link
Twitter link
Snapchat link

If you like our music, you'll love our Spotify playlist, which has our music mixed up with our personal selection of artists and songs on high rotation at [XYZ Record Label] HQ.

[Spotify playlist link]

[name]
[XYZ Record Label] Manager

4. Buy our latest release email [S2]

Subject line ideas:

- Get the latest
- Latest music for you
- New [Genre] EP out now

This email drives purchases. Begin with a question to maintain a personal tone rather than explicit marketing. Highlight a specific artist release or label compilation to showcase your catalogue. Bandcamp discount codes can effectively incentivise purchases.

TEMPLATE:

> *Hi [first_name],*
>
> *We hope you liked the free tracks we sent last week. Let us know which one is your favourite on [@Facebook_Page] so we know what you want more of.*
> *We have a great label compilation [EP/album] that features tracks from all our label artists called [album/EP name]. It's a great introduction to our [label/artist].*
>
> *If you want to check it out, just follow this [link] and we will give you a 30% discount since you already have a couple of our tracks. Just enter this code on the purchase page [code].*
>
> *Best*
> *[name]*
> *[XYZ Record Label] Manager*

STEP THREE – INCENTIVISE NEW FANS TO JOIN THE LIST

Exchange email subscriptions for musical value with these strategies:

1. **Early access to music** – Share releases, shows, and merchandise news first. Provide exclusive YouTube links to unreleased music by using 'Unlisted' settings before making them 'Public'.
2. **Curated mini-compilations** – Create special collections with unique artwork, available only to subscribers.
3. **Behind-the-scenes content** – Offer production tutorials, gear lists, or studio tours from your artists.
4. **Exclusive tracks** depending on genre:
    - Rock/Singer-songwriter: unplugged versions or covers
    - Hip hop/Rap: remixes, acapellas, instrumentals for sampling
    - Electronic: remixes, bootlegs, edits, or stem packages for remixing
5. **Subscriber-only contests** – Run competitions around releases, offering limited merchandise bundles, signed items, or exclusive packages.

STEP FOUR – SCHEDULE REGULAR NEWSLETTERS

As you grow your emailing list, you can further develop your relationship with them by sending regular updates. Schedule standard times throughout the year, for example, the first Monday of the month. Tell your community what is going on and how you feel about it by sharing stories, not just facts.

You want to share exclusive news that hasn't been shared anywhere else and give the label fans at least 24 hours exclusivity before posting publicly.

Every time you communicate with your community, it's an opportunity to ask your label fans to purchase something. Use your stories to tie in a subtle offer like pre-order of an EP or album, merchandise, or early-bird tickets to shows.

If you have been playing shows and have pictures of fans or fans wearing your label or artists merch, post them and share them in the newsletter. You want to make it a two-way conversation. Ask them to share photos of themselves with your music or with friends at your artist shows and tag it with relevant hashtags.

If you're an established label that releases music weekly, then you will have plenty to email about. Let fans know there is new music available, update on previous releases doing well, or share online articles about your artists' reviews or shows.

But what about when you are starting out, or you only release once every two months, and none of your artists plays regular shows?

If this is the case, here are some examples of what you can share in your emails

- New signings – introduction to a new artist, include all their social links or links to their music.
- Big album releases on the horizon.
- Seasonal newsletters, e.g. New Year's Eve.
- Behind the scenes of artists' recordings.
- If you are starting out, the record label's progress – got a new office, doing our first vinyl release, and hired our first intern.
- The reason you started the label, what the vision is for the following year.

- If you have a Spotify playlist, remind people when it's been updated with new tracks.
- Your favourite charity. Often record labels will donate a portion of profit to a local charity, highlighting who this is and link to them.

TEMPLATE:

Subject Line: News/Topic

Hi [first_name],

Greetings from [Record Label HQ]!

[News headline1]
The artwork for our tenth release (we made it to double digits) is nearly complete, and it's been designed by the super talented graphic designer Frobisa Metcalf. Please don't share yet as we are still tweaking it, but we wanted to give you a sneak peek.
[Image of artwork]

[News headline 2]
We have signed some new artists and are putting out an EP with new music from each of them. It's a five-track EP featuring our artists Qwerty, Asdf, Zxcv and Poiuy. It's set to be released in June, but you can find out more about the artists and pre-order it here [link]

[News headline 3]
With summer on the way, we have been cranking out new songs with big anthem vibes, perfect for the oncoming festival season. We have been loving new music from [Artist 1] and [Artist 2], and you can check them out with other music we've had on high rotation on our Spotify playlist here [link].

Best

[name]
[XYZ Record Label] Manager

PS Tag any artist you think we should check out on our @ FacebookPage so we can discover some new music!

RELEASE COUNTDOWN EMAIL SEQUENCE

Another essential email strategy for record labels is the release countdown sequence. This targeted series of 3-4 emails builds anticipation and maximizes engagement around new music drops.

Start with an announcement email 7-10 days before release, introducing the upcoming track or EP with artwork and a preview snippet. Include pre-save links for Spotify, Apple Music, and other platforms to boost day-one performance.

Follow with a "48 hours to go" reminder that creates urgency and excitement, reinforcing the pre-save call-to-action and perhaps revealing another teaser element like behind-the-scenes footage or artist commentary.

On release day, send a celebratory email with direct links to the music across all platforms, highlighting any positive early feedback.

Finally, about two weeks post-release, follow up with a "Have you checked it out?" email that shares streaming milestones, playlist additions, media coverage, and fan reactions—this encourages listeners who haven't engaged yet while reinforcing the success for those who have.

This sequence maximizes both the immediate impact of your release and its long-term performance.

USING AI TO ENHANCE YOUR EMAIL MARKETING SEQUENCE

AI assistants can transform how you create your email marketing sequences, offering efficiency without sacrificing your label's authentic voice. This approach allows you to develop cohesive, engaging email journeys that nurture subscriber relationships from welcome message through to purchase conversion.

When crafting your four-part email sequence (Welcome, Share with Friends, Connect on Socials, and Latest Release), consider leveraging AI to generate initial drafts that follow industry best practices whilst maintaining your unique label identity.

The complete AI prompt template for creating your email marketing sequences is available inside the Marketing Machine platform.

EMAIL TIPS

Use personalisation {subscriber_name} so your emails start with 'Hi Sam' instead of 'Hi everyone!'

Never write to a list. Don't write "to all our fans or subscribers". Write as if you were speaking to one person. You can do this by visualising your one ideal label fan and write as if talking to them directly.

Speak in your own voice. Talk about yourself and the label as 'I' and 'we' and label fans as 'you'. This is a crucial piece of advice for your autoresponder messages and broadcasts.

If you are promoting a release, you can place multiple links in your emails, but always to the one same destination. Do not send emails that have different links to different destinations.

Set up your signature to include your label website and your role. Make sure to include the following:

- Name
- Job title/position
- Label name (as a logo if possible)
- Label postal address
- Phone number
- Label website
- Label's social media links
- Terms and conditions

Here is an example you can copy:

--

Sam Pull
Label Manager

Ten 87 Studios | Wilcox, West W | Los Angeles | 90038
Tel: +1 97825 534086
ersatzrecords.com

This email and any files transmitted with it are confidential and intended solely for the use of the individual or entity to whom they are addressed. If you have received this email in error please notify the system manager. This message contains confidential information and is intended only for the individual named. If you are not the named addressee you should not disseminate, distribute or copy this email. Please notify the sender immediately by e-mail if you have received this email by mistake and delete this email from your system. If you are not the intended recipient you are notified that disclosing, copying, distributing or taking any action in reliance on the contents of this information is strictly prohibited.

Email Don'ts

Don't buy a list of email addresses and use that for your own business.

Don't scrape emails off the web and randomly email people. This is called SPAM.

Every time someone reports your email as spam, your sending reputation gets worse. As a result, future emails will end up in their spam box, even to people who actually subscribed to your list. This affects your open-rates, thus your record sales.

Alternative email addresses

It is also helpful to create separate communication channels. You can set up as many email addresses as you need for your domain, e.g. press@recordlabel.com and accounts@recordlabel.com.

In the early days of Never Say Die Records, when it was just the two of us, we created extra employees and names for the different roles. Jake handled accounts; Samantha was the social media manager. This helped organise other parts of the business and, in the case of Jake, helped when we wanted someone to chase up payments and play the bad cop.

Obviously, use discretion, but it can be convenient and gives the appearance of being a bigger label until you have more staff.

REGISTERING AS A COMPANY

When you register as a company, you form a limited liability company. In the UK, it's titled LTD; in the US, it's an LLC. If you're based elsewhere, check your country's requirements. I'll cover key points for the US and UK.

Why register my record label as a company?

PROTECTION

Registering your label as a company is vital for personal protection. Without this, you risk personal liability for any legal action against your business.

Here's an example of how being unprotected might affect you:

Verity Bright works daily in her studio on an EP for her label, Bright On Records. She hasn't registered it as an LLC.

One day, she opens her car door and a cyclist collides with it. The cyclist sues for £2 million and wins. Without an LLC, Verity's personal assets (home, car) aren't protected, forcing her to sell them to pay damages.

Had Verity registered Bright On Records as an LLC, only her business assets would be liable. If the company were worth £100K, she'd liquidate the company, but her personal assets would remain protected.

LEGITIMACY

Perception significantly influences reality in the music industry. When recipients see an LLC name in your email signature or receive messages from artist@companyname.com, it conveys legitimacy and professionalism.

This increases your perceived value and demonstrates dedication. While it doesn't guarantee responses, it's advantageous in the industry.

MOTIVATION

Starting a business requires ambition and self-belief. Setting achievable goals helps – if registering costs £400 annually, target at least that much profit in your first year, which is achievable and will motivate larger future goals.

GETTING IT DONE

To establish your label legally, register it as a company. While you can register directly with the government, I recommend using a specialist service to ensure everything is done properly and avoid administrative headaches.

Registering in the US

Popular online services include:

- legalzoom.com
- swyftfilings.com

US registration costs approximately $200 as a one-off fee, varying by state.

You'll need an EIN number (federal tax ID). Apply directly on the IRS website rather than through a service company: irs.gov/businesses/small-businesses-self-employed/apply-for-an-employer-identification-number-ein-online

Once you have your LLC and EIN, set up a business bank account. Chase is popular if your personal bank doesn't offer business accounts: chase.com/business

Registering in the UK

Popular UK services include:

- companiesmadesimple.com
- 1stformations.co.uk

UK setup costs range from £5 to around £50 for comprehensive service.

During formation, a typical share structure is 100 shares at £1 each (£100 nominal value).

Your SIC code will be 59200 – Sound recording and music publishing activities.

Then choose a business bank account. HSBC and Barclays are popular choices:

- barclays.co.uk/business-banking
- business.hsbc.uk

Registering elsewhere

If outside the US or UK, visit stripe.com/atlas to set up a company worldwide.

Other options

If you have an accountant, they can often set up your company at similar prices and with less hassle.

The exception is for artists releasing a single project through a 'vanity' label. In this case, you can operate as a sole trader, with money and registrations through personal accounts, using PayPal for most accounting.

CREATING A RECORD RELEASE

Once you've set up your record label, the next step is to release your music. The following chapters take you through all the tasks around preparing the music for release, arranging the recording agreements, preparing and creating the music assets, and distributing the music.

Once these tasks are complete, you'll then move on to promoting and marketing the release to ensure it reaches your target fan base.

This process repeats for every release, and as your label grows, you will tweak the processes to suit your label's ideal release schedules.

- Deciding on a single, EP, or album.
- Creating a release strategy.
- Getting music complete.
- Creating artwork.
- Creating a release schedule.
- Preparing metadata.
- ISRC, UPC, ISWC, CAE/IPI codes.
- ℗ and © symbols in music.
- Preparing label contracts.
- Uploading to distribution.
- Registering songs with PROs.

SINGLE, EP OR ALBUM?

Will you release a single, EP or album?

DISTRIBUTION

From a technical and distribution point of view, your releases can be one of three categories: single, EP or album.

- A single has one to three songs that are under ten minutes each.
- An EP has four to six songs with a total running time of 30 minutes or less.
- An album contains over 30 minutes of music, seven or more different tracks from the same artist, or a continuous DJ mix.

MARKETING

What is the best format for releasing music from a marketing and commercial perspective?

Today's music listening habits are heavily influenced by playlists and singles, thanks to the popularity of platforms like YouTube and Spotify. For new or less established artists, releasing singles and EPs is the most effective way to build momentum and maximize plays and sales.

This approach is also lower risk, requiring less investment from both the label and the artist to test new material.

If you're starting a new label, focus on releasing singles and EPs during the first two years to make the most of your initial music releases.

CREATIVE

From a creative point of view, albums are an important career milestone for professional artists. Albums give artists credibility due to the time and money it takes to produce and release a successful album. Fans will expect an album at some point, and most artists have a lifelong ambition of releasing a full-length album.

As a label, once you have an artist with a large and dedicated audience, work with the artist to record and release an album.

ARTIST STRATEGIES

A good release strategy from an artist's point of view is a combination of the above. The first release should be a single or EP, followed by a second single or EP. Then write an album, and release three singles from the album leading up to and following the album's release.

EP – Single – EP – Single – Single – Album – Single

Another technique I've seen recently is using the waterfall

strategy for music releases. This involves releasing a four-track EP as singles, one week apart, and then combining all the tracks into the full EP release.

This approach capitalizes on single-driven listening habits, keeping listeners engaged over a longer period while also catering to those who prefer experiencing an artist's complete body of work in the form of an EP.

RELEASE STRATEGY

RELEASE STRATEGY OVERVIEW

Three main elements work together to make up the overall release strategy when it comes to releasing music. For a record label run by one person, all of these elements would be the responsibility of that one person. In a small to medium-sized record label, each of these would be the responsibility of separate individuals, and in a larger record label, different departments.

RELEASE SCHEDULE

This is the timeline of organising and executing the actual music release:

- Getting masters ready.
- Signing off on the final artwork.
- Getting contracts signed.
- Uploading to the distributor.

Think of this as the administration part of the release. This is typically managed by the label manager.

MARKETING AND PR SCHEDULE

This is the timeline of organising and executing everything to promote the music release: sending a press release, promoting teasers on social media, arranging premieres on blogs. This would be run by a marketing specialist or head of the marketing department.

MARKETING AND PR ASSETS

These are the assets you build used in the marketing and PR schedule to promote the music release: press release, social media banners, teaser trailers and music videos. This area would be the responsibility of the designer or design department. Even in a small one-person label, it's often an external specialist freelancer that will create the assets.

BEGINNING OF THE SCHEDULE

The release schedule starts with getting the music and artwork complete. By complete, I mean signed off from the artist. No more revisions! Once these are complete, you can then create the marketing assets and the marketing and PR schedule.

You need approximately six weeks to do a good release strategy for a release. With this in mind, once you have the music and artwork done, you can set the release date six weeks away and then create the schedule to fit within these six weeks.

GETTING MUSIC COMPLETE

GETTING MUSIC READY TO BE RELEASED.

One of my favourite sayings is 'It all starts with good music'. But what is 'good' music? Essentially, music needs to connect with an audience. On the one side, you have the emotional reaction people have to music based on their upbringing or personal journeys as music lovers. For example, a certain track may bring back memories of a party when you were a teenager. On the other side, there is the technical aspect of the music, in which good mixing and mastering that brings out the right tones becomes a satisfying experience to hear.

Early on in my career as a DJ producer, I was given a book from my mate Patrick (from the production duo State of Mind) called 'Mixing with your Mind' by Michael Paul Stavrou. Admittedly, it's getting dated now; however, it is truly insightful into the magic of getting the music just right. Its theories are timeless and I highly recommend getting a copy.

The Label Machine was designed for working with artists that have already mastered the processing of producing music commercially, so I'm not going to include a section on how to actually make great music. However, if you are not at this point, there are hundreds of YouTube tutorials on how to make good music for every genre, which is a great place to start.

A&R

A&R means Artist and Repertoire. This is the person responsible for selecting the music for a label and is often someone that is or was previously an artist. If you're looking to get signed to a label, this is the person you need to impress. A good A&R will help shape your music, give you mix pointers, sometimes even sit in the studio and show you little tricks to make your music sound the best it can.

Suppose you are an artist running your own label with your team. In that case, you are essentially already the head of A&R. So, you want to ensure the final masters have been recorded and arranged professionally and, in the artist and producer's eyes, have been mixed and mastered to a satisfactory level.

Compare with contemporaries

Check the music against others in your genre and compare them sonically and musically. This is called A/B referencing.

To A/B reference, open up your track in a QuickTime player and then open up a track from a contemporary or another artist similar to you in a second player. Switch between them quickly to compare them sonically.

Alternatively, you can use your digital audio workstation, have each track in a separate channel and switch the solo button between them.

When switching between the tracks, consider the following:

- How loud are they in comparison?
- What is the balance of bass and treble?
- Do they have a similar length?
- How does the stereo width compare?
- How loud are the vocals?
- Do they have a similar rhythm?

For electronic music:

- Are the tracks sonically matched?
- Is the phrasing in 16 and 32 bar counts to make it easy for DJs to mix?

A/B referencing is especially important in electronic music as much of a track's success comes from DJs playing the music in sets where they blend many tracks together. If your music doesn't sonically mix with similar genre music, it won't get played! It's also why the structure of electronic tracks are phrased in even 16 and 32 bar sections for the intro, builds, and main drops so they can be easily mixed with other tracks.

MIXING HELP

If the music ideas are solid, but the mixdowns and mastering do not compare well to other tracks, you can pay someone to do a stem mix. This is where an artist or producer will mix down groups of tracks into the main parts; drums (usually separated again into kick, hats, snare, perc) and then bass, lead synth, atmosphere, lead vocal, backing vocal, etc.

These audio stems are then sent to a mix engineer who will mix these down into a finished track. You can usually get a decent professional stem mix for about £350/$500 a track, and if it features a full vocal track, the fee will be a little more.

MASTERING HELP

The mixing engineers can usually do your mastering as well, but if you have a track already as a finished mixdown, you can get masters done by a specialist mastering engineer.

Prices for professional mastering by a human engineer generally start around £30–£120 ($37–$150) per track, depending on the engineer's experience and reputation.

For a four-track EP, rates can range from about £112–£400 ($150–$500), with discounts often available for bulk orders

There is also a popular online mastering service that uses AI to auto-magically master your music. These companies master your music in the cloud and use data from analysing thousands of tracks to find the best way to master yours.

Three popular services are

- LANDR: landr.com

- Cloudbounce: cloudbounce.com
- Emastered: emastered.com

I have used these services in the past with great results. While they don't give the same tailored benefit of a professional, they are a lot cheaper, and when it comes to well mixed electronic music, they come close to the pros.

GHOST PRODUCTION

There is one final (controversial) topic to cover about getting music ready – ghost production. This is where someone else writes music for you. You might have a bit of input on the idea, but the ghost producer does all the hard work: coming up with lead lines, writing the chords, bassline, programming the synths, recording a vocal, and mixing the entire track down.

You can pay anything between £300 – £500 ($400 – $700) per track, and you get all the rights to release the music under your name. Once they develop their own sound, some well-established DJs use ghost producers to keep churning out similar music.

Ghost production is fairly popular in electronic music, and if you want to go down this route, there are a few options for you. Three of the most popular sites are

- edmghostproducer.com
- edm-ghost-production.com
- ghostproducing.com

With these sites, it's as simple as buying a track you like, downloading it, or downloading the individual parts, rearranging it to your liking, then adding your own artist name and, hey presto, you've got your own track.

Today, ghost producers often use advanced AI-powered tools to assist with sound design, mixing, and creative inspiration, speeding up production while maintaining quality. However, most platforms require that tracks be primarily human-created to ensure originality and authenticity.

Transactions and rights management are increasingly secured through blockchain technology and smart contracts, providing transparent licensing and instant, secure payments. Additionally, platforms now require detailed metadata, such as software versions, plugin usage, and sample clearances, to ensure all music is legally compliant.

I'm not going to debate the right/wrong merits of doing this; I am here only to show you the practical side and give you all the options.

Now you should have a good grasp of the tools and options you can use to help get the music completed and ready for distribution on your record label.

CREATING ARTWORK

ARTWORK

The artwork is a vital part of a release. It is second only to the music and highlights your individuality, your brand. If you are serious about making a successful record label, it will encourage your audience to identify with you, recognise your label, and build brand identity.

Good artwork is the foundation of your brand identity and often forms the basis that all your marketing media is created from. You can use artwork to create a moving representation of the release, such as video teasers to create powerful marketing assets.

In short, the visual elements are a big part of your marketing plan. Even going back in musical history, there has always been a strong relationship between artists and musicians.

You may not have been aware of the artists behind some of the most iconic album covers. End Times by Eels (Adrian Tomine), Artpop by Lady Gaga (Jeff Koons), Think Tank by Blur (Banksy), K by Kula Shaker (Dave Gibbons). All very iconic and unique pieces of artwork that are representative of the artist at that time.

All successful labels I have worked with have had a strong visual identity. Stepping back and looking at any project, even outside the music industry, branding has a big impact on its success. Well-marketed products, including music, films and books, can be very mediocre and still sell well.

FINDING A DESIGNER

So, where can you find great designers? As artwork is a matter of taste and style, you will have to research and find someone that fits the label and artist brand whose previous work fits your taste. Much like getting a logo designed, there are a few options.

Use a professional designer

Most labels I know pay typically £280/$400 – £350/$500 per cover design to a professional piece of artwork for each release. Seems like a lot of money for only the artwork, but it's worth it.

Here's why: using a professional means you can get redesigns, request deadlines and expect them to be met (and receive 'layered' files, which are essential for creating your other marketing assets).

You can find professional designers on these websites:

- illustrationweb.com
- jellylondon.com
- centralillustration.com
- lemonadeillustration.com
- folioart.co.uk

When sending the brief, always request that they send the final design as layered Photoshop or Illustrator files. This means that the key elements of the design (the foreground, background, and titles) are all separate layers that you can edit independently of each other, making it easier to create variations of the art for different digital platform sizes.

Finding talented designers and video editors can be difficult, so if you find one, treat them well and pay them on time. If you have a good relationship with them, it can make your life a lot easier when you need to turn the release artwork around quickly.

When starting a record label, my advice is when you find an artist you like, negotiate for them to do a series of five pieces for your first five releases. This will help establish a visual identity and template that you can use moving forward, even if you choose to use different designers in the future.

Other options

A good place to find new visual artists is Instagram, as you can use hashtags to search for terms to fit your project, e.g. #labelartwork #musicartwork, etc.

Two other popular sites that are dedicated to showcasing new talent are behance.net and deviantart.com.

If you reach out to someone on one of these platforms, you can use this template to contact the artist for the first time.

Hi [Artist Name]

We came across your profile on [website/platform] and really liked your style of artwork.

We are a record label with upcoming releases from [artist name/s].

You can listen to some music here [private SoundCloud link].

We are looking for cover artwork for singles and EPs and would like to know if you take commissioned work.

If so, please get back to us to discuss budgets and availability.

Kind regards

WHAT ARE LAYERED FILES?

These are the different elements of the artwork saved as separate layers in Photoshop or Illustrator. Essentially, it means you can edit the background separately from the design elements. This makes it easier to create bespoke banners for social media, using elements on merchandise should you want to create t-shirt prints at some point.

Most importantly, you can give the layered files to a video editor who can use them to animate the design with the music to create a teaser trailer for the music (they'll likely do this in Adobe Premiere or Final Cut).

AI DESIGN TOOLS FOR ALBUM ARTWORK

AI-powered platforms have revolutionised the accessibility of professional-quality album artwork. These tools offer a balance of customisation, speed, and affordability:

- midjourney.com

- leonardo.ai
- runway.ml

The album artwork creation process typically involves:

- Crafting detailed text prompts describing your desired visual aesthetics
- Generating multiple variations based on your descriptions
- Refining prompts to achieve more precise results
- Downloading high-resolution versions for around £10-30

While AI tools excel at creating unique visual concepts quickly, they sometimes require post-processing in design software to perfect typography or add finishing touches. Many independent artists have successfully created distinctive album artwork using AI tools as their starting point, especially for experimental or digital-first music projects.

TECHNICAL SPECIFICATIONS

Most platforms you will need to send your artwork to will only accept it at a size of 3000 x 3000 pixels as a minimum requirement at 72 dpi, which means dots per inch.

Ensure your artwork does not contain the following, or it will be rejected. Stores will reject artwork containing:

- A website address (URL).
- Twitter name.
- The terms' exclusive' or 'limited edition'.

- Any image that's blurry, pixelated, rotated or poor quality.
- Unlicensed/stock photography.
- Prices.
- Store logos (such as Apple Music or Spotify).
- Nudity.
- References to physical media (example: "CD" or "Compact Disc").

CONTRACT

It is advisabe if using a freelancer to sign a design contract that gives you total ownership of the artwork. This allows you to use the artwork for merchandise or tour posters without the designer requesting extra fees. The benefit to using a freelancer website is that they have these contracts built in, so you are automatically legally protected with your copyrights.

You now have a good selection of resources and options for creating the second most important asset to music, the artwork for your record label releases.

CREATING A RELEASE SCHEDULE

So, now you have your final masters and artwork ready, you can set up your release and marketing schedules. These schedules will contain the key tasks that need completing to ensure everything is done to make a successful music release.

Creating a schedule is best done by using a calendar to record the key events. The size and nature of your team, your budget and what technology you have at your disposal will determine which scheduling tools you use for this.

If you have access to Google Workspace, you can use Google Calendar to set your schedule. Other popular alternatives are project management services such as Asana, Basecamp and Monday. These are particularly useful for larger teams as you can also attach documents and send reminders.

The example we use for a release is a digital-only release, which most music releases are these days. An ideal timeline for a digital release schedule is six weeks. This gives plenty of time to plan for marketing and PR and any delays you might experience.

If you have music and artwork ready, you can turn around a release in one week with a good distributor. However, there would be no way to have a pre-order campaign set up or marketing and PR buzz leading up to the release so it is not advisable for your leading singles and big releases. There are exceptions, for example, sometimes remixes are put out in this way, or if an unreleased track is used in a big TV advertising campaign and the label wants to capitalise on its popularity quickly they may do a one week turnaround.

If you plan to release physical products such as vinyl or CDs, you need to factor in the manufacturing time. The longer you can allow for production, the better, and for vinyl, you need about six to eight weeks extra, and for CDs, about two to three weeks extra.

The following is an example of an eight-week single release strategy. This is a full release schedule for releasing a single with six weeks build-up and includes two weeks of post-release promo. It includes all the activities for both the Release Schedule and Marketing and PR Schedule.

It covers all the essential tasks for preparing the release for distribution, creating the marketing assets, activating your press and marketing campaign, including your Spotify playlist submissions and a paid advertising campaign.

We will break down each of these activities over the following chapters.

Week 0

- Prepare the artist deliverables.
- Get music ready.
- Save final artwork and masters to the release folder.

Week 1

- Record metadata.
- Create agreements.

- Send a recording agreement to the artist.
- Upload to the distributor.
- Write a press release.
- Create DJ/radio promo.
- Create teaser clips for SoundCloud.
- Prepare marketing assets.
- Create 'release date' banners for social media.
- Create a teaser trailer.

Week 2

- Submit the song to Spotify playlists via Spotify for Artists account.
- Send a pre-release press release out.
- Send DJ promo out.
- Curate blog and publications.
- Upload 'release date' banners to all social platforms.
- Create extra marketing assets.
- Create a YouTube video of the tracks.

Week 3

- Register tracks for PPL / SoundExchange.
- Register tracks with PROs.
- Secure music features.
- Confirm premieres with music channels.
- Upload the teaser trailer to each social media platform.
- Curate Spotify playlists.

Week 4

- Check artists have signed recording contracts.
- Upload Soundcloud teaser clips and share on socials.
- Build an audience on Meta.
- Build Meta Fan Funnel (ad campaign).
- Set up a WhatsApp group for the team involved in the single release.

Week 5

- (DJ releases) Upload DJ promo mix to SoundCloud.
- Post-interview premieres confirmed.
- Marketing assets check.
- Upload at least two extra marketing assets this week before release day.
- Post the pre-order link.

Week 6

- Create press release support, confirmed press, premieres and plays.
- Start a three-day countdown.
- Upload at least two extra marketing assets this week.
- Make sure everybody is ready to promote the song.

Week 6 – Release Day

- Check release is correct on all platforms.

- Update record label platforms with the single release.
- Post Smart Link release landing page.
- Update all social media banners with 'out now' artwork.
- Update label assets and email artist team.
- Create an email newsletter for label fans.
- Send an email newsletter to fan mailing list.
- Send the press release out to the database.
- Send individual messages to PR contracts.
- Send one-to-one messages thanking for the support.
- Create a live Zoom or YouTube launch party.

Week 7

- Start Spotify outreach method.
- Activate Meta fan funnel (ad campaign).
- Update your Spotify profile.
- Update your artist pick on Spotify.
- Upload at least two extra marketing assets this week.

Week 8

- Post playlist additions confirmed for this week.
- Post fan feedback on socials.
- Upload at least two extra marketing assets this week.

To set your schedule, decide the release date, which falls in week six. Standard release days are Mondays or Fridays. Labels usually set them depending on when their country's music charts start and finish the counting period. However, in recent years, most indie labels I work with set a release date on Thursdays, as chart positions aren't as important and online engagement is highest on a Thursday.

Next, open Google Calendar, or your project management software of choice, and enter the release date at 9am on the release day, for example, October 1st.

Then, working backwards from that date, fill in key tasks from the checklist as you work back through each week. For weeks with fewer tasks, you might enter the task on Monday at 10am and, on busier weeks, spread them out over a few days, depending on other commitments.

If you use Google Calendar, you can set all the release tasks to a certain colour, so it's easy to see. You can edit the task notification setting to email you ten minutes before the task is due and add a guest email to remind a colleague of the task. No excuses for missing a task deadline!

Inside The Label Machine platform is a dedicated release function called the DROP that allows you to enter your future release date and automatically be updated via emails with all the activities mentioned here. As well as this 8 week DROP we also have a 2 week DROP for last minute releases.

This list of activities is also available for download by visiting the Book Resources tab on The Label Machine website.

METADATA

"Metadata, metadata, metadata!" is a phrase that was yelled at me at a publishing conference I attended in LA. It was something the LA-based music supervisors – the people who put your music in films, TV shows, and video games – drilled into us.

So what is metadata, and why is it so important? Metadata is the information attached to music that allows it to be easily identified and tracked across the various platforms and databases that companies use for managing music.

It contains essential information about the music, such as track names, artist names, musical genre that allows your music to be identified and processed correctly by distributors and music platforms.

Metadata is important as it allows collection agencies to know who owns the rights for the masters and who owns the rights to the publishing so they can distribute performance revenues to the correct rights holder and artists when music is used.

Metadata is required when you register your music with the PRO collection agencies such as SoundExchange, RIAA and MPA in the US and PPL in the UK. If you or your artists have a publisher, they will also need this information.

It's imperative to manage your metadata professionally if you want to track your royalties around the globe and ensure you can pay your artists!

What is it exactly, though? An example of stored metadata can be seen in MP3 files. For example, on a Mac, if you right-click on a track and select 'Get Info', a tab opens up and displays fields such as the track name, authors, album, and musical genre. All of those pieces of data are the metadata of the track. The same information can be found if you right-click on a track and select 'Details'.

The minimum metadata information you need for uploading to a distributor is:

- Artist / band name.
- Release date.
- Record label.
- Catalogue number.
- Album title.
- Primary genre.
- Secondary genre.
- Track name(s).
- Songwriter(s) legal names.
- Artist's publisher.
- ISRC code.
- UPC number.

As of 2025, DSPs require minimum credit information at the track level.

- Main Artist.
- Composer & Lyricist. Both required for vocal tracks; only Composer for instrumentals.

- Performer. At least one performance role (e.g., vocals, guitar, drums)
- Additional Contributor or Remixer. Typically a producer, mixer, etc.

For composer and lyricist credits, full names are required:

- Bryan Adams = valid
- Beyoncé = not valid

However, for performer and producer roles, using the artist's stage name is totally fine.

SONG LYRICS METADATA

Recently, platforms have stated that having lyrics in the metadata is now a priority when pitching music releases for features or banner placements. While this isn't mandatory, it does have benefits for your fans.

Apple has the ability to search by lyrics in Apple Music. This allows fans to find songs more easily; for example, when a song title doesn't reflect the lyrical hook.

You want to keep all your metadata well organised and easy to access at short notice, and the best way of doing this is by keeping your records in a spreadsheet. There is a template with all the essential data points to download on the Book Resources tab on The Label Machine website.

ISRC, UPC, ISWC, CAE/IPI CODES

ISRC and UPC are international metadata codes used to identify the music masters. ISRC codes are used to identify individual tracks in a release, and UPC codes are used to identify a whole release, such as an EP or album. They are essential for record labels as they deal with the master recordings of music.

ISRC

An ISRC is short for International Standard Recording Code and uniquely identifies sound recordings and music video recordings. A track can only have one ISRC code assigned to it for a lifetime. If the track is remixed or a cover version is recorded, it will be assigned a new ISRC code.

The format for ISRC codes is US-TLM-20-00001.

The first two letters are the country of origin, and the next three are the owner's registration code which, if you decide to manage your own ISRC codes, will be assigned to you when you register. The following two digits are for the year the recording was released, and the final five digits are the designation code and what you, as the master rights owner, assign yourself.

A typical format for the last five digits is using the first two digits for the release number on your label and the last three for the track number in the release.

For example, a label with registration code TLM, based in the US, releasing its fourth EP that year, with three tracks on it, would have ISRC for each track listed as:

US TLM 21 04001
US TLM 21 04002
US TLM 21 04003

UPC

UPC stands for Universal Product Code and is used to identify the whole release as a collection of master songs, for example, an EP or album. They are sometimes referred to as EAN codes which stands for European Article Number.

UPC codes are 12 digits long and are used across all industries. The most common format you will see UPC codes are in the form of a barcode.

How do I get UPC and ISRC codes?

Most distributors these days can create and assign a UPC code and ISRC code to the tracks for your releases automatically when you upload your music to the distribution platform. This is the easiest and simplest way of obtaining these codes. Once assigned, simply make a note of them in your own metadata spreadsheet.

If you plan on releasing many songs, it's best to manage your ISRC codes in-house as your record label is given a unique identifier code to prefix all your tracks, making it easier to find and track your catalogue around the world in the future.

Each country manages ISRC codes differently, and you can search isrc.ifpi.org to find out how to obtain one for your country. In the US, they use RIAA and, in the UK, they use PPL.

For UPC codes, unless you plan on releasing your music in multiple different physical formats that require individual UPC barcodes, then simply use the UPC code assigned by your distributor.

If you eventually create physical products that need a UPC, the physical distributor will usually assign these for you.

PUBLISHING CODES

There are two other codes you will find used in the music industry that you will use as an artist and you should be familiar with as a record label.

ISWC

The first is the ISWC code which is short for International Standard Musical Work Code. This is a unique 10 character code assigned to a musical work or composition.

ISWC codes are used to identify information such as song title, songwriter(s), music publishers and song splits.

If you are an artist who writes their own music, you will need to keep a record of your ISWC codes to help link your song back to you and your publisher so people know who to pay when your music is used commercially.

A song receives an ISWC when it is registered at a Performing Rights Organisation (PRO). So, if you are an artist, ensure you have signed up to a PRO in your country to register your songs.

CAE/IPI

CAE and IPI are the same. It is a unique identification number assigned to songwriters and publishers to identify rights holders. IPI is short for Interested Parties Information, and CAE is short for Composer, Author and Publisher. The IPI system replaced the CAE system in 2001, but the numbers are used interchangeably.

The number will typically be a 9 to 11 digit number, and it is assigned to a writer when they sign up to a PRO in their country. This number connects writers to compositions so they can be tracked and paid.

If you are signed to a PRO, you can find your CAE/IPI number by doing a repertoire search on your PRO (such as ASCAP, BMI or PRS), and your number will come up next to your name.

It is not the responsibility of a record label to manage the publishing and ISWC codes for artists; that is a publisher's role. Some labels offer registering songs as a service, but as an artist this should be treated and accounted separately to your master recordings.

℗ AND © SYMBOLS IN MUSIC

Sound Recording Copyright ℗
This symbol represents the sound recording copyright for the release and identifies the sound recording's copyright owner. If the artist has signed the recording to a record label, it will be the record label name.

Copyright Owner ©
This symbol represents the copyright of the whole release and identifies the copyright of any other material for the release, such as the artwork used on the cover, and the copyright owner will typically be the record label as well.

Both copyright terms are recorded with the year in which the material was created and is also considered the copyright and phonograph year.

If you submit a release in November 2024 to be released in January 2025, then 2024 is the copyright and phonograph year. (Because that's when the content was created).

If the release is part of a back catalogue, you must select the year it was originally copyrighted.

RECORD LABEL CONTRACTS

Recording contracts and agreements are the legal documents that detail the terms for copyright ownership between the artist and record label, the terms of payment for the copyright, and any exclusivity.

Agreements and contracts come in all shapes and sizes. The three main contracts or agreements that a record label will create and engage with are the Recording Agreement, the Remix Agreement and the Split Sheet.

Throughout the industry, you may find variation in the names of these agreements. For instance, the Recording Agreement is sometimes called a Recording Contract, Music Contracts, or Music Agreements. Some are very long and detailed, some are just two pages.

Regardless of name or length, these contracts and agreements' main purpose is to lay out the details for who owns the copyright of the music masters and how the royalties from sales of the masters will be paid.

The label's responsibility is to arrange and ensure the contracts are signed before a record release is made public.

If you're an artist starting a label to release your own music, then signing a recording contract with yourself might seem pointless. However, if you want to do everything professionally, it's good practice (especially if you want to sell your label, as you will need these contracts signed to hand over the company).

Let's break down the main types of deals found in record label agreements so you can understand how your record label can create a fair deal for your artists.

MASTER LICENCE AND MASTER OWNERSHIP

A master license deal is signing over the masters for a set period, for example, a term of five to seven years. When we talk about contract templates in the following chapters, this would be in the form of an Exclusive Licensing Agreement.

A Master Ownership deal is where the masters are signed for perpetuity, aka forever. When we talk about contract templates, this would be in the form of a Recording Agreement.

Many modern record deals sign exclusive master licence deals for a limited time. However, it is not uncommon for smaller indie labels that support a particular genre of music and/or new artists to sign in perpetuity.

TERMS OF PAYMENT

Most indie labels offer net profit deals where the artist gets a percentage of net profits after the label has deducted release expenses. This is typically 50%, so the label and artist share net profits 50/50. This is the deal we use in our template contracts.

Traditional recording deals, especially at major record labels, use a PPD deal which means Published Price to Dealer. This is when the artist is paid a percent of each record sold to the dealer, which is usually around 12 to 20% of the PPD.

EXCLUSIVE OR NON-EXCLUSIVE

Most indie record deals are non-exclusive deals. Meaning you sign the rights for a particular single, EP or album, but the artist is free to sign their other music to other labels.

An exclusive deal means that the label owns all the music an artist writes for a set time, defined in the deal. These deals are more common with major record deals.

Sometimes a record deal might have an option clause. This means the record label has the first option to sign the artist's next single, EP or album before any other label when certain conditions are met, such as reaching a certain level of sales.

EXECUTION

When it comes to signing, digital signatures are the easiest and quickest way for both parties to sign. Some of the most popular applications for signing digital contracts are docusign.com, and hellosign.com, and the Marketing Machine has this function also built in for contacts (including the drafts contracts mentioned here).

It's worth re0membering that the record agreement will be referred to if a dispute can not be handled civilly between each party. For example, if the masters are delayed and sent to a label after 30 days, you don't need to march the artist off to court; you will simply agree with the artist when they will be sent.

As an independent record label, your contracts don't need to be overly complicated, and if you have read the other sections about the music industry, you will be able to grasp what each section means in the following chapters and the variations you might include for your record label requirements.

AI FOR CONTRACT REVIEW

AI tools now offer indie labels a cost-effective way to review and update contracts. These platforms can analyse agreement language, highlight potential issues, and suggest industry-standard clauses. While not replacing legal counsel, AI can help labels spot discrepancies, ensure consistency across agreements, and generate draft contracts based on specific parameters. This technology particularly benefits small labels with limited legal budgets, though final contracts should still receive professional legal review. Popular AI legal tools include Spellbook, Harvey AI and Contract Companion, which can dramatically reduce contract preparation time whilst improving accuracy.

You can use the following templates for your own record label, but remember, these have been used for educational purposes, and we recommend getting a consultation with an attorney/lawyer to get a stamp of approval on your version of the contracts before signing any agreements.

DISCLAIMER

Nick Sadler, The Label Machine, and any of its employees are not attorneys at law, and this should not be taken as legal advice. We cannot be held liable for any ramifications of your use of the information in this book.

RECORDING AGREEMENT

As mentioned, recording agreements come in all shapes and sizes. As many modern independent record labels will typically sign singles, EPs or albums once they have heard the final product or at least substantial demos of the final product, we have taken this approach for our agreements.

This is different from major record labels where an artist might be signing future recordings or albums that have not been created yet. These types of deals are more complicated and would require input from legal professionals.

The following is a template of a master recordings agreement for an independent record label that is signing the finished masters. Anything in [**square brackets**] indicates sections that need to be reviewed and edited depending on the release's specifics.

[Record label logo]
[Record label name]
[Record label address]

This Agreement is made the **[date day]** of **[month date 20XX]**.

Parties:

(1) [Record label name] of **[Address]** ("Label") and

(2) [ABC] professionally known as **[DE]** of **[Address]** **["Artist"]** or **[jointly and severally "Artist"]**
1. Type of Agreement: [Recording Agreement] or **[Exclusive Licensing Agreement]**

2. Territory: [World]

3. Term of Agreement: [Life of copyright together with all renewals and extensions]

OR

[Period of X years commencing from the date of this Agreement plus a non-exclusive six month sell-off period]

4. Product:[X Singles (two tracks per single)]

[Names of tracks]

Each track must be a new and original studio performance **[comprising Artist's vocal and instrumental performances]** and feature a different musical composition. Track cannot be a "live" performance or recorded for a film soundtrack.

5. Delivery Materials: Final WAV version together with separate vocals (if applicable) instrumental and acapella. **[Any remixes, club mixes, radio edits videos, artwork etc]**("Masters").

6. Delivery: Within 30 days from the date hereof.

7. Advance: [$X payable within 7 days from receipt of Delivery Materials and valid invoice. Advance recoupable from Artist's share of Net Receipts] or [$1 receipt of which is acknowledged].
8. Royalty Rate: 50% of Net Receipts.

Net Receipts means 100% of all income Label receives directly from the exploitation of Masters after deducting all costs and expenses Label incurs in connection with such exploitation including without limitation recording costs, advances to third parties, remixers fees, manufacturing, distribution, sales, marketing, promotion, artwork, and VAT or similar taxes and mechanical copyright royalty payments.

If a Master is remixed by a third party, any royalties payable to remixer shall be deducted from Artist's share of Net Receipts.

9. Mechanical Royalties: Statutory rate payable in each country or (if none) the customary rate in force at the relevant time except for sales inUSA and Canada where rate shall be 75% of the minimum statutory rate in force at the date of delivery without regard to playing time subject to a maximum of two tracks per Single and ten tracks per Album.

10. Release Commitment: Within six months from receipt of Delivery Materials. Label will use reasonable endeavours to procure international release.

11. Grant of Rights: Artist hereby assigns the copyright and all other rights of a similar nature in the Masters all copies and derivatives thereof, all production parts and all audio and audio-visual recordings manufactured therefrom

together with the performances embodied therein to the Label with full title guarantee (including without limitation performers rights and exclusive rental and lending rights). Label shall be entitled to exploit such rights free from restrictions in Label's absolute discretion throughout the Territory for the full period of copyright and all extensions and renewals thereof.
Label and any party authorised by Label shall have unlimited exclusive rights throughout the Territory to exploit the Masters in any manner and in any form and by any method now known or hereinafter invented, including without limitation public broadcast, electronic transmission, and synchronisation.

Artist hereby grants all necessary consents to enable Label to fully exploit the Masters including without limitation all consents required under the Copyright Designs and Patents Act 1988 and any amendments thereof, all consents required pursuant to any performers property rights and all consents required by any EC Directives on rental and lending rights and any present or future legislation passed for the protection of performers.

12. Warranties: Artist warrants, represents and agrees that:

Artist has the right to enter into this Agreement and to grant the rights granted in this Agreement;

Artist has the ability to perform the obligations required in this Agreement and that there are no subsisting licenses for the Masters in the Territory nor will Artist grant the same;

Artist has obtained all waivers, clearances and consents

necessary for Label to exploit and utilise the Masters in any way, including without limitation sample clearances;

Delivery Materials shall be original and shall not be obscene, defamatory, nor infringe the rights of any third party;

Artist is over the age of 18 years and shall be responsible for Artist's own tax and national insurance contributions; Artist has been advised to seek legal advice prior to signing this Agreement;

Artist shall not for a period commencing from the above date and expiring five years after the initial commercial release each track re-record or record for any third party or authorise the recording of such track;

Label has the right to use Artist's name, individual name, biographies, photos, and any logos, designs and trademarks relating to Artist or Artist's name in connection with Label's business and exploitation of the Masters; and

Label shall be able to obtain without delay mechanical reproduction and synchronisation licenses in respect of each composition embodied in each Master to enable Label to release and fully exploit each Master in the Territory.

13. Indemnity: Artist agrees to indemnify Label and its licensees against any loss and damages (including legal fees) arising out of or in connection with any claims, actions, or demands by any third party which is inconsistent with any warranties and/or representations Artist has made under this Agreement. Pending determination of any claim Label may withhold a reasonable sum Label deems sufficient to meet such a claim.

14. Accounting: Label will account to Artist on a semi-annual basis within 90 days after the end of 30 June and 31 December in each year.

15. Audit: Artist may audit Label's books and records relating solely to the exploitation of Masters once per calendar year. Statements shall not be capable of challenge or objection by Artist within 2 years after the relevant statement was rendered. If audit reveals an underpayment exceeding 10% or $2000, whichever is the greater, of the amount due to Artist for the audited period, Label shall reimburse Artist's reasonable costs of such audit (excluding travel, accommodation, and subsistence) up to a maximum of 1,000.

16. General: Label may license, assign or otherwise transfer all or any of its rights under this Agreement to any third party. Artist may not assign or license the benefit of this Agreement. This Agreement shall be binding upon each of the parties and their respective successors and assigns.

This Agreement is not a partnership, joint venture, or contract of employment between Label and Artist. Neither party shall be bound by any representation, act or omission of the other.

[This Agreement shall apply to and bind Artist jointly and severally]

If any provision of this Agreement is held by a court or other body of competent jurisdiction to be void or unenforceable but would be valid and enforceable if a part(s) was deleted or modified, such provision shall apply with such deletion or modification to make the Agreement valid and effective.

This Agreement is the entire agreement between the parties relating to this subject and may only be varied or modified by a written document signed by both parties.
17. Jurisdiction: [This Agreement shall be governed and construed in accordance with the laws of England whose courts shall have exclusive jurisdiction.]
OR

[This Agreement shall be governed by the laws of the State of California and any dispute shall be settled in the state or federal courts located in the city of Los Angeles, CA.]

The Parties confirm their acceptance of the above terms by signing below where indicated.

____

For and on behalf of
[Record label name]

____

[Artist's full name]

Let's break down and explain each section in detail.

Name and date

This is where you put the record label logo, name and address and the date of the contract.

Parties

Here is where you detail the legal names of each party the contract is between. As the label or music company you need to list your legal company name. If your label name is different from your legal company name you can use T/A for trading as. For example 'Music Company Name Ltd T/A Sureshot Records'

The address is the physical address of each party. For a solo artist, you end it with 'Artist'. If the artist has multiple members, you need to write each of the individual's full legal name and address here and then include the term 'jointly and severally "Artist" at the end.

Type of Agreement

States what kind of agreement this is, a Recording Agreement or Exclusive Licensing Agreement.

If a label wants to sign the final masters of music to the label in perpetuity, then state Recording Agreement. This may be the case with newer artists where the investment risk from the label is higher.

If the artist wants to license the music for a set period to the label, this will be an Exclusive Licensing Agreement, which may be the case with more established artists that have a track record of generating substantial royalties.

Territory

Most digital releases on an independent label will be for the entire world. If you are only signing for one country or territory, amend this section to the appropriate details.

Term of Agreement

If this will be a Exclusive Licensing Agreement then you need to add in the Term of Agreement clause. The term Period can be negotiated with the artist, but from a label's point of view, try not to go lower than seven years. If this is a Recording Agreement, then use Life of Copyright together with all renewals and extensions.

Product

This section is to detail the names of the tracks (if known) and the formats. By formats, I mean single, or EP or album. If the artist uses their own vocals and instrumental performances, then include the wording "comprising Artist's vocal and instrumental performances", which will be the case most of the time.

If you know the names of the tracks because the music is finished, then list them here. If they are unknown, list what they intend to be, for example, two EPs of three tracks minimum each.

Delivery Materials

This details what the final master format should be sent to the label as, typically WAV format, and if you want any alternative versions included, such as the instrumental, radio edits, or a music video edit.

Delivery

States the time the label needs to receive the masters after the artist signs the agreement.

Advance

An advance is an amount of money paid in advance of the artists' future royalties. You might pay an advance if an artist has a successful career and already a substantial fanbase; as you know you will be selling enough music to cover the future royalties.

If you're not paying an advance (for example, working with a less established artist), you need to include the wording' $1 receipt of which is acknowledged', which needs to be included to make the contract binding. If in another country, use the currency format of your country.

Royalty Rate

The royalty rate defines what percentage of the royalties the artist receives after all releases expenses have been deducted. Most independent record labels share 50/50 between artist and label. However, as the royalty income from music sales has been declining slightly in recent years, some more established independent labels may assign a lower royalty rate of 40% or 30% for signing new, unproven artists. And large independent labels or majors, the overall royalty rate goes down to between 18% to 15%.

If you are a label that will be producing remixes, the last clause states that remix expenses are deducted from the artist's share of the net receipt, as usually the royalties are split between the artist and remixer.

For a more detailed breakdown of royalty rates, expenses, and net income, refer to the Music Copyright section of this book.

Mechanical Royalties

This defines what the label will pay in mechanical royalties to the copyright owner of the composition. This is a statutory rate for each country (or in the case of the US and Canada, it will be 75% of this rate). This is an industry-standard across most recordings agreements.

If you are only putting out digital releases, the mechanicals will be paid from the platforms such as Spotify directly to the rightful copyright owner. Many distributors will also be set up to pay this directly to the copyright owner also.

However, if you will be releasing physical formats, you will need to make sure you account for this in your release budget.

Release Commitment

This clause states the label will release the music within six months of receiving the final masters. If you sign the tracks and don't release the music, the artist can take the music elsewhere to release, giving them a way out and ensuring they can still release the music to the public.

Grant of Rights

This clause assigns the rights from the artist to the label to sell and exploit the music. It states that the label is free to do this with all copyrights associated with the masters and that it is free to do this throughout the territories defined in the territories clause, without any limitations.

The second part of the clause states the right to sell and exploit the music across all known formats and any formats yet to be invented in the future. So if a new format is invented, a label still has the rights to sell the music in the new format when it becomes available. For example, when MP3 became a format, any agreements signed before MP3 was invented would have been covered with this clause.

Warranties

In this clause, the artist provides warranties that they have the rights to the copyright, the ability to sign over the copyrights, and there are no other licenses already existing for the masters. The artist won't be signing the copyright to anyone else.

It states that if any clearances required for the music or any samples used, that the artist has cleared these for legal use already and that there is no obscene material or material that infringes a third party's rights, for example, hate speech.

The artist must be over the age of 18 and is responsible for their own taxes, and that you, as a label, advised the artist to take legal advice before signing the contract. The artist also agrees to not re-record or allow anyone else to re-record the masters for five years after the release.

The AI clause protects the Company from legal risks tied to AI-generated music by ensuring the Artist used only human-created elements and takes full responsibility for any related copyright issues.

Finally, the last two paragraphs state that the label has the right to use the artist's name, logo, press pictures, and the like for promoting the music for sale and that the label will be able to obtain mechanical licenses for the release as well. This last point applies if an artist has a major publisher who needs to grant the mechanical license. It's simply saying that an artist's publisher can't delay the label releasing the music by holding back a mechanical license.

Indemnity

This clause states that if the artist did something against what they agreed in the warranties above, for example, not clearing a sample, that the label has the right to be compensated for any costs associated with dealing with the issue as paying for the sample rights. The label can hold back an amount of royalty money the label believes it will cost to cover dealing with an issue.

Accounting

This states when the label will send a royalty statement to the artist. 90 days gives the label time to collect royalties for the last accounting period as many platforms can take up to 60 days to pay the distributor, and distributors often only report every 30 days to the label.

Audit

This clause outlines the details of how the artist can audit the royalty statements of the label. This is rarely required between independent artists and labels, but if it is required, a specialist accountant is usually assigned to audit the books.

General

The first clause gives the right to assign the copyright to other parties, for example, licensing the track to a music compilation. The second part means the artist can't license this agreement to a third party and benefit from selling the royalties this agreement generates to a third party. The last part means that the agreement is still valid even if the rights are assigned.

The next clause states that the agreement is not a partnership, joint venture, or contract of employment between the label and artist. This is to prevent the artist from claiming any legal rights that fall under any of these types of relationships, such as employment rights.

If the artist is more than one person as stated in the parties section, you need to include the clause 'This Agreement shall apply to and bind Artist jointly and severally'. If the artist is only one person, then delete this clause.

The next clause states that if some terms are held to be illegal or otherwise unenforceable, the remainder of the agreement should still apply. For instance, if, for some reason, it became illegal to pay mechanical royalties, it would not void the whole agreement. It would be deleted or modified, and the rest of the agreement terms would still apply.

The last clause states that if either party wants to change any part of the agreement, it must be agreed by a written document signed by both parties.

Jurisdiction

The final clause states which country the jurisdiction of the agreement and any disputes which court of law they will be settled in. Change this depending on the country or state your record label company is based.

The final section is for signing. Edit to state your record label name, your legal name, the artist's legal name. If there is more than one member for the artist, add each member's legal name.

FEATURED ARTISTS AGREEMENT

If the main artist on a recording has collaborated with other producers or a featured artist, then the label will need to know who these collaborators are and if master royalties are being paid to them.

And from the artist's point of view, they will all need to decide what the writer's share will be between each artist.

To do this, collaborators or featured artists work with the main artist to sign an agreement that documents the royalty and writer splits. Some names for these agreements are the Producer Agreement, Featured Artist Agreement or a Featured Artist Split Sheet, which all fundamentally do the same thing.

It's important that all the writers and artists agree to the splits before releasing the record to avoid a dispute later, especially if the track is a runaway success.

These agreements will usually offer a share of the royalties and sometimes an upfront fee to the collaborators. In the case of a 'buy-out', the featured artist would be bought out of all master royalties for a set fee. However, they would still be entitled to a share of the publishing, which would be agreed upon.

In most cases, for independent labels and artists, a simple Split Sheet made between the main artist and featured artist detailing the percentage splits for the recording master rights (recording) and the writers share (publishing) with any advance paid will suffice.

The Split Sheet, along with the Recording Contract, would then have all the details for who gets paid what and what the writers share between all parties involved.

Typically, if the track has been recorded with collaborators before the record label is involved, it will be the main artist's responsibility to arrange a split sheet and for reporting record royalties to contributors and producers. However, as a record label, it's good practice to ensure that these have been signed and to assist artists if they are unsure of how to do this.

Below is a typical split sheet you can use as a template for a featured artist. Anything in [square brackets] indicates sections that need to be updated depending on each release's specifics.

Main artist name
Main artist address

This Agreement is made the **[date day]** of **[month date 20XX]**.

Parties:

(1) **[Main legal name]** professionally known as **[Main artist name]** "Main Artist" and

(2) **[Featured legal name]** professionally known as **[Featured artist name]** "Featured Artist".

1. Type of Agreement: Masters and Writers Split Sheet

2. Product: The master recording "(the Master)" and the musical and lyrical composition ("the Composition") for **[Main artist name] - [Track name] ft. [Featured artist name]**

3. Royalties

3.1 Master Rights shares:

In full and final consideration of the provision by the Featured Artist services hereunder and of the assignment contained hereunder, Main Artist agrees to pay Featured Artist the following Master Royalties on income received:

[Featured legal name]: X%

3.2 Writers shares:

The Artists hereby agree that the writing shares within the track are as follows:

a) **[Main legal name]**: X%
CAE/IPI: **[XXXXXXXXXX]**
Publisher: **[Publisher Name]**

b) **[Featured legal name]: X%**
CAE/IPI: **[XXXXXXXXXX]**
Publisher: **[Publisher Name]**

3.3 Advances

Any advances on Master Royalties shall be shared on a prorated basis in accordance with clause 3.1

3.4 Advance of $500 will be paid upon the execution of this agreement in accordance with clause 3.3 and will be considered recoupable against future master earnings.

[This Agreement shall be governed and construed in accordance with the laws of England whose courts shall have exclusive jurisdiction.]

OR

[This Agreement shall be governed by the laws of the State of California and any dispute shall be settled in the state or federal courts located in the city of Los Angeles, CA.]

Read and Agreed	Read and Agreed
________________	________________
[Main legal name]	**[Featured legal name]**
Date:	Date:

Let's break down and explain each section in detail.

Name and date

This is where you put the artist's name, address and date of the agreement.

Parties

Here is where you detail the legal names and the artist names of the main and featured artists on the track.

Type of Agreement

This states what kind of agreement this is: a Masters and Writers Split Sheet.

Product

Write the full name of the track here, including all featured artists as it will be listed when released publicly.

Royalties

This states what percentage of the royalties the featured artist is receiving from the artist's share of master royalties from the track's sales. If it's an equal split between the main artist and featured artist, you will list 50%.

Writer's Share

This states how the writer's share will be split amongst the writers. Ensure you record the artist's CAE/IPI number (obtained from the artist's PRO) and their publisher, so it's easier when registering with the PROs.

If an artist is unpublished, then use the term 'Copyright Control' for the publisher. This means the artist controls their own publishing and is the default term for artists that have not signed to a publisher.

If there are more than two writers, copy and repeat this section for each writer.

Advances

This states that if the track receives an advance from a label then it is shared equally between all parties. Also, if the main artist has agreed to pay a separate advance to the featured artist on the execution of the agreement, this is stated here. In this instance, $500. If no advance is to be paid, remove this clause.

Jurisdiction

The final clause states which country has jurisdiction over the agreement. This will determine where any disputes that reach a court of law will be settled. Change this depending on the country or state the main artist is based.

The final section is for signing. Edit to state each of the artist's legal names. If there are more than two writers, then copy and repeat a signing section for each extra writer.

Note: You can also edit this template to remove any reference to masters, and then the agreement is just a 'Writers Split Sheet' for the writer's share of the track. You may want to do this if the other writers of the track will not be having any share of the master royalties.

REMIX AGREEMENT

A remix of a song is used to create a version of the original song that is appealing to a new audience, typically a version that can be played in a club or for fans of electronic music. Even within electronic music, different remixes are done for the various genres (for instance, a house remix of an original drum & bass song). If you are an electronic record label, you'll frequently sign and release remixes as part of your catalogue.

If you are an aspiring DJ producer, remixes are a fantastic way to start your producing career, and many producers have launched their careers off the back of a great remix. For instance, the producer Kygo did a remix of "Sexual Healing" by Marvin Gaye, which was initially an unlicensed remix. It became so popular, the remix was eventually made official, and he now has a huge career.

There are three different ways to approach the remix fee.

You can pay a work-for-hire remix fee. This is essentially a buy-out for creating the remix and is paid on delivery. This is the simplest approach, as there is no ongoing accounting, and the remixer knows they will be compensated for their work.

You can agree to a royalty rate on the sales of the remix. Typically, 50% of the artist's share of the remix sales. This means ongoing accounting to the remixer; however, there is no upfront fee for the record label to pay. Sometimes with popular remix artists, they may want to negotiate a share of the track's publishing. This is more common in the US, and if the artist is published, it requires more paperwork and ongoing accounting.

Finally, you agree to a remix swap. This is common among electronic artists that are at similar levels in their career. Each artist agrees to remix one of the other artists' tracks. In this case, the artist may agree to a share of each other's remix sales.

If you are looking to request a remix from another artist, then these are the things you need to know and share:

- Link to the original track.
- Remix budget.
- Which label is releasing it.
- When the deadline for the remix is.
- When the proposed release date is.
- Are there other confirmed remixes? (Is it part of a remix EP?)
- Confirmed promo for the release (music video, radio plugging budget, etc).

Send the above information to the remixer directly or their manager via email. Once you agree to the deal points, you can send over a remix agreement.

Below is a typical remix agreement you can use as a template for your own remixes. Anything in **[square brackets]** indicates sections that need to be updated depending on the deal point specifics to each remix.

[Record label logo]
[Record name]
[Record label address]

This Agreement is made the **[date day]** of **[month date 20XX]**.

Parties:

(1) [Record label name] of **[Address]** ("Label") and
(2) [ABC] professionally known as **[DE]** of **[Address] ["Artist"]** or **[jointly and severally "Artist"]**

Remixing as: [Artist Name]

Type of Agreement: Remix Agreement

Track (S) Title: [Full Track Name]

Territory: World

Term: Life of Copyright

Formats: Vinyl, CD, digital and mobile (all formats known or hereafter created)

Remix Fee: [$500] [if paying royalty rate remove this section]

Royalty Rate: [50%] share of net receipts on revenue derived from sales of remix only **[if paying a remix fee then remove this section]**

Publishing: No publishing share

Accounting: Ninety (90) days after 30 June and 31 December

Compilation requests: It is agreed that artist and artist management will be informed of any compilations prior to approval. If the artist or management does not reply within 72 hours of the notification, the label has consent to secure the deal in good faith.

Release Commitment: Within six months from receipt of Delivery Materials.

Auditing: You will have the audit Label's books and records relating solely to the exploitation of Masters once per calendar year. Statements shall not be shall not be subject to challenge or objection by Artist within 2 years after the relevant statement was rendered. If the audit reveals an underpayment exceeding 10% or $2000, whichever is the greater, of the amount due to Artist for the audited period, Label shall reimburse Artist's reasonable costs of such audit (excluding travel, accommodation, and subsistence) up to a maximum of $1,000 **[If Artist is paid upfront Remix fee, remove Auditing section]**

Grant of Rights: You grant and license to us all copyright and any other rights in all singles or other recordings ('The Masters') made hereunder to include the right to manufacture, sell and otherwise exploit and license to others the same audio and audio-visual devices (whether known or hereafter created) embodying the Masters ('Record(s)') and to perform and broadcast the Masters in any manner and in all media (whether now known or hereafter created) and to recompile, remix and re-edit the masters.

Warranties:

The Artist warrants and agrees that:

1) You have the right to enter into this Agreement and to grant the rights granted in this agreement.

2) You have the ability to perform the obligations required in this agreement and that there are no subsisting licenses for the masters in the territory, nor will you grant the same.

3) You have obtained all waivers, clearances and consents necessary for us to exploit and utilise the Masters in any way.

4) You understand that you are not entitled to mechanical or performance related royalties under this agreement, and you waive the right to collect any if applicable.

General:

1) We shall initially release the single on the Label. However, we may at any later date release the remixes under any name, trademark or label which we or our subsidiaries, affiliates or licensees may select.

2) Neither Artist nor any other person shall release the remix.

3) We have exclusive and unlimited rights throughout the Territory to use and publish, and to permit others to use and publish, Artist's approved name (including any professional name heretofore or hereafter adopted by Artist), and approved photographs, portrait, likeness, and biographical material concerning Artist for advertising and trade purposes solely in connection with the Remixes, including, but not limited to, in the marketing, sale or other exploitation of remixes.

4) You hereby understand the above terms and enter this agreement having been advised by Label to seek legal advice.

5) This Agreement is the entire agreement between the parties relating to this subject and may only be varied or modified by a written document signed by both parties.

Jurisdiction:

[This Agreement shall be governed and construed in accordance with the laws of England whose courts shall have exclusive jurisdiction.]

OR

[This agreement will be governed by the laws of the State of California and any dispute shall be settled in the state or federal courts located in the city of Los Angeles, CA.]

Please confirm your acceptance of these terms by signing below where indicated.

____

For and on behalf of

[Record Label Name]

____

[Artist's full name]

Let's break down and explain each section in detail.

Name and date

This is where you put the record label logo and the date of the contract.

Parties

Here is where you detail the legal names of each party the contract is between. The address is the physical address of each party. For a solo artist, you end it with 'Artist'. If the remix artist has multiple members, you need to write each of the individual's full legal name and address here and then include the term 'jointly and severally "Artist"' at the end.

Remixing As

The name that the remix artist is remixing as. This is the name that will be listed on the official remix release.

Type of Agreement

This states what kind of agreement it is: a Remix Agreement.

Territory

Most remixes released on an independent label will be for the entire world. If you are only releasing the remix for one country or territory, amend this section to the appropriate details.

Term and Formats

Remixes will be for the life of the copyright. Format lists the expected formats the remix may be released on.

Remix Fee

If this remix has been agreed for a fee, state this here. If you have agreed to a royalty rate, then remove this section.

Royalty Rate

If this remixer is being paid a share of the royalties, state the percentage here. If you have agreed to a remix fee, then remove this section.

Publishing

This states that there will be no publishing share of the remix.

Accounting

If a royalty rate has been agreed upon, this will state when royalty reports are sent. If you have agreed to a remix fee, then remove this section.

Compilation Requests

If there is a request for the remix to be licensed to a third party compilation, the label agrees to notify the remixer about the deal and give them 72 hours to respond.

Release Commitment

This clause states that the label will release the remix within six months of receiving the final masters.

Auditing

This clause outlines the details of how the artist can audit the royalty statements of the label. This is rarely required between independent artists and labels, but if it is required, a specialist accountant is usually assigned to audit the books. If you have agreed a remix fee, then remove this section.

Grant of Rights

This clause assigns the rights from the artist to the label to sell and exploit the music. It states that the label is free to do this with all copyrights associated with the masters, and that it is free to do this throughout the territories defined in the territories clause, without any limitations.

Warranties

In this clause, the artist provides warranties that they have the rights to the copyright, the ability to sign over the copyright, and there are no other licenses already existing for the masters, and that the artist won't sign the copyright to anyone else.

It states that if any clearances are required for the music or any samples used, then the artist has cleared these for legal use already, and that there is no obscene material or material that infringes a third party's rights (for example, hate speech).

The remixer is not entitled to any mechanical or performance related royalties.

General

This clause states that the remix will be released on the label, and it can be released in the future on other labels that the label controls or licenses too. The following section states that the remixer or any other person is not allowed to release the remix.

The next section states that the label can use the artist's name, logo, press pictures, and other materials for promoting the music for sale.

The last points state that the label has advised the remixer to get legal advice and that any changes to the agreement can only be made through a written agreement between both parties.

Jurisdiction

The final clause states which country the jurisdiction of the agreement is in and, if there are any disputes, which court of law they will be settled in. Change this depending on the country or state where your record label company is based.

The final section is for signing. Edit to state your record label name, your legal name, and the artist's legal name. If there is more than one member for the artist, add each member's legal name.

UPLOAD TO DISTRIBUTION

Uploading your release to your distributor is very straightforward as all the hard work is getting the assets and metadata together, which you would have already done.

If you haven't decided on a distributor yet, go back to the Distribution chapter and use the distribution chooser link on the Book Resources tab on The Label Machine website to help pick your preferred distributor.

It does depend on whom you use for distribution as to what you need to do next. However, in general, the next steps are:

- Enter the metadata (including individual track level credits).
- Upload the WAV files and artwork.
- Submit the release.

Usually, within 72 hours, you will get an email notification of the release and a chance to check it over and send any edits. Always double-check the spelling as it's been known for names to be misspelt by accident, so always check.

Most problems usually arise if the artwork is not in the right format and size or the music files are not in the correct format.

Ensure artwork is 3000 x 3000 pixels in size at 72 dpi (dots per inch) and the music is a WAV file in 16-bit format. Some distributors will allow for 24-bit file uploads, and if you get errors, check which format they require.

If, for some reason, your release has a special consideration that doesn't fit the criteria for a release, such as an artist name that needs ALL CAPS (which normal rules won't allow), you can send a request to your distributor to make this change.

Each of them are different, so check the FAQ or ask your distribution representative on the best way to ensure the release is set up properly.

IS YOUR RELEASE A SINGLE, EP OR ALBUM?

An album that contains one to three tracks, with each track being less than ten minutes, will automatically be identified as a single. The term "- Single" will automatically appear after the album title. Releases that do not meet these criteria will not be recognised as a single.

To be identified as an "EP" and have "- EP" after the release title, the release must have one to three tracks, one or more tracks with a running time of ten minutes or more, a total running time of less than 30 minutes, or four to six tracks, with a running time of fewer than 30 minutes.

An Album will need to have seven or more tracks to be identified as an album.

REGISTER SONGS WITH PROS

As a record label, you will have to register the song masters with your neighbouring rights collection agency for each release. If you are an artist or manage an artist, you will need to register the song compositions with your PRO.

REGISTERING MASTERS

Ensure your mastered songs are registered with your neighbouring rights agency, also known as a Digital Performance Royalties collection agency.

If you are based in the US, you need to register your songs with SoundExchange.

Record Labels based in Canada register your songs with Re:-Sound.

If you are based in the UK, register your songs with PPL.

NOTE: PPL will also take registrations from any label based anywhere in the world, so if you are outside the US or UK, you can still use PPL to collect and pay your digital performance royalties.

REGISTERING COMPOSITIONS

If you are an artist, you will need to register as a writer with your Performance Right Organisation (PRO) in your country.

If you are an unpublished artist, you can claim the publisher's share of the music by also registering as a self-published artist.

If you are based in the US, you need to register your songs with one of the PROs, either ASCAP, BMI, or SESAC, to collect your performance royalties.

If you want to register with ASCAP as a self-published artist, follow these steps:

Join ASCAP as both a writer and a publisher. It's free to join as a writer, and if you join as both simultaneously, ASCAP will waive the publisher application fee as well.

To become an ASCAP publisher, you'll need: A mailing address

You don't need to set up a corporation or fictitious business name to join as a publisher. You can simply use your Social Security Number if you select the "Individual/Sole Proprietor" option.

Once you've joined, sign in to ASCAP Member Access and click "Register a Work" under the "Works" menu on the left navigation bar to start using ASCAP's Online Work Registration system.

Register your music through this system. This is crucial because ASCAP needs this information to identify your works and pay you correctly when they're performed.

If your music is used in television, cable, or audio-visual streaming services, ensure that cue sheets are submitted. These are usually provided by the producer of the film or TV program.

By joining ASCAP, you'll also be able to collect rights payments worldwide, as these organisations have reciprocal arrangements with most other countries' equivalents.

Remember, by registering as both a writer and a publisher, you'll be able to collect both the writer's share (50%) and the publisher's share (50%) of your royalties. This setup allows you to maximize your earnings and maintain control over your music publishing rights.

Mechanical Royalties (The MLC)

The MLC (Mechanical Licensing Collective) collects streaming and download royalties from platforms like Spotify and Apple Music under the US Music Modernization Act. To access these royalties, you'll need to complete a straightforward two-step process: first, sign up at The MLC Portal providing personal information for identity verification, then create a Member profile, which is required for receiving all US digital mechanical royalties. This ensures you receive the compensation you're entitled to from digital music distribution.

If you're a UK-based artist looking to self-publish your music, the easiest way is with PRS. Here are the key steps you should take:

Register with PRS for Music (Performing Right Society):

PRS collects royalties for you when your works are performed or communicated to the public. Upon registration, you'll receive a unique CAE number, which you'll need to register all works you've written or co-written.

Register with MCPS (Mechanical-Copyright Protection Society):

MCPS administers the fees you receive on physical sales, including download sales.

Register your works:
For each piece of music, you'll need to provide details such as the title, writer(s), publisher(s), and performer(s). You'll receive a unique tune code for each work, which is important when submitting your music to distribution services.

Register with PPL (Phonographic Performance Limited):
If you're a session musician or perform your own work in recordings, register with PPL to receive payments when those recordings are broadcast or played publicly.

Register each performance:
After every gig, make sure to submit your playlist (including composers) to the appropriate Performing Rights Organisation. This ensures you receive your fair share of royalties, even for performances of your own material. You can do this as a DJ also. The platform allows you to save your performance to use again, so if you play the same set (mostly) at each gig, so it's a very quick process.

By joining PRS and PPL, you'll also be able to collect rights payments worldwide, as these organizations have reciprocal arrangements with most other countries' equivalents.

Remember, it's crucial to register all your music and performances. By following these steps, you'll ensure that you're set up to receive royalties from various sources, including live performances, radio play, streaming, and physical sales.

If you are outside the US, Canada, or the UK, and your country supports music copyright, register with your local PRO.

For more information on this, please refer to the Collecting Royalties and Registering with PROs chapter.

MARKETING: PROMOTING THE RELEASE AND THE ARTIST

The following chapters will cover preparing and creating marketing assets and then marketing and promoting the release to fans. Marketing your music is what makes the difference between having a few hundred people listening to your music and hundreds of thousands of fans both listening and buying.

Marketing also covers promoting an artist consistently between music releases, which we will explore further in the 360° Music System chapters.

The digital marketing landscape is constantly changing; however, the principles say the same. While I'll focus on marketing the music from a label's point of view, everything covered can be applied to promoting an individual artist self-releasing.

- Music marketing principles
- Create marketing and PR schedule

- Create marketing assets
- Press release
- Creating The EPK (Electronic Press Kit)
- DJ promo
- Getting on blogs and publications
- Secure music premieres
- Curator Submissions
- Create pre-saves
- Facebook and Instagram ads
- Spotify playlists
- Release day
- Post-release activities

MUSIC MARKETING

Marketing and promotion. This is where you can really make or break a release. Subpar music can still rise up the charts and gain listens, followers and plays with a solid marketing plan. If you have great music and a solid marketing plan, it won't be a question of whether you will succeed; it will be a question of how much of a success it will be.

Aside from creating great music, understanding marketing principles is one of the most essential aspects of being a successful artist and label. All successful labels have a good brand

and marketing strategy, even if your marketing is anti-branding (intentionally avoiding traditional branding).

The key to being a successful record label or artist is ensuring people know about and hear your music. We will break down the practical steps to marketing in later chapters, but for now, we will provide an overview of the different marketing types available to artists to reach as many potential fans as possible.

INBOUND AND OUTBOUND MARKETING

When we first started marketing our records at Never Say Die Records, I came across a company called Topspin. This company introduced me to outbound and inbound marketing and the marketing funnel, or 'fan' funnel. These funnels were crucial to our early success with growing our email fanbase.

Outbound marketing is when you use strategies like influencer marketing to get people listening to your music on various channels, which you can manage in-house or via a PR/ marketing agency.

Inbound marketing is when you convert people who have connected with your music into fans and followers on social media and then into consumers of your music via purchasing albums, tickets to gigs and merchandise.

You need to employ both inbound and outbound marketing to grow your audience and thus enhance your label and your artists' success.

INBOUND MARKETING

A great way of explaining and implementing inbound marketing is using the marketing funnel, which demonstrates how you should aim to convert people from being strangers to being fans (or advocates).

In traditional marketing, it's called the sales funnel, and in the music industry, it's called the fan funnel.

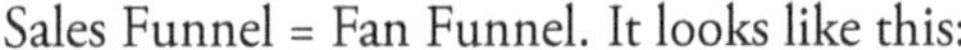
Sales Funnel = Fan Funnel. It looks like this:

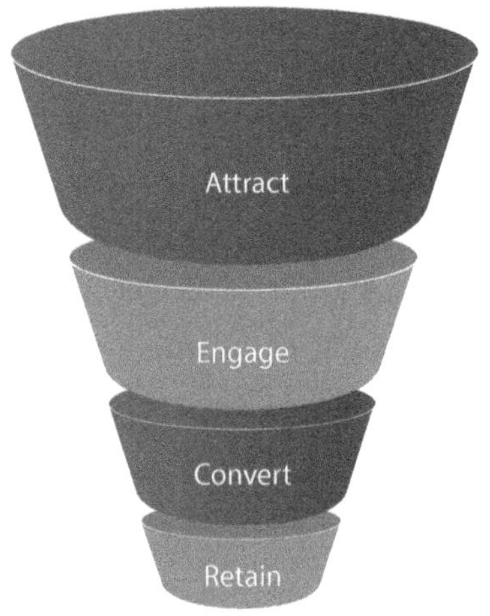

The top of the funnel is where you ATTRACT potential new fans who discover you via your website, social media, Spotify playlist, mainstream media, live shows and paid traffic (Facebook ads).

Next is the ENGAGE section, where the fan will subscribe to your email list, become a YouTube subscriber, Spotify follower, Facebook like, and Twitter follower.

Following this is the CONVERT section, where the casual fan becomes the actual fan by purchasing physical products, vinyl, digital download, merchandise, and tickets to live shows.

Finally, the RETAIN section is where you create your Super Fans, those that buy frequent purchases, subscriptions, or crowdfund an album project.

When you have a fan following and subscribing to you, they give you permission to keep marketing. You're going to keep these super fans by giving them more great music and engaging content and encouraging them to keep building a relationship with you and your label.

So you need to release amazing music and content.

- Actively engage with your fans by interacting with them and sending them great content via your email list structured around your releases schedules.
- Put out engaging content across all the different social platforms.
- Allow fans to purchase your creativity, whether it be free music downloads for an email address, merchandise or ticket sales to your gig.

The way we manage our music marketing funnel is by using our Marketing Machine software with social media schedulers and paid ad triggers to ATTRACT at the top of the funnel. We use email sequences and social media automations to ENGAGE, the shop and purchase funnels for the CONVERT section, and community tools for the RETAIN section. The Marketing Machine handles everything from top to bottom of the funnel.

OUTBOUND MARKETING

Your outbound marketing is what you do to push your music and marketing outwards from your label. It is any activity when you reach out to get people talking about your record label, music, or artists. Generally speaking, the term PR, which stands for Public Relations, means outbound marketing.

A PR agency's job is to spend their time reaching out to media outlets to try and get them to talk about your music.

In music, examples of outbound marketing could be:

- Reaching out to a blog and getting an interview for one of your artists.
- Getting your music reviewed on a music blog.
- Having an album review or artist interview published in a magazine or local newspaper.
- Securing the premiere of a music video on a YouTube music channel with thousands of subscribers.
- Reaching out to a Spotify playlist and securing a listing.
- Getting a TikTok influencer to do an original dance routine to your music.

INTERACTIVE MARKETING

There is a new form of marketing that sits between inbound and outbound, interactive marketing.

As mobile, web, and immersive technologies advance, brands have more opportunities than ever to create media with spatial, multisensory, and participatory elements. These experiences are especially powerful, as our brains naturally respond more strongly to interactive and immersive content.

Some examples of interactive marketing include:

- Augmented Reality (AR) Filters on Snapchat and Pinterest: Brands and artists use these channels to create engaging AR effects and filters for fans.
- Immersive Web and Web 3.0 Experiences: Embracing Web 3.0, brands and creators are building interactive 3D environments, virtual tours, and metaverse spaces.
- Virtual Reality (VR) for Exclusive Fan Content: VR is increasingly used to deliver VIP experiences for superfans, such as behind-the-scenes access, virtual meet-and-greets, or immersive concerts.
- AI-Driven Personalization and Gamification: Advances in AI allow marketers to deliver highly personalized interactive content, while gamified experiences like interactive challenges, boost engagement and provide valuable insights into audience preferences.

Now you have an overview of marketing theory and the different types of inbound, outbound, and interactive marketing. In the following chapters, we will look at the different ways you can set up your inbound marketing with fan funnels and outbound marketing with PR.

MARKETING AND PR SCHEDULE

A marketing and PR schedule is a timeline of releasing your marketing assets to build up a buzz for the release. For singles and EPs, use an eight-week release plan that starts on the first day of the announcement and ends two weeks after the release date.

For most releases, this is plenty of time to announce the music is coming and build momentum without drawing out the release date and losing the attention of fans. The minimum is about four weeks, and sometimes less if it's a quick turnaround, but the visibility will decrease with less time spent on the release.

There has been a move in recent years towards starting your marketing on the day of release. The idea is that fans want instant access to music when they know it is available, and having to wait a few weeks before they can listen is a waste of promo.

My take on this is that you need a balance between the two. When you have a solid fan base, it makes sense to let your core fans know what's going on, as they are part of the journey. And when you hit release day, that's when you spend most of your marketing budget on promoting posts and PR and attracting new fans.

We will use the same eight-week release example discussed in the Creating a Release Schedule chapter to highlight the Marketing and PR Schedule activities. You will notice it is almost the same, with the exception that there are no admin tasks listed below. That is because the majority of activities when releasing a record are marketing and PR activities.

If you already entered all these activities into your calendar when setting up your Release Schedule then you can use the below list to recap.

MARKETING AND PR SCHEDULE

Week 1

- Write a press release.
- Create DJ/ Radio promo.
- Create teaser clips for SoundCloud.
- Prepare marketing assets.
- Create release date banners for social media.
- Create a teaser trailer.

Week 2

- Submit songs to Spotify playlist via Spotify for Artists account.
- Send out the pre-release press release.
- Send DJ promo out.
- Curate blog and publications.
- Upload release date banners to all social platforms.
- Create extra marketing assets.
- Create YouTube video of tracks.

Week 3

- Secure music features.
- Confirm premieres with music channels.
- Upload teaser trailers to each social media platform.
- Curate Spotify playlists.

Week 4

- Upload SoundCloud teaser clips and share on socials.
- Build an audience on Meta.
- Build Meta fan funnel (ad campaign).
- Set up a WhatsApp group for the team involved in the single release.

Week 5

- (DJ releases) Upload DJ promo mix to Soundcloud.
- Post interview premieres confirmed for this week.
- Marketing assets check.
- Upload at least two extra marketing assets this week before release day.
- Post pre-order link.

Week 6

- Create press release support, confirmed press, premieres and plays.
- Start a three-day countdown.

- Upload at least two extra marketing assets this week.
- Make sure everybody is ready to promote the song.

Week 6 – Release Day

- Post Smarturl release landing page.
- Update all social media banners with 'out now' artwork.
- Update label assets and email artist team.
- Create an email newsletter for label fans.
- Send email newsletter to fan mailing list.
- Send out press release to the database.
- Send individual messages to PR contacts.
- Sending one-to-one messages thanking for support.
- Create a live Zoom/Google Hangouts launch party.

Week 7

- Start Spotify outreach method.
- Activate fan funnel (ad campaign).
- Update your Spotify profile.
- Update your artist pick on Spotify.
- Upload at least two extra marketing assets.

Week 8

- Post playlist additions confirmed for this week.
- Post fan feedback on socials.
- Upload at least two extra marketing assets this week.

This list of key marketing tasks is available for download by visiting the Book Resources tab on The Label Machine website.

A good idea to communicate with everyone involved in the release is to create a WhatsApp group with everyone involved. You want to add people on the team involved in promoting the single release: band members, managers, PR company contact, and close friends.

Alternatively, this can be set up as a Messenger Group or a Slack group; it doesn't matter what app you use, so long as there is a place for everyone to communicate instantly and share assets and information easily.

MARKETING ASSETS

When you write your marketing schedule, it is the marketing assets that you have available or intend to create that will largely shape your plan. To quickly summarise, a marketing schedule is essentially a timeline of when you release your marketing assets, build up awareness of the track or EP towards the release day, and follow up promotion in the first month the music is released.

So for your marketing schedule to work, you need to build the basic marketing assets. As they say, "content is king", and you want as many digital assets as possible to build up to the music release and follow it to keep the momentum going. The more people who hear about or see your release, the more traction it gets.

A famous marketing theory called the 'Rule of Seven' originated in the early 2000s, stating that someone needs seven touchpoints to make a buying decision. However, today's saturated social media landscape has transformed this into the 'Rule of Twelve'.

Consumers or fans, now require approximately twelve touchpoints with your name/logo/brand before developing sufficient familiarity and trust to make purchasing decisions or, in our context, to buy or listen to your music.

You use assets to create these touchpoints. Some assets are valuable enough that you can use them to secure exclusive exposure, for example, a premiere of a track on a blog. So creating assets are vitally important to get as much exposure for your music release.

I'll describe the essential marketing assets you need in this chapter and then describe some optional extra marketing assets in the following chapter.

Refer back to the 'Design Tools and Assets' chapter to recap the different tools and resources you can use to create these assets.

ESSENTIAL MARKETING ASSETS

Social Media Banners

There are two variations of banners you want to create for the release, formatted for each of the platforms listed below. When formatting the sizes, you want to edit the original artwork and add the release name and the release date on the artwork, e.g. 'OUT MARCH 5TH'.

Then duplicate each of the banners, update the release date to 'OUT NOW', and upload them on release day.

And remember, you can also use tools like Canva and Adobe Express to create the different sizes as they have these preset sizes available as template defaults.

Banner Format Sizes:

- Facebook Cover Photo – 820 pixels by 312 pixels (landscape) on computers and 640 pixels by 360 pixels (landscape) on smartphones.
- Facebook Event Photo – 1920 x 1005 pixels.
- Facebook Group Photo – 1640 x 856 pixels.
- SoundCloud – 2480 × 520 pixels.
- X – 1500 x 500 pixels.
- Instagram – 1080 x 1080 pixels.
- Instagram Stories – 1080 x 1920 pixels (portrait).
- YouTube – 2560 x 1440 pixels.

Teaser trailer

This is a short video of the music, artwork, and release and track titles edited together into an animation to create a teaser trailer. It's used to hype the release and is usually the first public asset showcasing the upcoming release.

It will usually end with the full artwork and the release date. If the release is more than one tune, get the producer to edit a small section of each track into a tiny mix that the video animator can use in the teaser trailer.

If you have an album, you can break up the album into smaller part teasers to use across the campaign. These have become very popular in recent years.

Video size formats:

- Square version: 1080 x 1080 pixels
- Instagram Stories / TikTok Vertical: 1080 x 1920 pixels

Teaser edits of the music

Create 40 second edits of the tracks that have the intro with a small bit of the drop or main chorus. Upload these to Soundcloud and use them three to four weeks before the release to tease the music for the core fans.

YouTube Video

On release day, you will need to upload the single to YouTube as a video, so you will need a full-length video of the track. If you have a music video or a lyric video, you can use those as the video to upload.

If you're not releasing any of these, you need to create a simple video with the static artwork, or maybe a looped part of the teaser trailer video over the top of the track. These can be made in the channel that is available inside your YouTube account.

Top ten playlists from the artist

Ask the artist to create a top ten list of favourite tunes. They need to be already released, as you will use a public playlist to create them. Use the list to create a Spotify playlist for the artist, and for electronic artists, use the Beatport Top Ten submission tool to create a Top Ten list there.

Ensure that the track in the release is included in the top ten too! Release this on the week of the main release, as the music will need to be out to be submitted.

DJ promo mix for electronic releases

This is a DJ mix set that showcases the type of music the artist would play in a DJ set or the music that inspires them to make the music they do. When dealing with dance music producers, 99% of them will also DJ or have some sort of live show, and this is a great way to show what to expect when you see them live.

Mixes are typically 40 to 60 minutes long. When you have a roster of artists, you can have the DJs playing each other's music in their sets, pushing the sound of the label together.

This is a good asset to implement from the first release as you can build up a mix series, which can later become a collector's item for fans.

Ensure the tracks in the release you are promoting are included in the mix. This is also an excellent place to drop in IDs, unreleased tunes that are often playable demos or unreleased music from the artist – a great way to tease future releases for the artist into the mix.

You'll want to upload the mix to SoundCloud and Mixcloud. However, be mindful of using tracks released on major labels and indie majors. SoundCloud uses audio detection software to find uploads of the label's music, including detecting them in DJ mixes. You can have a mix taken down automatically from SoundCloud for this, so be careful with these tracks.

PR assets

There are three main assets you will need to create that are focused on PR. This is the Press Release, the EPK (Electronic Press Kit) and DJ & Radio promo. How to make and use these assets will be covered in more detail in the following chapters.

Bigger budget assets

These are not essential, but if you have the budget and feel like you have a strong enough release, these are all good assets to have, the music video being the strongest.

Music video

Music videos make great assets, but they can be expensive to make one that is of good enough quality that it helps promote the music, and you will want to upload to YouTube.

I've seen decent videos built around a cheap-to-film concept and using loads of favours, but I've also seen cheap videos built around favours fail completely.

If you want something decent with minimal risk, it's best to get a decent budget and pay a professional crew. Here are some great resources for finding music producers.

- filmtank.co.uk
- genero.com
- rotorvideos.com
- lutimedia.com
- epikmusicvideos.com
- needafixer.com

AI Music Video Generators

AI-powered tools are now a significant part of the music video landscape, especially for independent artists and those on a tight budget. These platforms allow you to create high-quality, customizable music videos quickly and affordably.

- klingai.com
- runwayml.com
- shaicreative.ai
- neuralframes.com
- pika.art

Merchandise + merchandise gimmicks

Using a merchandising gimmick, by which I mean some piece of merchandise that's related to the music release, you can really get people talking about an artist. Which is the whole point, right?

When we released Skrillex ft. Foreign Beggars – Still Getting It, we decided to release it on a USB credit card. The artwork was on the front of the card, and you plugged the card into a computer and could download full and uncompressed versions of the tracks and remixes as well as other bonuses.

We built an interactive graphical menu where you could watch music videos and download desktop-sized artwork too. No one had done this before, so it was a real talking point. We packaged it up in a nice metal tin with the label logo engraved on the top. We saw plenty of times people found alternative storage uses for this neat little tin as well.

Other examples I've seen are sunglasses, which are popular for summer releases. Creating one-of-a-kind skateboard designs featuring the album artwork. Custom artwork on craft beer is becoming popular these days. Artists are creating NFTs (Non-Fungible Tokens) offering digital ownership of exclusive artwork or content connected to the release too.

You can, of course, release merchandise alongside the release, which can become part of the press. For instance, in the case of vinyl picture disks, making an event of signing the fresh vinyl, or making a video of playing the first test press.

There are many ways to create assets, and you should now have a good understanding of what you can use to create your own assets to market and promote your music releases.

EXTRA MARKETING CONTENT

Every time you post new content, you create an opportunity to make another conversation around you and your music with your existing and potential new fans. That's why it's essential to create as many extra content assets as possible to increase these conversations around your music.

The following is a list of 20 ideas you can use to create extra content. Go through these ideas and pick out as many as are suitable for you.

Then open up the calendar you created earlier with the critical release schedule dates and add when you plan to make each piece of content, release each content piece, and on what platform. You want to focus on these different content assets the week before and the weeks following the release day.

This is the nitty-gritty of marketing, but time well spent here will pay dividends on connecting with a larger audience.

Important note on content formats

When creating content as either stills or videos, remember to always make two versions of the content – one in landscape view and one vertical (aka portrait) view. Viewing content on mobile portrait view is becoming the default format on apps like TikTok, Snapchat and Instagram stories, so make sure you're creating content that fits how your audience will experience it.

EXTRA CONTENT ASSETS IDEAS

Vertical video

Platforms like TikTok, Instagram Reels, and YouTube Shorts are now the primary discovery channels for new music. Prioritize these extra content ideas that fits these formats. Always film in vertical format as the default. Think quick, visually engaging snippets, trends, or challenges.

Release date photo

Create a photo of you or your band holding up a card with the release date on it. Keep it simple with a marker pen on a sheet of printer paper with the date in bold. Use the comments section when you post to add more detail, such as the single name.

Who are you?

Create a simple website landing page that tells the story of what the artist has been up to up to this point in time. Essentially this is an updated bio that is as current as possible and mentions the new single. Point new fans to this page to discover more about the artist and their story.

Create Spotify video canvas

Engage your fans in a whole new way with a Spotify Canvas, a short looping visual you can add to each of your tracks on Spotify. It's album artwork for the streaming age. You can easily create one using videos from Mixkit or the Rotor Video app.

Lyric Video

If you have lyrics, create a lyric video. The easiest way of doing this is to look for a freelancer on a site like Fiverr.com. There are plenty of options available, as lyric videos have become popular over the years. Or create one yourself using Rotor Videos or learn how to make one using a video editing app like Adobe Premiere.

New Press Picture

Take new press pictures of you or your band. Nowadays, the cameras on modern phones allow you to take professional photos, and there are plenty of editing apps to get the final pic looking just right. Even using the built-in Instagram filters can allow you to create some awesome new pictures.

Equipment run down videos

Create a video of all the equipment you use to create music in the studio or the equipment when you play live. Or create both. These are easy to film and edit together with a voice-over. These are great for TikTok as you can list your equipment in quick rapid-fire shots.

Create an interview

You don't need a publication or blog to request an interview with you or your band. You can create one yourself to share online. Prepare questions ahead of time and record answers to the camera. Then edit the video with the question popping up for a few seconds on screen, followed by your response.

Cover song of your own track

Get a cover done of your track. Swap with another band or get a cover version done from someone on Fiverr.com. Or Use AI to create a cover version of your own track, which can be done with text prompts in Suno.ai

Remixes

If you are doing remixes, this is an opportunity to use these different content ideas to further create more videos of how the remix was made, a video of the remixes drop, or an interview with the remix artist.

Performance video

Create an acoustic version of the track or a full band performance in the studio. Set up each band member's mobile phone to record a different angle of the band to create a dynamic video of the song. If it's a club track, record a live DJ set, opening with the new single.

Live stream event

This is ideal to do on the evening of the release day on Instagram Live, YouTube Live, or Twitch. Create an event and share. Like the performance video idea above, do an acoustic version of the track or a full band performance for an extended live version of the song. For club music, do a DJ set. Break out the drinks and celebrate, and don't forget to encourage everyone on the stream event to go and buy or add the track to their Spotify playlist.

How the track was made

This can be a simple explanation of how the track was produced. Simply open up the DAW project file and use Zoom or QuickTime to record your screen capture video with audio. You can break down each of the track's plugins, go in-depth about what synths were used, how the synths were programmed, and any special mix techniques used.

Fan video

Get your fans to record and upload videos of them lip-syncing to the track or, for club music, fans doing a bass face for the music on the drop or doing a dance routine. For posting on TikTok, the idea here is to get a particular move popular and everyone to record and post their version of it to your music.

Quote video

This is a video where you share supporting quotes as text over a 30-second clip of the song playing. These can be fan supporting quotes or, if you have done a DJ campaign, supporting quotes from the DJs that have given feedback.

Behind the scenes video

This is where the artists talk about how the song came into existence. What is the story? Where did the original idea come from? What other bands or artists inspired them? Was it created in a day or over weeks? What do they love about the track? Was it easy to write and record? Who produced it, what other music have they produced? Who mastered it, and what other artists have they mastered? This is similar to the "interview" asset, but instead of answering questions, the artist will be talking in a conversational style about themselves and their process.

Radio DJ targeting

If you have sent the single to a local radio station, get your fans to tweet, tag, and message the radio DJ to play the track. If enough people message them, they will play the track on their show. This works well with college radio stations that are more supportive of local indie music.

Picture in billboard

Get a still of a public billboard (somewhere famous) and superimpose the release date artwork over it using Photoshop. There are mobile apps that will automatically create these, such as the app 'Billboard Photo Frames Effects'.

Re-record the vocals in a different language

Do you or someone in your band speak another language? If so, translate, sing and record the lyrics in a different language. You can also use sites like Fiverr to find a non-native English speaking singer to do this for you. Get your track in Spanish, French or German.

Create a Spotify Playlist

Create a playlist of your favourite music and add in your single and own tunes too. Bear in mind this should be a reoccurring content asset to do throughout the year. Set a schedule to update this at least once a month and alert fans the playlist has been updated.

New merchandise

Set up a direct-to-fan merchandise page using free print-to-order solutions from companies like Printful and run a competition for fans to win a t-shirt by voting on their favourite designs. These are free to set up and also great for kick-starting your merchandise store.

These lists with links to examples are available for download by visiting the Book Resources tab on The Label Machine website.

PRESS RELEASE

CREATING A STORY

It's about taking your fans on a journey. It is a journey that goes from discovering the artist, to falling in love with their music and supporting them.

And to take someone on a journey, you have to tell them a story. And it is essential at the beginning that you have a story because that is one of the easiest ways that people can emotionally connect with you.

There is a great marketing author called Seth Godin, who often talks about the importance of stories. I highly advise reading his Purple Cow book. I once heard him on a podcast interview, and he said something that always stuck with me, which was...

> **"You need to be able to tell a story that people can tell other people about you, and then those people can tell that story to other people too."**

Having a simple, unique story that people can remember and recall to others easily is hugely powerful. This story will be in your press release, which is the basis of which journalists and bloggers will write about you.

So ensure you have a great story developed around you, or

your artist, as it's the basis for everything else you will do when reaching out to fans.

To read about examples of artist stories, go to NME.com and read the NME Radar section. Every headline is an opening line into a back story about the artist.

There are three main press releases in a PR music campaign.

Pre-Press Release

This press release goes out first, approximately four weeks before the release date.

Post-Press Release

This press release is sent out on release day.

DJ Promo

This is sent out approximately four weeks before the release date to DJs only. I will cover this in more detail in the 'Create DJ Promo' chapter.

A press release is a one-page document containing all the relevant info about the release saved as a PDF file.

Whether you are doing PR in-house or using an external press company that will craft the press release, you need all the information below. If you are using an external press company, you can send the information as text, and they will edit it into the format they use to send out their press contacts.

Your press release should contain:

- Artist/band name.
- EP name.

- Track names.
- Release date.
- Record label name.
- Artwork.
- Artist background, bio and recent news.
- Artist online links: Website, SoundCloud, Facebook, Spotify, TikTok, Instagram, X and other relevant links like Snapchat.
- Link to artist's EPK (Electronic Press Kit)
- Contact information (phone number and email address).

When it comes to writing the story around the artist's background, bio and recent news, you can break it down into three paragraphs.

Paragraph One

This should include the most essential information about the release. If the artist has had a previous release, mention this here, and if this is a debut release, give a brief introduction to the artist instead. Keep it short; detailed artist information can go in the EPK.

This is where you should also mention any interesting key information:

- Support from a well-known artist, producer or radio DJ.
- If it was recorded or mastered in a famous studio.
- Produced by someone with known credits to renowned artists.

You should also give a description of the music. Using comparisons to other artists is usually the most useful way of doing this, so people get a quick idea of what to expect.

Paragraph Two

If you have a quote from the artist already, start the second paragraph with this quote. Include details of where the artist is based, who their influences are, or any other projects they have been involved in.

For a new artist, use this space for extra biographical information. For an established artist, you might want to talk about previous releases that have done well or recent tours or gigs they have played.

Paragraph Three

This is where you mention how the release will be promoted. This might include any DJ promo or other PR companies you are working with, if there is a music video or any already secured support such as a premiere on a blog or YouTube channel. People need to know how you are actively working on selling the release.

You need to spend time creating a good press release, which is why you might hire a PR company. However, if you put the time in and follow the guide, you can get a great press release yourself.

Two Press Releases

A lazy option is to create one press release with the info you have ahead of the release and send it a month beforehand and again on the release date. Don't be lazy. You should have two press releases for your single/EP.

Pre-Press Release

The first is the Pre-Press Release, which will be sent about four weeks ahead of the release date. You likely will, at that point, have little or no press about the upcoming release. So the pre-release Press Release is sent to publications/blogs/DJs, aiming to generate a buzz around your release and gain some premiers, write-ups, and interviews.

Post-Press Release

The second Press Release is the general public release. This goes out on release day (or just after) and includes DJ support and any mentions from premiere channels, plus any other notable news around the release gained from your first Press Release, such as radio support.

Creating Private SoundCloud links

At this point, upload the release to SoundCloud and set it as private. You can attach the private SoundCloud link to the release so that people can check out the music to see if they want to support it.

Always make sure you test the link on a browser that is not logged into your SoundCloud account first! This is to make sure that the private link opens properly. There is nothing more unprofessional than someone clicking on a dead link because you hadn't checked that the privacy settings were accurate.

You should now be able to write and publish your own press release and have a good idea of what content it should include.

You can download a press release template or use our custom-built AI PR writing assistant by visiting the Resources tab on The Label Machine platform.

THE EPK (ELECTRONIC PRESS KIT)

EPK, short for electronic press kit, is a pre-packaged set of an artist's promotional materials distributed to the media for promotional use. It's a place where promoters, venue managers, journalists, and music supervisors can find all the info they need to promote the artist.

Most info that goes in a press release also goes in an EPK, so if the artist doesn't have this already, this is an excellent time to create one.

An artist's EPK typically is the responsibility of the artist and the artist's management team. If your artist does not have one, it can be helpful for the label to create one for its artists. Some labels also have a label EPK, which is useful if the label is being profiled in a publication or running an event promoting its music.

An EPK is often a dedicated webpage on the artist's or label's website, designed with a mobile-responsive layout to ensure smooth access across all devices. The EPK includes clear navigation and interactive elements such as embedded audio and video players, allowing users to engage with the content directly without needing to download files.

You can create a zip download on a publicly shared Google Drive or Dropbox link that contains PDF documents with all the vital material as a supplementary option.

The important thing is that it's easily accessible via just one link. A concise list of what needs to be included in an EPK is:

Marketing assets

Press pictures, hi-res logos saved as PNG format, the latest music release artwork, and direct streaming links and ensure you include vertical image & video formats.

Artist bio

The biography, or bio for short, is your story. To recap, "You need to be able to tell a story that people can tell other people about you, and then those people can tell that story to other people too."

It's super important, so spend time making sure you get it right. This is a good chance for people to form a super quick opinion of you, so you want to make sure it's punchy, clear and exciting.

Press quotes

If you've already had some reviews or have some positive quotes, then these need to be included (making sure you provide a link to the original quote so people can check). Do not make one up. You don't want to garner that kind of negative attention. If you have any press clippings, save these here as well.

Social media and music platform links

Add links to the artist and label's website, Facebook, Instagram, X, SoundCloud, YouTube, Spotify Artist Link, TikTok, Snapchat accounts. Include social media metrics showing audience engagement.

Contact details

This may seem obvious, but do not forget to put the contact details down! Make sure you have up-to-date information for the label contact and the artist manager. If there are multiple contacts, specify the preferred one.

DJ PROMO

DJ Promo is typically sent out to only DJs that play in clubs and festivals. It's usually sent out three to four weeks before the release date to build a buzz, and also because DJs like to play the freshest music, so having music before a release date is a massive plus.

Depending on how established you are as an artist or label will reflect on the amount of DJ contacts you have. If you are starting out, I recommend paying a DJ PR company to send out your promo as they have a trusted list of DJs that will open and listen to the promos.

While you can send out DJ promo via simple emails, this is usually done via specialist software with unique functions. For example, allowing track downloads once a rating has been recorded and allowing the collection of written feedback on tracks.

To create a DJ Promo, you will need artwork, the release date and a short blurb text about the release. This is a brief description of two or three sentences that tell the reader something about the artist, the style of music and any support the music or artist already has from other DJs or labels.

Try to keep the description that goes with the DJ mailer to simply be a quote from the artist about the music, as it's primarily other DJs who will be reading this. There is no point in a lengthy description of what the music sounds like, e.g. 'earth-shattering bass' when they just need to click the play button and hear what it sounds like themselves.

A list of DJ mailer services:

- promopush.com
- promo.ly
- label-worx.com
- inflyteapp.com
- fatdrop.co.uk
- label-engine.com

Each of these services has a slightly different way of managing the promos. Of course, you will need DJs' email addresses to send the promos to, and if you don't have them, it's best to use a PR DJ promo company. Some of the established promo companies are:

- reaktion.net
- promoonly.com
- your-army.com
- globalprpool.com
- getinpr.com

- infectiouspr.com
- power.co.uk
- promopush.com
- listen-up.biz
- biz3.net

There also Record Pools, which are subscription services offering DJs curated libraries of high-quality music, exclusive tracks, remixes, and edits for performances and promotion. They help DJs stay current, discover artists, and maintain a unique sound with genre-specific selections, DJ tools, and legal music access via cost-effective monthly or yearly memberships.

- BPM Supreme
- DJ City
- Digital DJ Pool
- ZipDJ
- Club Killers
- Headliner Music Club
- Promo Only

These lists are available for download by visiting the Book Resources tab on The Label Machine website.

GETTING ON BLOGS AND PUBLICATIONS

To get your music heard on blogs and digital publications, you need to utilise outbound marketing in the form of PR.

In this chapter, I'll look at how to run your PR in-house. For bigger music campaigns and albums, you might hire an external PR company. However, many indie labels will run PR in-house to keep costs down and to have more control over ensuring the music is being pushed out to the right blogs, websites, and influencers.

If you are interested in using a PR company, you can find links to the most established companies by visiting the Book Resources tab on The Label Machine website.

THE MODERN APPROACH TO BLOG SUBMISSIONS

Whilst the traditional approach to blog submissions involves building your own database and individually contacting writers, a far more efficient method exists today. Database submission platforms have revolutionised the process, saving time and increasing your chances of success.

The most effective platforms include MusoSoup, SubmitHub and Groover.

These platforms consolidate thousands of blogs, YouTube channels, Spotify playlisters and influencers in one place, allowing you to submit directly to relevant curators who are actively seeking new music.

MUSOSOUP

Musosoup is a music promotion platform where artists submit their music once and get exposure to over 400 vetted curators, including blogs, playlists, radio stations, and influencers. For a one-time fee ($40 for a 21-day campaign), your release is reviewed and, if approved, shared with all curators on the platform.

Curators who are interested will send you offers for reviews, interviews, playlist placements, radio play, and social media promotion. Each paid offer always comes with a free alternative, so you can choose the coverage that fits your budget. You can accept or decline offers, and manage your campaign through a live dashboard with messaging and coverage tracking.

Musosoup's approach ensures guaranteed coverage or your money back, making it a straightforward and affordable way to promote singles, EPs, or albums to a wide music industry audience.

- musosoup.com

SUBMIT HUB

SubmitHub connects artists, labels, and publicists with over 1,750 active music blogs, playlist curators, and social media influencers on platforms like YouTube, SoundCloud, Instagram, and TikTok. Artists purchase credits to submit music, and curators are paid to listen, increasing the likelihood your track gets heard.

Premium credits guarantee a response within 48 hours, at least 20 seconds of listening, and feedback or approval for posting. Standard credits offer no such guarantees. You can filter curators by genre and platform to target your submissions.

With new curators and influencers added monthly, SubmitHub remains a transparent and effective tool for music promotion and outreach.

- submithub.com

GROOVER

Groover is a music promotion platform that connects artists with over 3,000 curators, including playlist curators, labels, radio stations, and bloggers. Artists buy credits called "Grooviz" to submit their tracks directly to targeted curators filtered by genre and goals.

Curators are required to listen and provide guaranteed feedback within seven days, or the credits are refunded. This ensures transparency and increases the chances of meaningful exposure. Groover streamlines music outreach by offering direct access to industry professionals and reliable responses, making it an efficient tool for growing your audience and advancing your career.

- groover.co

Submission Best Practices

When using these platforms, follow these guidelines for maximum effectiveness:

1. Only select curators who genuinely support your genre
2. Read curator profiles carefully to understand their preferences
3. Craft personalised submission notes referencing their previous coverage
4. Send your absolute best, release-ready tracks
5. Include a professional press kit with high-quality artwork
6. Be specific about what you're looking for (premiere, review, playlist add)

Remember that most platforms offer both free and paid submission options. Paid submissions typically guarantee feedback and have higher response rates, whilst free submissions often have longer wait times and no feedback guarantee.

WHEN TO USE TRADITIONAL PR METHODS

Despite the convenience of submission platforms, traditional PR outreach still has its place in certain circumstances. Consider building your own contact database when targeting very niche or specialised publications that might not have a presence on mainstream platforms.

Traditional outreach is also valuable when focusing on building long-term relationships with key journalists who might become champions of your music over time. More complex or conceptual projects that require detailed explanation often benefit from the personalised touch of direct communication.

High-tier publications that don't accept platform submissions or maintain a more exclusive approach to coverage will typically require conventional PR methods. If you do choose to build your own database, follow the approach outlined below.

BUILDING YOUR PR DATABASE

Whilst building your own PR database is the traditional approach, it's time-consuming and often less effective than modern methods. However, if you choose this route, there are two main paths forward.

From Scratch vs Purchased Database

Starting from scratch requires identifying artists similar to yours, then researching which blogs and publications feature them through Google searches. Use tools like Music-Map and Last.fm to expand your list of comparable artists, then methodically find the websites covering them. The objective is to create a comprehensive list of tastemakers relevant to your music style.

Using a purchased database from freelance platforms like Fiverr offers a more efficient alternative, as much of the laborious contact-gathering has been done for you. When using a database or similar resources, simply review each contact to confirm they support your genre and transfer relevant details to your customized spreadsheet. For publications with multiple contributors, focus exclusively on writers who cover your specific genre rather than targeting general editors.

Essential Contact Information

For effective outreach, maintain a thorough record of each contact including their website, email, name, role, genre specialisation, country, social media accounts, and a detailed history of your interactions.

Note when you first reached out, through which medium, when you followed up, and any relevant comments that might help personalise future communications.

Finding Contact Details

When contact information isn't immediately available, conduct targeted searches for writers' names on Google, often pairing them with "LinkedIn" "Twitter/X" or "contact" to find their public profiles. Most writers have an email address published somewhere, though you may need to dig deeper.

Tools like findthat.email and hunter.io can identify common email patterns across domains, useful for difficult-to-find contacts. As a last resort, social media platforms offer alternative contact routes, though email remains the most professional and effective approach for music submissions.

SENDING OUT THE MUSIC

Whether you're using submission platforms or direct contact, you need to contact blogs professionally. Here is a template to use when reaching out:

Hey XXXX,

In short, my name is [name] and I represent a [style of music] artist out of [city/country name] called [artist name] (website link). I found [blog] because of a post you made a few weeks back about [example: DJ Qwerrty's new EP, Sun King]. I wonder if [blog] would be interested in premiering a new single from [your artist's name] upcoming EP? It's reminiscent of [two other artists the blogger has reviewed].
soundcloud.com/[artist name]/new-song

Here is a link to the press release about the upcoming LP and a link to the artist's EPK [Dropbox links]

Thanks for listening, XXXX!
Nikki

This simple email works because it accomplishes a few different things in the course of three sentences:

1. It tells the blogger you took the time to read the blog, find their name, and figure out what kind of music they like
2. It tells the blogger exactly what type of music the artist you're pitching makes by relating it to past content they've covered
3. It includes an easy-to-use listening link
4. It directly asks the blogger what course of action you'd like them to take after reading your email (in this case, premiere a new EP from the artist)

Essential tips for submissions

1. When creating your private SoundCloud link, check it can be viewed by anyone. Open a separate browser window in private mode. In Google Chrome, go into 'incognito' mode and check you're not logged into SoundCloud. If you can still hear the track, then you know the link works. There's nothing worse than someone clicking a dead link – your first impression and chance are potentially blown.
2. Do not spam! Spam is sending impersonal emails to multiple email addresses at once using the BCC field in an email. It does not work ever, and you'll just get blocked. And what's the point?
3. You have one chance to make a good impression, so make sure that the music you send is the best it can be. You must be able to play your track side by side with music that is currently being supported by the tastemaker you are reaching out to, and sonically and musically, they are comparable.
4. Never ever send demos to blogs. Unless you are at the point where they have supported much of your previous music, you're great friends, and you are just looking for feedback.
5. Ensure you have created a press release and an EPK pack and saved both as a public Google Drive or Dropbox link.

SECURE MUSIC PREMIERES

Music premieres are when curated music channels play a track first exclusively for a length of time. Premieres are usually focused on a YouTube or a SoundCloud channel and sometimes a radio show.

The advantage of premieres on curated channels is that you tap into a built-in audience. A prominent channel with thousands of subscribers will instantly give you an audience, and via the comments section, you'll quickly get feedback too.

Securing a premiere is an extension of PR, so you need to approach it similarly to get featured. Research the best channels, find the contact details, and send them your pitch.

If you want to secure a premiere with a very established channel, a PR company can make that connection easier, which is why it is worth using them if you can afford the cost.

When you get a premiere, send them a WAV file, artwork, and short info text (including the release date and all your social handles) that will be added to the description text. If you have a pre-order available, include this link too.

WHEN IS THE BEST TIME TO PREMIERE A TRACK?

There are two options. The first option is before the release date to get a buzz going. However, if new fans can't buy the tracks or add them to their Spotify playlist, you could be missing a trick.

Therefore, the second option is to premiere on release day with a buy/stream link, so it's instantly available for fans to add it to their Spotify playlist or buy in the Apple Music store.

Sometimes you can't choose; the channel will tell you when they have a slot, and you work around it. However, if you have a choice, a good balance is to secure a premiere the day before a release, so you can build some buzz before the music comes out, but still take advantage of new listeners that like the track adding it to a playlist or downloading it.

YOUTUBE

Getting on a big YouTube channel with an excellent track suited for its audience can give millions of plays over a year.

All channels have an email address listed, and most of the established channels will have instructions for a formal submission process.

Curators look for tracks with a buzz that suit their audience. If there is already some decent news or support for the track, then definitely include that in the submission. It shows it is worth listening to, as verified by someone else in the industry.

Do your research and only send relevant music. It's pretty obvious, but you'll be surprised how many people ignore this advice, and you can guarantee your music won't get played. This isn't a scattergun approach. Be sensible with who is likely to be interested in your music.

If you email the channel curator, use this template:

Hey XXXX,

My name is [name] and I represent a [style of music] artist out of [city/country name] called [artist name].

We are big fans of your YouTube channel [channel name], and I was wondering if you would be interested in premiering a new single from [artist's name] upcoming EP?

soundcloud.com/[artist name]/new-song

The track is the same style as [two other tracks on the channel], and it's been supported already by [support news]. The press release and artist EPK is here [Dropbox links].

Cheers, Nikki

Another way of using YouTube is offering your music as backing tracks to channels that need music. For singer-songwriter guitar music, make-up channels are a good fit. For electronic or rock music, approach extreme sport channels requiring backing music for their footage.

SOUNDCLOUD

A premiere on a highly subscribed SoundCloud channel is a great look too. People can repost the music on their own channels easily. You can message a channel using the messaging system built into SoundCloud, but most of the established channels will have a formal submission system to follow.

Approach the SoundCloud curator in the same way as discussed previously in the YouTube submission and adjust the template to suit the SoundCloud channel.

Some channels will ask for a 'donation' to host on their channel. Is this worth it? Do your research. If it looks like they get the plays, their audience suits your music, and they charge no more than £40/$50, it may be worth it.

PRE-SAVES

A pre-save or pre-order is a link you can promote to your audience before release day, which will boost first-day sales or streams and give something actionable to promote to your fans.

As Spotify is the leading platform for streaming, most people will set up and promote a pre-save campaign for their music release. When a Spotify user pre-saves a song, it will automatically appear in their song or album list on the release day.

You can incentivise your fans to pre-save your release by running contests or giving access to exclusive material, which will ensure your music has a high listenership on the first day of release.

If you can drive Spotify listeners to your pre-save campaign and have a high stream count on release day, it indicates to the

Spotify algorithm it's a song worth sharing. This will increase your chances of getting onto Spotify algorithmic playlists such as Discover Weekly.

For electronic music, if the focus is on getting a Beatport chart position, then setting up a pre-order campaign that can boost first-week sales on the platform will be a priority, making it more likely to get a top chart position.

Either way, pre-saves and pre-orders are a great way to help build pre-release momentum and incentivise people to hear your music on release day.

HOW TO SET UP PRE-SAVES AND PRE-ORDERS

To set up your Spotify Pre-Save, you need your Spotify URI. You can get this by asking your distributor. Some distributors will automatically email this to you when it becomes available.

For pre-orders on Apple Music, Amazon or Beatport, you will need the URL for those stores. Again, you can ask your distributor for these.

There are a few tools you can use to set up your pre-save page.

Automatic set up

Some distributors will automatically create a pre-save page for you. The Label Machine Distribution has a free service, Distrokid has a free service available to its members, called HyperFollow, which creates a unique pre-save page once the release is scheduled for distribution.

Paid Versions

There are paid versions that give detailed analytics and can have multiple pre-save and pre-order links on one page (helpful for promoting to a broad audience or non-Spotify users). Two examples are:

- show.co
- linkfire.com

Once you have your Pre-Save link set up, add this to your marketing and release schedule. Typically we start promoting the pre-save one week before the release, so usually the Friday before release day.

PAID ADS

Paid advertising on social media is one of the best ways of reaching an audience for a music brand. This is an area where the more you put in, the more you get out in terms of both money and time.

It's incredibly powerful. Never in history have you been able to find fans of your music on such a granular level and interact with them. And unlike most other types of marketing, it's highly measurable and quantifiable.

Right now, we are in a golden age of paid advertising, where clicks are cheap, and the majority of music fans are not put off by ads. However, this won't last forever, and as prices go up, and more people get savvy to ads, it will become more challenging to get the desired results.

Now is the time to capitalize and build an army of fans for your music.

AD STRATEGIES

In this chapter, when I refer to paid ads, I'm specifically referring to ads on Facebook and Instagram both owned by Meta. These two platforms are managed by the same advertising platform, the 'Meta Ads Manager', and it's straightforward to reach a large audience this way.

Other social media platforms have paid advertising services such as TikTok, X, LinkedIn, Reddit, and Spotify, and you can use these same strategies on their platforms.

Spotify's Campaign Kit offers advanced tools to target listeners based on their streaming behavior. Features like Discovery Mode, Playlist Pitching, and Marquee allow artists to reach new audiences, reengage past fans, and deepen connections with existing listeners.

And TikTok has gained significant ground for music promotion, especially for reaching younger demographics.

However, real-world testing by music marketing experts in recent years demonstrates that Meta ads still deliver competitive results at reasonable costs, particularly with conversion-based campaigns.

The most basic version of advertising is promoting an existing post on your timeline using the boost post feature. This ensures your post is seen by more of your existing fans.

However, to grow your fan base, you need to reach out to a new audience, which our strategies will focus on.

Paid advertising follows classic marketing principles used across industries:

- Find your audience
- Craft a message that connects with them
- State a clear call to action

You'll follow these same principles for your ads.

This chapter outlines how the system works with useful starter strategies. The fundamental mechanics remain valuable despite the emergence of AI-driven campaign optimisation tools since 2023.

It's worth noting that paid platforms such as hypeddit.com and feature.fm simplify this process through streamlined interfaces and integration with streaming analytics.

The best way of learning is by creating your own ads following tutorial videos. Find the most recent and up-to-date videos on the Resources tab on The Label Machine platform.

SETTING UP

To get started, you'll need the following:

- A music release.

- A Facebook account and an Instagram account.
- A Meta Ads Manager account.
- Video content of some kind (music video, release trailer etc.).
- A defined audience of eight to ten similar artists, records labels or brands.

Music release

By music release, I mean that you have uploaded a track to the distributor and have a release date that you are working towards. You can also use these strategies for an already-released track for which you are working towards an 'impact date', for example, promoting a post-album single release.

A Facebook and Instagram page for the label or the artist

To run the ads manager for your campaign, you need to have a Facebook Business page and Instagram account, so ensure you have set up your record label as a business page and any artist pages you manage. You also want to link your Instagram account to your Facebook to display ads across both platforms. Ensure your artist profile is credible and active before running ads, as this can improve ad approval rates and results

Ads Manager

Ad campaigns for both Facebook and Instagram are managed from the Ads Manager. Once you have a business page set up, you can access your Ad Manager from the main menu. There is also a Business Manager which is used by companies that manage multiple Facebook pages and ad accounts. As you advance in your paid ads success, you may want to use this too.

Video Content

To promote your music, you will need some video content to go with the music. You want to have enough content to create a video approximately one minute long and a shorter 15-seconds piece. The audio you cut to the video will change depending on the music style, but try using the most energetic or catchiest part.

Some examples are:

- Stock video footage – There are free or paid stock videos available, and they are great for creating videos to connect with music related brands.
- Short lyric video – good for singer-songwriter songs.
- Teaser trailer of the artwork animated – great for electronic music.
- Clip of a music video – suits all music but requires a bigger budget.
- Clip of live music – great for bands.
- Simple static artwork – not ideal as it's a static picture, but it can be used.

If you don't have professional editing software, you can edit something together for free using your smartphone using the following tools:

- CapCut.
- Adobe Express.
- Youtube Studio.
- Canva.
- iMovie.

Or you can use a service like Fiverr.com to edit something together for you.

Defining your audience

Targeting the right audience is essential when setting up your ads. To do this effectively, you'll need to research eight to ten artist names similar to your music, eight to ten similar record labels, and eight to ten brands that your ideal music fans connect with.

To start gathering a list of similar artists and labels, think of one artist that you think is similar to yours, Google them and note down other artists in the 'people also search for' section. Or use Music-Map and Last FM to find similar artists. When finding similar brands, start by thinking of an activity your ideal fans would do, and then look at brands that make products, clothes, and shoes in that activity.

Now we have covered what you need to get started, let's look at how Meta Ads Manager is set up.

Meta Ads Manager

Ads you create in Meta Ads Manager have three parts. The individual ads, ad sets and campaigns. Collectively, this is called the campaign structure.

Campaign level

The Campaign Level is the top level of consideration for your campaign. It is the level at which you think about your overall advertising objective, the end goal of all your ads. Popular music objectives are:

- Drive traffic to an email to download.
- Pre-save the track on Spotify.
- Play the track on a particular platform such as Spotify or YouTube.
- Build up followers on a Spotify Playlist
- Promote an upcoming event or gig

Ad sets level

At the ad set level, you define your target audience, budget and schedule, then create and save multiple ad sets for different audiences. For example, targeting specific genres of music, artists, labels, brands or particular countries.

Ad level

At the ad level, you design the ads themselves, choosing the videos and the call to action text that your audience will respond to.

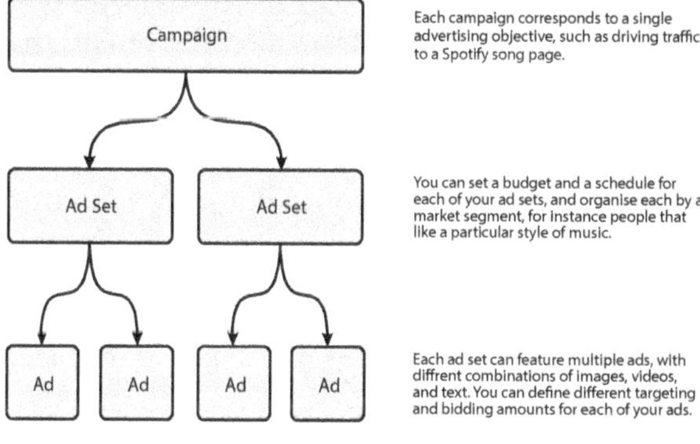

Meta Pixel

The Meta pixel (previously known as Meta Pixel) remains a crucial code snippet that tracks fan interactions after engaging with your Facebook or Instagram content. When installed on your website, it records visitor activity, enabling retargeting through subsequent ad campaigns. It can still track when users click buttons to listen to your music on streaming platforms.

Due to Apple's privacy updates and browser cookie restrictions, Meta now relies on combined pixel and Conversions API tracking for more privacy-compliant data collection, though with reduced precision compared to previous years.

Now you have a good understanding of the basics of how ads work, let's look at some strategies around a music release and growing an audience of fans.

MUSIC RELEASE STRATEGIES

I'm going to tell you about three useful strategies, the first two of which work together for promoting a single song music release.

The first strategy is called the 'Custom Audience Builder', and the goal is to find and build an audience of fans that will most likely connect with your music. You activate this strategy in the weeks leading up to your music release, and ideally, you need a minimum three weeks to do this, and most artists are starting eight weeks before a release.

The second strategy is 'Music Release Promoter', and the goal is to get an audience of fans most likely to connect with your music to take action, for example, give you an email address in return for a music track, pre-save the track on Spotify, or to promote an upcoming event or gig. You get the cheapest and best results when used with the Custom Audience Builder.

The final strategy is using 'Custom Conversions' and this strategy is used to be focused on a particular action you want a fan to take outside the Meta platforms, such as listening to the single on Spotify, or to build up followers on a Spotify playlist.

CUSTOM AUDIENCE BUILDER

The secret to getting this to work effectively is to think about an audience interest or brand that your music fans would also like and then target them. For example, many hip-hop, grime, and EDM fans also like extreme sports such as snowboarding, skateboarding, and many indie rockers like surfing.

In this instance, by having your music edited to extreme sports videos and showing these videos to fans of extreme sports brands, you link your music to the sport. This will work even if you have a tiny audience, as you are tapping into the fan bases of other brands on Facebook to build your audience.

For example, let's use an organic house single called 'Deep Dreams' by Kyries and a release date of April 1st. The artist knows that rock climbers enjoy this style of chilled out music, so we use them as an audience interest to base our first custom audience on.

To find out what brands to target, simply Google 'rock climbing brands' and make a list of the top ten, which a blog has already listed for us. They are Arc'teryx, Edelrid, Black Diamond, Five Ten, Granite Gear, Mammut, MSR, Osprey, Scarpa and North Face.

To find videos for the ad content, go to Pixels.com or Pixabay.com, search for rock climbing and mountain climbing and download a few epic looking videos. Use CapCut to edit one minute of the music's main section with the climbing videos. Create both landscape and vertical videos, so your content works in the Facebook and Instagram Stories format. Get a pro to do this on Fiverr.com if you struggle to do it yourself.

We can now open up Meta Ads Manager and create the ad campaign by completing each of the three levels. It can look complicated as there are many options, but we will explain the important ones you need to set below.

Campaign level: We want to show this to as many fans of rock climbing as possible. We set our objective to video views which will default to 'ThruPlays', which is defined as when someone watches 15 seconds or more of a video.

Ad sets level: On this level, set the daily budget, starting at $2 a day to test. Set the target countries, for instance, the US, Canada, and Europe and then in 'Detailed Targeting', search and add the ten rock climbing brands.

Ad level: This is where to create the ad. Ensure your Instagram account is selected in the 'Identity' section. Upload the video you created and add simple text like 'Epic!' or three fire emojis in the 'Primary Text' space. As we are interested in people watching the video, we don't have a call-to-action, so there's no need to add an address in the website URL.

Once done, click 'Publish' and let the ad run, checking back every 24 hours on the progress. The more money you spend, the more people will see the video and the larger your custom audience. But even running the campaign for two weeks at $2 per day at 0.001 cost per ThruPlay, we would get 14,000 people listening to more than 15 seconds of the music!

These 14,000 people are most likely to like rock climbing and the music, so they are primed to target with the music promo on release day. This is a powerful strategy because you target people who clearly like the music; otherwise, they would have skipped past and not bothered to watch and listen for 15 seconds or more. You are filtering down to true fans of the music.

MUSIC RELEASE PROMOTER

This next ad strategy starts on release day, when the music is available to download and stream. Our goal is to get fans to respond to a call-to-action, such as listening to the track on Spotify or downloading the single from Beatport.

When used with the Custom Audience Builder, you can get very cheap clicks on the call to action as the audience is already primed. We can also run this strategy targeting a new audience of similar artists and record labels, so ensure you have done your research and have these ready.

We need to create a shorter 15-second long video ad, which works best on these call to action ads. You can edit the earlier one minute videos into a 15 seconds version. You can also use a video of the band playing the track live, the chorus of a lyric video, or 15 seconds of the teaser trailer.

You want to spend most of your budget at the start of the campaign and tail it off towards the end. This is especially important for Spotify. The algorithms look for activity at the beginning of a release that shows it's popular as it will then promote it to more playlists. If you have a $200 budget for two weeks, set $25 per day for the first four days and adjust it to $10 a day for the next ten days.

In Meta Ads Manager, create the ad campaign by completing each of the three levels.

Campaign level: We want to drive people to listen to or buy the track. So we set the objective to 'Traffic'. For more advanced ads, you could also set the objective to 'Conversions', which we will cover later in the chapter.

Ad sets level: Set the budget to maximise your daily budget for the campaign's start, as explained earlier.

If you have a custom audience, choose 'Create New Audience' and choose 'Custom Audience'. From here, pick ThruPlay Video views and select the video created in the last campaign.

Alternatively, if you want to target similar artists and labels, select target countries (for instance, the US, Canada, and Europe). Then in 'Detailed Targeting', search and add the artist names and labels you have selected as most relevant to your music.

Ad level: This is where we create the ad. Upload the 15 seconds video and in the 'Primary Text' section, add 'Listen to the New Single Deep Dreams from Kyries – Out Now'. In 'Website URL', add the link to the music destination (for example, the Spotify URI) and change the 'Call to Action' to 'Listen Now'.

Click 'Publish' and let the ad run. Log back in after four days to edit the daily budget to suit your budgeting plan. Again, the more money you spend, the more plays, followers and sales you make. Every campaign you run, you learn more, and the cheaper and more efficient ads become.

Now you understand the two main ad strategies that promote your music release, let's look at some advanced techniques.

ADVANCED ADS WITH CUSTOM CONVERSIONS

The more data you can give Meta, the more efficient it will be at placing your music in front of your ideal audience that is more likely to take action, and thus the cheaper your campaigns will become. A vital data metric is called the 'Custom Conversion', set up with a Meta Pixel. The pixel allows us to know when someone has completed the custom conversion goal, for instance, listening to the single on Spotify.

Before starting, ensure you have set up a Meta Pixel and a custom conversion event. These are created in the Events Manager section of your Ads Manager account. The Pixel should be installed on a landing page (using platforms like SubmitHub.com or Hypeddit.com) that tracks when someone clicks through to listen to your music.

In Meta Ads Manager, create the conversion ad campaign by completing each of the three levels.

Campaign level: Set the campaign objective to 'Conversions'. This tells Meta to optimize your ads for people most likely to complete a specific action, such as listening to your track on Spotify.

Ad sets level: Set your daily budget according to your overall campaign plan.

Under 'Conversion Event', select the custom conversion you set up (e.g., 'Spotify Listen'). Choose your audience:

If you have a custom audience (such as people who watched your previous videos), select 'Create New Audience' and add your custom audience.

To target new listeners, use 'Detailed Targeting' to add relevant artist names, labels, or genres, and select the countries where you want your ads shown.

Ad level: Create your ad by uploading your chosen creative (e.g., a 15-second video or image). In the 'Primary Text' section, write a compelling call to action, such as: *"Listen to the New Single Deep Dreams from Kyries – Out Now."* In 'Website URL', enter the link to your conversion-tracked landing page (e.g., your SubmitHub or Hypeddit page).

Set the 'Call to Action' button to 'Listen Now'. Click 'Publish' to launch your campaign. Monitor your results and, after a few days, adjust your daily budget or targeting based on performance data. Over time, as Meta gathers more conversion data, your campaigns will become more efficient and cost-effective.

SPOTIFY PRE-SAVE STRATEGY

Spotify pre-saves are essentially the digital streaming equivalent of pre-ordering an album. When fans pre-save your track, it automatically appears in their library upon release.

Accumulating pre-saves boosts day-one stream counts, signalling popularity to Spotify's algorithm. This increases chances of placement on algorithmic playlists like Discover Weekly and editorial playlists.

Pre-save pages are now integrated with most distributors including DistroKid (Hyperfollow), and The Label Machine Distro. Third-party services like Presave.io, Feature.fm and Linkfire continue offering enhanced pre-save functionality with better analytics. For maximum impact:

- Set up your pre-save page
- Create short-form vertical video ads targeting custom audiences
- Run campaigns 7-14 days before release
- Share pre-save links across email and social channels

If you have 5,000+ monthly listeners, create a Spotify Countdown Page, Spotify's native pre-save landing page. This powerful tool automatically converts to a streaming link on release day, integrates merch sales and exclusive content, and supports Spotify Clips (short video previews) to engage fans effectively.

MUSIC COVER, BOOTLEG, AND REMIX STRATEGY

A very popular way of using the Custom Audience Builder strategy is to create a cover of a current popular song (or a bootleg if you are an electronic producer) and target the audience of the artist you covered. This way, you ride on the coattails of an already popular song.

I have seen hundreds of artists use this strategy to quickly build up an email list because it works so well. In this case, when targeting similar artists, using a superstar artist works well as you're appealing to the largest audience.

Create a campaign for video views, and then create a custom audience of fans that watch more than 15 seconds (ThruPlay) to download the track or watch a cover version on your YouTube page in exchange for an email address, which you can then link into your middle of funnel automation inside the Marketing Machine.

SPOTIFY PLAYLISTS

Getting on the right Spotify playlist these days can make or break the success of a record. And with Spotify being the most popular listening platform today, it's a vital way of promoting your music and earning revenue.

Apple Music is also a very popular platform; however, their playlists are all managed in-house, and there are not the same opportunities to pitch your music to their playlists.

There are three different types of playlists: Personalised, Editorial and Listener. Let's look at each one in detail and the various ways you can ensure you are added to them in the first 2 weeks of your release, to help encourage the algorithms to pick your music for the editorial playlists.

PERSONALISED PLAYLISTS

These playlists are created for individual listeners based on their listening tastes and habits. Examples are Discover Weekly, Release Radar, DJ, Smart Shuffle, and Blends. They are generated by algorithms that look at the user's listening habits (and habits of similar users) and recommend music it thinks they will like. Habits are things like plays, shares, skips, and adds to playlists.

The more followers you have, the more of these playlists you will be featured on. Spotify also monitors the internet for conversations about your music, so the more people talking and sharing online, the more likely your tracks are to be added to these playlists. Any new music you release will feature in your followers' Release Radar Playlists. So building up followers is critical.

EDITORIAL PLAYLISTS

These are playlists created by the Spotify editorial team. You can tell these playlists by the Spotify logo in the top left corner of the playlist. There are thousands of these playlists, and the editors have different genres, styles and cultural backgrounds to help create them.

If you get on one of these playlists, you can use a unique link to share it, which means that whoever clicks on it sees your track at the top of the playlist for the following 24 hours. You can pitch one song per upcoming release to be considered for an editorial playlist, which we will discuss later.

LISTENER PLAYLISTS

These are playlists created by everyone and include private Spotify curated playlists that have large follower counts that you can pitch to yourself. Music publications and blogs such as Pitchfork, Stereogum and Data Transmission also have playlists with large followers you can pitch to.

As a label, you should also create your own playlist and encourage your fans to follow this as it's a great way of keeping them updated with your latest music. If you are an artist, make sure you create your own playlists (that features your music!) and add the playlist links to your artist profile using the Artist Pick.

There are millions of personal playlists generated by fans as well. It's important to get your fans to add your music to their own personal playlists as they can influence other people's playlists. When a fan saves it to their playlists, it's an indicator of the type of music they like, which Spotify uses to generate recommendations.

PITCHING TO PLAYLISTS

There are three different ways to pitch your music to playlists as a record label and as an artist.

- Spotify Editorial.
- Paid Pitching.
- Spotify Outreach Method.

How to pitch to Spotify Editorial

By using Spotify for Artists as an artist or label, you can pitch an upcoming, unreleased song to the playlist editors. The track you submit also gets added to your followers' Release Radar playlist, so it's essential to do so for every release you have.

As a record label, you will have to request access to the artist's account. Likewise, if you are an artist manager, you can request access too. This allows you to pitch songs on behalf of the artist as a label or manager.

To get access to an artist as a record label in Spotify for Artists, you need to have access to the artist's name, X account, and evidence (such as being published on your record label's website), and/or a Google or Dropbox link to a signed recording contract.

When pitching a track via Spotify for Artists desktop, select PITCH A SONG under the UPCOMING section.

Complete all fields thoroughly: Main Genre & Sub Genres, Music Cultures (for regional styles), Moods (helps match to mood-focused playlists), Song Styles, Languages (up to three), song type specifications (cover/remix/instrumental/live), featured instruments, your identified city, and a compelling description including featured artists, marketing plans, existing press, and upcoming video releases.

Comprehensive submissions significantly improve your chances with playlist curators.

IMPORTANT NOTES

This only works for unreleased music.

You must submit this at least seven days before the release, but for the best results, submit it at least three weeks before it comes out.

Ensure the artist avatar, bio, and press pics are up to date. Spotify uses this when they share your music.

You can only pitch one song per artist at a time.

You can't pitch if you're a featured artist or a remixer.

If you get playlisted, Spotify will send an email to let you know. You can also check the Playlists tab in Spotify for Artists when the release goes live and explore detailed stats about it.

HOW TO PITCH TO SPOTIFY PRIVATE CURATED PLAYLISTS

There are two ways of pitching to Spotify curated playlists.

Pay a playlist pitching service

The first option is using an online playlist pitching service. Reputable companies worth considering include Playlist Push, SubmitHub, Musosoup, PlaylistSupply and Indiefy, alongside established services like YouGrowPromo and the free-to-use DailyPlaylists.

These companies connect artists, labels and publicists with playlist curators across streaming platforms. Many now offer expanded services including TikTok creator outreach, music blog features, and podcast placements to create wider digital footprints.

Playlist pitching services provide an excellent way to kickstart momentum for new releases. When you find a service that works well with your genre and audience, it becomes a valuable component of your overall paid marketing strategy, complementing your direct advertising efforts and organic growth tactics.

Testing different services with your music remains the only reliable way to determine effectiveness for your specific sound.

The Spotify Outreach Method

I've included this here for the true DIY artists, however, using a paid playlisting service like the companies mentioned above that have updated active databases, is far easier and quicker. If you can, spend the money.

But for the artist or label looking for the cheapest way to get onto private curated Spotify playlists that are not controlled by Spotify, follow this simple three-step method.

Discover

Either open up Spotify and search for genres of music that your music fits, or use a Spotify database such as The Label Machine's Spotify Playlist to find relevant playlists.

Research

Visit the playlist and find artists similar to your music. Note five songs on the playlist that are the most similar to the music you are pitching.

Contact

Now you have found playlists relevant to your music, you need to contact them in a professional manner using email or over DMs on social media.

Through Email

If you have the curators email address, then use the following template to reach out to them.

> *Hey [playlist curator name],*
>
> *My name is [name] and I represent a [style of music] out of [city/country name] called [artist name] [link to Spotify artist profile].*
>
> *As your playlist [playlist name] supports the artists [at least three supporting artist names] who have similar music to [artist name], I was wondering if you would be interested in adding the new single from [artist name] upcoming EP. It's reminiscent of [two other artists the playlist supports].*
>
> *open.spotify.com/track/xxxxxxxxxx [link to Spotify track]*
>
> *Here is a link to the press release about the upcoming LP and a link to the artists EPK [Dropbox links].*
>
> *Thanks for listening, [playlist curator name]!*
> *[Your name]*

This simple email works because it accomplishes a few different things in the course of three sentences. It tells the Spotify curator you took the time to research and understand their playlist. It tells the curator exactly what kind of music the artist you're pitching makes by relating it to past content they've playlisted before. Likewise, it includes an extremely easy-to-use listening link. It directly asks the curator what course of action you'd like them to take after reading your email (in this case, add to their playlist).

Through social media

If the curator has an Instagram account, you can use it to build a relationship to request an addition to the playlist.

Follow the playlist curator on Instagram.

Share their playlist as a story post and tag them in it.

Then, after a few weeks, do the ask.

'I like your Spotify playlist, and my music sounds like [two of the artists on the playlist], and I think my track [your track name] would sit well between them.'

If the curator likes your music, they will add it. They always look for new music, so by contacting them, you have made their job easier to find you and add your music. If they add you to a playlist, send an email of thanks, or shout out to them on social media to show your appreciation.

NOTES

- Do not spam.
- Be realistic; target the right playlist that will play your music.
- You have one chance to make a good impression, so make sure that the music you send is the best it can be. You must be able to play your track with music that is currently being supported side by side, and sonically and musically, they are comparable.

- Make sure you have set up your Spotify profile all OK.
- Be patient, build up a relationship. You might not hear back from the playlists.

SPOTIFY SOCIAL SHARING RECOMMENDATIONS

Spotify encourages you to share your music on their platforms, and their algorithms monitor the internet for evidence of external linking to Spotify artist accounts and songs. If they see you actively promote your Spotify links, they are more likely to feature your music in the curated playlists. Some specific sharing tips are:

- Add your Instagram, X, Facebook, and/or Wikipedia links to the about section of your Spotify artist profile.
- Ask fans to save your music in their own playlists. Mention on social media those that do to encourage it further.
- Since playlists drive the maximum amount of streams per listening session, share any playlists that feature your music over direct links,
- Use the Spotify Codes on visual media such as flyers, merchandise, and posters.

We recommend submitting to the official Spotify playlists through Artists for Spotify three weeks before the release date and then using the Spotify Outreach Method to connect to private Spotify playlists curators. Finally, implement as many of the Spotify recommended tips and tricks to share your music.

If you follow these methods and take action, you are dramatically increasing your chances of being featured on multiple playlists and driving up your monthly listeners and followers.

THE TRUTH ABOUT PAYING FOR SPOTIFY STREAMS

Spotify clearly states on their website: *"Always avoid services that guarantee streams or playlist placement. Their unlawful practices could result in your music being removed from Spotify. It's important to know you're putting your career at risk any time you engage with one of these bad actors."*

These "bad actors" are companies bombarding your Instagram feed with adverts promising 10,000 streams for £20 or 50,000 streams for £30. They genuinely deliver these streams, but they're worthless and dangerous to your career.

Why? Their methods are problematic:

They utilise streaming farms, similar to click farms, operating on remote servers behind IP walls with thousands of fake Spotify accounts playing your track repeatedly. They purchase or rent existing popular Spotify playlists and add your track to them. Both methods fail to generate real fans. These aren't listeners who will play your music again, purchase merchandise, attend your gigs, or follow your social platforms. They're simply artificial numbers that create a false impression of popularity without building a genuine audience that supports your career.

For legitimate playlist promotion, I recommend YouGrowPromo, Playlist Push, Musosoup, PlaylistSupply, Indiefy, and the free-to-use DailyPlaylists. These platforms connect you with real playlist curators and listeners who might genuinely appreciate your music and become long-term fans.

RELEASE DAY

It's release day! If you have prepared your marketing assets and emails ahead of time, today's activities should be fairly straightforward.

If you have set up a WhatsApp group or communication channel with your team, you will want to update the group the day before release day with the content assets you are uploading and instructions for how and when to share across their channels. Check that everyone has access to the banner artwork for different media platforms too.

DSP CHECK

The first thing you need to do is check the release is on all the digital service providers (DSPs) such as Spotify, Amazon, Apple Music and Beatport.

If anything is incorrect (such as spelling mistakes or the artwork is wrong), contact your distributor immediately through a change request on the help section, detailing the issue and requesting an edit. Changes take around 24 – 48 hours to remedy.

UPDATE RECORD LABEL PLATFORMS

Most distributors don't distribute your music to your own SoundCloud, YouTube or website pages, so you will need to upload the music to these platforms on release day and update the description and about sections with the Smarturl link when it is ready.

Ensure you update the following:

- SoundCloud
- YouTube
- Bandcamp
- Label and artist website

CREATE SMARTURL LINK

Now these platforms are updated, we are ready to add them to your Smarturl page. A Smarturl is a single short form unique link and landing page that combines the links from all the different platforms into one place, which gives fans the option to choose their favourite platform for streaming or buying your music.

Many distribution platforms will create a Smarturl page for you, such as DistroKid and The Label Machine distribution. Some music marketing platforms offer this functionality as part of their paid promotional tools, and the following have a free option, PUSH.fm, Feature.fm, and Soundplate Clicks.

You can only create this on release day as the release needs to be live on the main platforms:

- Spotify
- Apple Music
- Amazon
- Beatport (electronic music)
- Deezer
- Tidal
- SoundCloud
- Youtube
- YouTube Music
- Bandcamp

UPDATE SOCIAL MEDIA BANNERS

It's time to announce that it's release day! Update all platforms with 'out now' artwork and Smarturl links. For Beatport focus, share only the Beatport link; otherwise use Smarturl.

Facebook: Update banner, add Smarturl to description, post in feed tagging artists.

Instagram: Add Smarturl to bio, post in feed and stories tagging artists.

X: Update banner, add Smarturl to About section, post in feed tagging artists.

SoundCloud: Update banner and About section, add Smarturl to preview clips, make release public, spotlight at top position.

YouTube: Upload tracks with Smarturl in descriptions, make videos public, add comments.

Spotify: Add tracks to label playlists, optionally update artist profile pic and highlight release.

UPDATE ARTIST AND TEAM

Now you have updated all the label platforms, created the Smarturl link and posted on all social media platforms; it's time to add this information as well as a link to all the marketing assets into a concise email. Then send it to the artist and team members so they have everything in one place, and it's easy for everyone to share the release across their own platforms.

EMAIL YOUR FAN LIST

Create your newsletter email in your emailing provider platform and send it to everyone on your subscription list. Have the artwork, brief description of the single, keypress support and DJ feedback quotes, and one link to the Smarturl. If you are focused on one particular DSP, then use that link only. Remember to keep this simple, with one call-to-action in the email to drive traffic.

SEND PRESS RELEASE

Be sure to let your key press contacts know it's the release day and send the updated press release that contains all the updated support for the single.

The best practice is to send individual messages to PR contracts that you have built up a relationship with and let them know it is out today, and encourage them to share on their social media platforms.

If the press contact has already posted and supported the single, send a simple personalised email saying thanks for the support. This earns great karma for future press releases.

UPDATE SPOTIFY PROFILE AND ARTIST PICK

Make sure your artist's Spotify bio contains the latest information about the new single. Log on to your Spotify account and update this. You can also update your Spotify Artist Pick. Spotify For Artists' Artist's Pick gives artists control of the music at the top of their artist profile. Get them to pick any track, album, or playlist, and add a short message about why they love it.

ONE-TO-ONE MESSAGING

Sending one-to-one messaging thanking for support is super important on release day, both as a label and as an artist.

Spend the afternoon reaching out to everyone and personally thank them for supporting this release. Not just blogs or radio DJs, but all the fans that have supported the release. DM them on each platform that they have interacted with you. Ask them to listen and share your music. Ensure the artists are doing the same on their channels too.

This also acts as a subtle reminder to download or stream the single if they haven't already. You only have one release day, so make the most of it.

You can download a release day checklist by visiting the Book Resources tab on The Label Machine website.

POST RELEASE ACTIVITIES

Now the music is public for everyone to hear, it's crucial to promote the track and build momentum.

EXTRA ASSETS

Upload at least two different marketing assets the week after release day and two extra marketing assets two weeks following the release date to keep driving conversations about your release. Depending on what else you have going on will depend on which days are best to do this or what platform you will post on.

A terrific extra marketing asset to update this week to drive Spotify algorithms is to create a Spotify video canvas.

Engage your fans with a Spotify Canvas, a short looping visual you can add to your tracks on Spotify. It's album artwork for the streaming age. You can easily create one using videos from Mixkit or Capcut templates.

- mixkit.co/free-vertical-videos
- capcut.com

As you will have generated new fans over the last few weeks of the campaign, another extra content idea could be finding out and getting to know more about the artist.

Create a simple website landing page for the artist telling the story of what they have been up to prior this point in time. This is essentially an updated bio that is as current as possible and mentions the new single – pointing new fans to this page to discover more about the artist and their story.

REMINDERS

Spend time replying to feedback across socials and watch for mentions of the release online to repost and share. An easy way to do this is to set up a simple Google Alert for the release to email you daily with mentions.

- google.com/alerts

If you creep into the top ten in specialist charts such as Beatport's for electronic music or are featured on a Spotify editorial playlist, do a screen grab and share on socials. Encourage any fans that haven't bought/streamed to support the release and help climb up the charts, as every bit helps.

You can also use apps like Chartmetric, Viberate, and Songstats to monitor your releases, track playlist placements, and receive alerts for music trends or spikes in activity around your tracks. This gives you early insights into how your release is performing globally and across different platforms.

- chartmetric.com
- viberate.com
- songstats.com

THE 360° MUSIC SYSTEM – BUILDING A SUSTAINABLE MUSIC CAREER

Now that you've got your label up and running and have released music, the next part of the journey is looking at how to apply everything long-term from an artist's perspective. In other words, how do you create something that repeats, grows, and scales using the label as a platform to continuously develop and grow the artists on your roster? That's what the 360° Music System delivers.

I've spent years studying how the most successful independent artists operate. This system distills their approach into a clear, actionable framework. It shows you how to apply everything you've learned in this book to build momentum, not just moments.

Whether you're an artist or a label, the principles stay the same: build a strong brand, create compelling content, use social media with intent, distribute music across key platforms, and develop a funnel that turns casual listeners into lifelong superfans.

At the center is your community. A loyal fanbase gives you freedom from gatekeepers, sustainable income, and a buffer against industry shifts.

Each stage in the system connects back to chapters in this book. What follows is a breakdown of those stages, with pointers to the tools and tactics you've already learned. Use the system to zoom out, assess your progress, and plan your next moves with clarity.

UNDERSTANDING THE 360° FRAMEWORK

The 360° Music System consists of eight interconnected components that work together to create a comprehensive music career strategy:

1. **Artist/Label Foundation** – The starting point and driving force
2. **Brand Development** – Your identity, story, and tone
3. **Content Creation** – Organic and paid content pillars
4. **Social Media Distribution** – Platform-specific strategies for engagement

5. **Music Distribution** – Getting your music to fans across all channels
6. **Fan Funnel: Discovery (Top of Funnel)** – Attracting new fans
7. **Fan Funnel: Nurturing (Middle of Funnel)** – Building relationships
8. **Fan Funnel: Monetization (Bottom of Funnel)** – Converting fans to supporters

Each component feeds into the next, creating a cycle where success in one area amplifies results in others. The revenue generated at the bottom of the funnel gets reinvested back into the artist or label, allowing the cycle to expand and grow stronger over time.

THE ARTIST/LABEL FOUNDATION

Every successful music career begins with a solid foundation: good music, the right mindset, commitment, and a strategic approach to building a sustainable career.

Core Requirements

Before implementing the 360° system, ensure you have these fundamental elements in place:

Music Readiness: You must have music that you're genuinely proud of and ready to share with the world. This means professionally mixed and mastered tracks that represent your best work. Having at least three releases planned gives you the momentum needed to maintain audience engagement.

Clear Aspirations: Define your specific goals for growing a fanbase and monetizing your music career. Vague ambitions lead to unfocused efforts. Be specific about what success looks like for you, whether that's selling 1,000 copies of your next release, booking 50 shows per year, or building an email list of 10,000 dedicated fans.

Commitment to the Process: Building a music career requires consistent effort across multiple areas. You must be prepared to develop marketing skills, engage with fans regularly, create content beyond just music, and treat your artistic career as a business.

The Mindset Shift

Success in the modern music industry requires thinking beyond just creating music. You're building a brand, developing music products, nurturing fan relationships, and creating experiences. This doesn't diminish the artistic aspect of your work, it ensures your music reaches the people who will value it most.

Example: Ashley Wilde's Foundation Ashley Wilde, an emerging synthwave artist, exemplifies this foundation approach. Before launching her 360° system, Ashley ensured she had three complete synthwave tracks professionally mastered, each showcasing different aspects of her retro-futuristic sound. She set specific goals: build an email list of 2,000 fans within six months, sell 500 vinyl copies of her debut EP, and book 20 live performances in neon-lit venues across major cities. Most importantly, Ashley committed to treating her music as both art and business, dedicating specific hours each week to marketing and fan engagement activities.

For more detail refer to Part Three: The Set-Up (Mindset, Goals and Missions, Business Plan, Choosing a Label Name, Record Label Backbone)

BRAND DEVELOPMENT: YOUR FOUNDATION FOR EVERYTHING

Your brand serves as the foundation for all content creation and fan interaction. Without a clear brand identity, your marketing efforts will lack focus and consistency, making it difficult to build a loyal following.

The Three Pillars of Brand Development

Identity Archetype: Choose one of four core archetypes that best represents your artistic persona:

- **Leader**: You guide others through your music and message
- **Adventurer**: You explore new sounds and take your fans on journeys
- **Educator/Reporter**: You share knowledge and insights through your art
- **Reluctant Hero**: You create music that helps others through difficult times

Your Unique Story: Identify what makes you distinctive both musically and personally. This might include your background, influences, creative process, personal interests, or the communities you're part of. Your story should answer why fans should care about you specifically among countless other artists.

Communication Tone: Decide how you'll convey your message to fans. Your tone might be professional and polished, humorous and playful, raw and authentic, or informative and educational. Consistency in tone across all communications builds trust and recognition.

Benefits of Strong Branding

A well-defined brand eliminates uncertainty in content creation. Instead of wondering what to post or how to present yourself, you have clear guidelines that make decisions easier and faster. This consistency also helps fans understand what to expect from you, making them more likely to engage and support your work.

Example: Ashley Wilde's Brand Development Ashley positions herself as an **Adventurer** archetype, taking fans on nostalgic journeys through retro-futuristic soundscapes. Her story centers on being a software developer by day who discovered her passion for recreating the sounds of 80s sci-fi films and video games. This unique combination of technical precision and artistic vision sets her apart in the synthwave scene.

Ashley's tone is **mysterious yet approachable** – she shares insights into her creative process while maintaining an air of intrigue about her upcoming projects. This tone is consistent across all her communications, from social media posts to email newsletters, creating a cohesive brand experience that fans recognize instantly.

For more detail refer to Part Three: Label Branding, Design Tools and Assets, Logo, Website, Social Media Handles

CONTENT CREATION: THE TWO ESSENTIAL PILLARS

Content creation forms the bridge between your brand and your audience. The 360° system relies on two distinct types of content, each serving different purposes in your overall strategy.

Organic Content: Building Authentic Connections

Organic content showcases your personality, passions, and music without direct promotional intent. This content builds genuine connections with your audience by providing value and entertainment.

Key Types of Organic Content:

- **Behind-the-Scenes Content**: Share your creative process, studio sessions, equipment setups, and the daily life of being an artist
- **Music Snippets**: Post teasers of new tracks, live performance clips, or acoustic versions of your songs
- **Music Commentary**: Explain the meaning behind your

songs, discuss your influences, or share what inspires specific tracks

- **Personal Interests**: Share content about hobbies, causes, or interests outside of music to connect with fans on multiple levels
- **Blog Content**: Write detailed posts about your journey, creative process, or topics related to your genre

SEO Benefits of Blogging: Regular blog posts improve your website's search engine visibility, helping new fans discover you through organic searches. Write about topics your target audience cares about, incorporating relevant keywords naturally.

Paid Content: Strategic Audience Growth

Paid content reaches new audiences and brings them into your fan funnel through targeted advertising and PR campaigns.

Advertising Strategies:

- Promote free downloads or exclusive content in exchange for email addresses
- Use cover songs or remixes as ad content to attract fans of established artists
- Target audiences based on similar artists, genres, or interests
- Create compelling calls-to-action that encourage immediate engagement

PR Campaigns:

- Invest in features in music publications and blogs
- Secure interviews and podcast appearances
- Build relationships with music journalists and influencers
- Coordinate PR efforts with release schedules for maximum impact

Example: Ashley Wilde's Content Strategy Ashley's organic content includes weekly studio vlogs showing her analog synthesizer setup, posts explaining the sci-fi films that inspire specific tracks, and shares about her vintage gaming collection. Her blog features posts about the history of synthwave and tutorials on analog synthesis techniques, which rank well for searches related to "synthwave production" and "analog synthesizers."

For paid content, Ashley creates cover versions of iconic 80s songs with her synthwave twist, using them as Facebook and Instagram ads to attract fans of artists like Depeche Mode and New Order. She also invests in PR campaigns targeting retro-gaming and synthwave blogs, securing features that align with her brand identity.

For more detail refer to Part Three: Marketing Assets, Extra Marketing Content, EPK, Press Release, DJ Promo

SOCIAL MEDIA DISTRIBUTION: PLATFORM-SPECIFIC STRATEGIES

Once you've created content, strategic distribution across social media platforms maximizes your reach and engagement. Different platforms serve different purposes in the 360° system.

Organic Content Platforms

YouTube: Your primary platform for long-form content including music videos, behind-the-scenes vlogs, and educational content. YouTube's algorithm favors consistent uploading and audience retention, making it ideal for building a dedicated subscriber base.

Vertical Video Platforms: Distribute shorter, engaging clips across YouTube Shorts, Instagram Reels, and TikTok. These platforms offer massive reach potential and help introduce your music to new audiences through algorithm-driven discovery.

Platform-Specific Optimization:

- Create platform-native content rather than simply reposting the same content everywhere
- Use trending hashtags and sounds on TikTok and Instagram Reels
- Optimize YouTube videos with compelling thumbnails and SEO-friendly titles
- Engage with comments and messages daily to build community

Paid Advertising Platforms

Meta Advertising (Facebook and Instagram): These platforms provide the most effective paid advertising for musicians, offering sophisticated targeting options and reliable performance tracking. Meta's advertising platform handles approximately 90% of effective music advertising.

Alternative Platforms: While you can advertise on YouTube, TikTok, and Reddit, Meta platforms typically provide better return on investment for music marketing.

Example: Ashley Wilde's Social Media Strategy Ashley posts full music videos and production tutorials on YouTube, creating a consistent weekly upload schedule. She adapts her content for vertical platforms by creating snippet videos showcasing her synthesizer in action, often featuring recognizable 80s movie quotes as captions.

Her paid advertising focuses entirely on Meta platforms, targeting fans of synthwave artists, retro gaming enthusiasts, and 80s nostalgia groups. She uses video ads featuring 30-second previews of her tracks overlaid with retro-futuristic visuals, driving traffic to landing pages offering free EP downloads.

For more detail refer to Part Three: Marketing – Social Media, Facebook/Instagram Ads, Spotify Playlists

MUSIC DISTRIBUTION: MAXIMIZING ACCESSIBILITY

Getting your music to fans across all possible channels ensures maximum accessibility and revenue potential. The 360° system emphasizes comprehensive distribution rather than relying on a single platform.

Streaming Platform Strategy

Major Platforms: Distribute to all mainstream platforms including Spotify, Apple Music, Amazon Music, and Deezer. These platforms provide global reach and are where most music discovery happens today.

Genre-Specific Platforms: For specialized genres, include platforms like Beatport (electronic music) or Bandcamp (independent music) that cater to dedicated fan communities.

Alternative Distribution Channels

Digital Downloads: Maintain presence on Bandcamp and Amazon Music for fans who prefer to own their music digitally.

Physical Products: Offer CDs, vinyl records, and even cassette tapes for collectors and fans who value tangible music products.

Live Performance Integration: Use live shows to introduce new music and drive streaming platform follows.

Sync Licensing Opportunities: Pursue placements in films, TV shows, advertisements, and video games for additional revenue and exposure.

Example: Ashley Wilde's Distribution Strategy Ashley distributes her synthwave tracks across all major streaming platforms while also offering limited-edition vinyl releases through Bandcamp. She creates special cassette tape versions of her EPs, appealing to synthwave fans' love of retro formats. Ashley actively pursues sync licensing opportunities with video game developers and retro-themed advertisements, leveraging her music's nostalgic appeal for placement in indie games and 80s-themed commercials.

For more detail refer to Part Three: Upload to Distribution, Register Songs with PROs and *Part One: Distributors, Aggregators, Self-Distribution*

FAN FUNNEL: DISCOVERY – TOP OF FUNNEL

The discovery stage is where potential fans first encounter your music and brand. Your goal is to capture their attention and bring them into your marketing ecosystem where you can build a relationship over time.

Creating Awareness and Interest

Content Strategy for Discovery: Create captivating content that showcases both your music and personality. Use engaging short videos, performance clips, and behind-the-scenes content that resonates with your target audience.

Free Value Offerings: Provide exclusive content in exchange for contact information:

- Free downloads of unreleased tracks, remixes, or cover songs
- Exclusive access to live streams or virtual listening parties

- Behind-the-scenes video content or production insights
- Early access to new releases or pre-order opportunities

Capture Systems

Landing Pages: Create visually appealing, conversion-optimized pages that clearly communicate your offer and include simple forms for email and phone number collection.

Lead Magnets: Develop compelling reasons for fans to share their contact information:

- Free EPs or compilation albums
- Production tutorials or educational content
- Virtual meet-and-greet opportunities
- Exclusive remix packages

Social Media Integration: Use targeted ads on Meta platforms to promote your offers and guide fans to your landing pages. Create ads that feel native to each platform while clearly communicating value.

Example: Ashley Wilde's Discovery Strategy Ashley creates Instagram Reels featuring 30-second snippets of her tracks paired with vintage sci-fi movie clips. She runs Facebook ads targeting synthwave and retro gaming groups, promoting a free download of her "Neon Dreams" EP in exchange for email signup. Her landing page features retro-futuristic design elements consistent with her brand, and her lead magnet includes bonus tracks and production notes explaining her creative process. New subscribers receive a welcome email series sharing her journey from software developer to synthwave artist.

For more detail refer to Part Three: Marketing Strategy, PR, Ads, Fan Funnel Overview

FAN FUNNEL: NURTURING – MIDDLE OF FUNNEL

The nurturing stage focuses on building deeper connections with fans who have already shown interest in your music. This is where casual listeners become dedicated supporters through consistent value delivery and authentic relationship building.

Email Sequence Development

"Get to Know You" Series: Create a comprehensive 12-16 email sequence spread over several weeks or months. Each email should provide value while deepening the fan's connection to your story and music.

Content Structure for Each Email:

- Personal stories about your musical journey
- Insights into your creative process and inspirations
- Links to specific tracks with context about their creation
- Behind-the-scenes content from recording sessions or performances

- Your perspectives on music, art, or topics relevant to your brand

Exclusive Content Strategy

Fan-Only Access: Provide content that's only available to your email subscribers or community members:

- Demo versions of unreleased songs
- Acoustic or alternate versions of existing tracks
- Extended behind-the-scenes video content
- Early access to new releases, merchandise, or ticket sales

Interactive Engagement: Create opportunities for fans to influence your work or feel personally connected:

- Q&A sessions via email, live streams, or social media
- Polls about cover art, setlists, or merchandise designs
- Fan shoutouts and user-generated content features
- Virtual listening parties for new releases

Example: Ashley Wilde's Nurturing Strategy Ashley's 14-email welcome series shares her transition from coding by day to creating synthwave by night, includes production tutorials for her signature synthesizer sounds, and provides exclusive downloads of instrumental versions of her tracks. She maintains a private Discord server called "The Neon Underground" where fans share retro gaming experiences and discuss 80s sci-fi films. Ashley hosts monthly listening parties where she previews new tracks and shares stories about their creation, creating intimate connections with her most dedicated supporters.

For more detail refer to Part Three: Emails and Email Marketing, EPKs, Post-Release Activities

FAN FUNNEL: MONETIZATION – BOTTOM OF FUNNEL

The monetization stage converts loyal fans into financial supporters through strategic product and experience offerings. A well-structured value ladder ensures you have appropriate offerings for fans at every level of engagement and financial commitment.

Value Ladder Development
Low-Ticket Offers ($7-$15):

- Digital album downloads with bonus content
- Stickers, buttons, or small merchandise items
- Individual track downloads with stems or remixes
- Digital wallpapers or artwork collections

Mid-Ticket Offers ($25-$75):

- Physical albums (CD, vinyl, cassette)
- Branded merchandise like t-shirts, hoodies, or posters
- Signed copies of releases or merchandise
- Small merchandise bundles or gift packages

High-Ticket Offers ($100-$500):

- Limited edition box sets with exclusive content
- VIP concert/gig experiences or meet-and-greet packages

- Private online concerts or personalized song dedications
- Exclusive merchandise collaborations or artist-designed items

Ultra High-Ticket Offers ($1000+):

- Weekend experiences or retreats with the artist
- Collaboration opportunities on writing or recording sessions
- Private concerts for special occasions
- One-on-one mentoring or production coaching sessions

Recurring Revenue Streams

Membership Programs: Create tiered subscription offerings that provide ongoing value:

- Basic tier: Monthly exclusive tracks and updates
- Premium tier: Video content, early access, and merchandise discounts
- VIP tier: Direct access to the artist, exclusive events, and personalized content

Example: Ashley Wilde's Monetization Strategy Ashley's value ladder starts with $10 digital EP downloads including bonus instrumental versions, progresses to $45 limited-edition vinyl releases with holographic covers, and reaches $250 for VIP synthwave concert experiences with 80s costume contests. Her highest tier offers $1,000 weekend retreats where fans collaborate with Ashley to create custom synthwave tracks using her vintage synthesizer collection. She maintains a $15/month "Neon Archive" subscription providing monthly exclusive tracks, production tutorials, and retro gaming soundtrack covers.

For more detail refer to Part Four: Merchandise, Live Shows, Sample Libraries, Publishing, Compilations

BUILDING AND MANAGING YOUR COMMUNITY

Community represents the heart of the 360° system – the element that ties everything together and ensures long-term sustainability. A thriving community provides independence from external gatekeepers and creates a foundation for sustained growth.

Defining Your Community's Purpose

Core Focus Areas: Clearly define what your community centers around:

- Exclusive access to your music and creative process
- Shared interests beyond music (gaming, fashion, causes)
- Educational content related to your genre or production techniques
- Fan interaction and connection with like-minded individuals

Platform Selection and Setup

Platform Evaluation: Choose platforms based on your community's needs:

- **Discord**: Best for active, real-time conversations and structured community management
- **Facebook Groups**: Ideal for ongoing discussions and easy content sharing
- **Patreon**: Perfect for monetized communities with tiered access levels
- **Marketing Machine:** Similar to Patreon but linked to your website and funnels
- **Instagram Broadcast Channels**: Great for quick updates and exclusive announcements

Content Strategy for Community Engagement

Regular Content Schedule:

- Weekly discussion topics or questions
- Monthly exclusive content releases
- Quarterly virtual events or live sessions
- Annual special events or celebrations

Interactive Content Types:

- Live Q&A sessions and AMAs (Ask Me Anything)
- Polls and votes on creative decisions
- Challenges or contests for user-generated content
- Collaborative projects involving community members

Example: Ashley Wilde's Community Building Ashley creates "The Neon Underground," a Discord community focused on synthwave culture, retro gaming, and 80s nostalgia. Members gain access to exclusive track previews, monthly production livestreams, and collaborative playlist creation. She implements a leveling system where active members earn badges like "Synth Explorer" and "Neon Legend." Ashley hosts quarterly virtual events where members share their own retro-inspired creations, from music to art to gaming mods, fostering a creative community that extends beyond just consuming her music.

MEASURING SUCCESS AND OPTIMIZING THE SYSTEM

The 360° system requires ongoing monitoring and optimization to ensure each component performs effectively and supports overall growth objectives.

Key Performance Indicators

Content Metrics: Social media engagement rates, website traffic, email open rates, content reach and sharing

Funnel Metrics: Lead generation rates, email list growth, conversion rates, customer lifetime value

Community Metrics: Active member counts, engagement levels, growth rates, user satisfaction

Revenue Metrics: Revenue distribution across streams, customer acquisition costs, monthly recurring revenue

Optimization Strategies

Regular Review Cycles: Establish quarterly review processes to analyze performance data and identify improvement opportunities.

A/B Testing: Continuously test different approaches to content creation, email marketing, community engagement, and monetization strategies.

Fan Feedback Integration: Regularly survey your audience to understand their preferences, needs, and suggestions for improvement.

Example: Ashley Wilde's Complete System Results After one year of implementing the 360° system, Ashley has built an email list of 3,500 synthwave enthusiasts, a TikTok following of 25,600 followers, maintains an active Discord community of 800 members, and generates $4,000 monthly through a combination of streaming revenue, merchandise sales, and subscription services. Her "Neon Underground" community has become a hub for synthwave culture, with members creating fan art, sharing vintage gaming content, and collaborating on retro-inspired projects. This community-driven approach has led to organic growth through word-of-mouth, reduced her customer acquisition costs, and provided a sustainable foundation for long-term career growth.

Most importantly, Ashley has achieved creative independence – she no longer needs to rely on external validation or gatekeepers to build her career. Her dedicated community provides the support, feedback, and financial foundation necessary to continue creating the music she's passionate about while building a sustainable business around her art.

The 360° Music System provides a comprehensive framework for building a sustainable music career in today's industry. By implementing each component systematically and maintaining focus on community building, artists and labels can create self-sustaining cycles of growth that provide independence, financial stability, and creative fulfillment.

PART FOUR

BECOMING ESTABLISHED

OVERVIEW

This section is about activities for creating a record label that goes beyond a few releases. I once heard a saying that once your label has had its tenth release, you're established and most likely to succeed.

With more than ten releases, you'll have built a substantial back catalogue to monetise through additional channels like sync licensing and music compilations. You'll need to ensure you have robust accounting services as your catalogue grows. You might consider investing in merchandise for both the label and signed artists, or releasing special-edition vinyl records.

As artist relationships mature, you could offer management services and expand into publishing administration for unpublished artists and music on your roster.

These strategies will help transform your record label into a sustainable, multi-faceted music company with diverse revenue streams.

ACCOUNTING

Label accounting is the management of your record label income and activity across your streaming royalties, physical sales, music sync, and merchandising. This is separate from your company accounting, which deals with your overall income and expenses such as office rent, salaries and paying your tax.

If you put out more than five or six releases a year, you will need a label accounting system in place.

To recap from the budgeting chapter:

> Gross Royalty Income – Release Expenses =
> Net Royalty Income

And

> Net Royalty Income = Artist Royalties Payments +
> Label Royalties Payments

With the percentage split between artist royalties and label royalties defined by the Royalty Income Split.

The label accounting software will allow you to calculate these amounts for each of your releases based on the complex royalty reports sent from your distributor and automate the process of sending the royalty statements to artists.

RUNNING A LABEL FOR YOUR OWN RELEASES

If you are running a label purely for our own releases, this will be pretty straightforward as all money coming in will go directly to you, so there won't be a need to create payment accounts for each artist you release.

You will only need to consider splitting payments and accounting to others if you collaborate, are in a band and are splitting payments between band members, or have agreed to a percentage split with a producer.

For instance, if you have a track remixed and agree to 50% of sales to go to the remixer, you will have to split your royalties. A simple spreadsheet that you update with royalty income every six months will work fine in these cases. It's worth noting here why a buyout fee for a remix or a beat for a track can be a preferred arrangement, as it means less paperwork and ongoing accounting in the future.

RUNNING A LABEL FOR OTHER ARTISTS' RELEASES

If you plan to release other artists' music, you will need to use label accounting software to split multiple revenue streams into various payment accounts.

Likewise, if you plan to release compilations, you'll need to account for each track on the album. In a nutshell, you'll need some sort of system for accounting.

Software solutions

When we first started Never Say Die, we used a spreadsheet to calculate royalties which worked fine for the first year of releases, when we had only five releases.

However, as the accounting periods rolled on and we released more EPs and singles with remixes, calculating the splits and emailing everyone statements and collecting invoices started becoming very time-consuming and cumbersome to do. Besides, accounting sucks. A lot.

However, DJ Lazy Rich started Label Engine for this exact problem and after using it for a few releases, doing the accounts became much more straightforward.

There are a few different online platforms for calculating royalties for labels and some distributors have this functionality built into the distribution system, which can make doing accounts far easier.

Platforms offering payments splits alongside the distribution platform are Label Engine, Amp Suite, Distrokid and Label Worx.

You can also use standalone accounting software platforms, and some of the most popular ones available to independent labels are Infinite Catalog, EddyApp, Curve Royalty Systems, and SR1.

Some distribution platforms (such as our own Label Machine distribution) allow you to do auto royalty split payments at source, which means you won't have to do royalty accounting on music releases, a real time saver!

It's worth noting if you are releasing electronic music, you'll want to use a system tailored for electronic music, specifically dealing with the issue of accounting individual tracks within a release with separate splits for collaborators and remixers. Label Engine, Amp Suite and Label Work all have these tailored solutions.

Accounting periods

Typically record labels will calculate royalties for a set period and then account to artists 60-90 days later after that specified period. This is because there is a delay between when a distributor or aggregator collects money from customers and when the money is received in a record label's bank account.

Typically label's account using one of the following accounting periods:

Twice a year on 30 June and 31 December.

In this case, all the royalties in the six months between 1 January and 30 June are calculated as one period usually called H1, which means Half 1 of the year. And 1 July to 31 December is called H2, the second half of the year.

The label then sends the statements 90 days later, so for H1, that would be 30 March. Artists get a statement, and royalty money is transferred to the artist's bank or PayPal account.

Four times a year on the 31 March, 30 June, 30 September and 31 December.

In this instance, the accounting periods are called Q1, Q2, Q3, Q4, short for quarter 1, quarter 2, etc. Again, the accounts will be sent to the artist 90 days later, so for Q1, the artist would get a statement on 30 June.

Twelve times a year, on the last day of every month.

Similar to the other accounting periods, but each period is titled for the month. This is becoming more commonplace as labels go to all digital releases, and payments between distributors and labels speed up.

How do you decide which one works for you?

If you're a small team working part-time on the label, you might want to account twice or four times a year. However, if you have a dedicated team member working full-time with more resources, you might want to do this every month. Your artists will appreciate it, that's for sure!

If you use a distribution and accounting all-in-one platform, I suggest four times a year or once a month as it's just a few clicks at the end of the month and then transferring the money. I know that larger and very well-run indie record labels such as Monstercat account every month.

Most importantly, send statements when they are due. You'll keep a good rep in the industry for sending statements on time, and the artists will appreciate you. A gripe a lot of artists have with labels is that they don't pay on time, and I know it has been something that has pushed artists over the edge and led to artists subsequently leaving a label.

MERCHANDISE AND PHYSICAL DISTRIBUTION

There are two good reasons to focus on merchandise, aka merch, for your record label and your artists: free advertising and another income stream.

If someone is wearing your logo on their shirt, you're getting free advertising, right? And seeing your logo or brand on a fan in the audience is pretty great too.

Many artists and labels who are starting out classify merchandise as a marketing cost (small batches of merchandise often only break-even) as it creates physical content to help promote releases. Having physical merchandise gives you flexibility to create video and photo content based around the merchandise, such as photoshoots, or creating design contests with fan voting.

Whether it's a vinyl, CD or limited edition cassette tapes, having something physical adds a layer of value to a release. Everyone knows digital music is almost 'free' to distribute, but with merchandise and vinyl, someone has put their hard-earned cash behind the project, giving it a layer of value.

You can also make a good side income when you have built your brand and have a solid following. If you have a strong brand identity, it works really well. The best example that I have seen is when the artist has a natural flair for what looks good.

Producer and designer Alix Perez is an excellent example of this. He designs all his own clothing styles, and it's extremely popular, with every one of his merch ranges selling out. Producer and illustrator Eptic designs all his own artwork and merchandise and, again, it's very popular.

If you don't have a natural flair for design or style, you can reach out to design artists online. We have done this not just for merchandise but also for EP and single artwork, which we covered in the Creating Artwork chapter.

Alternatively, you can use a freelancer website to find a designer that suits your style. Great websites are:

Coroflot.com
This is a platform for professionals that work exclusively in the design and creative industries. Very high quality.

Behance.net
This is a creative platform designers use to build their portfolio, and you can see in-depth the way they work before sending a message to someone you like.

Dribbble.com
Highly curated creatives database as designers need to be invited to the platform and is thus a very personalised service.

Fiverr.com
The Pro section of this platform has verified exceptional talent, handpicked for quality and service, and offers freelancers outside the creative sectors.

It can take some time to find a good artist that fits with your branding, but if you find someone, treat them well. They can become part of your team long-term and make a big difference to your branding and overall success in your merch efforts.

Let's look at the practicalities of creating, selling and shipping your merchandise. There are two ways you can go forward with this: bulk manufacturing or made-to-order (aka print-on-demand). I have tried both ways and a mixture between the two.

BULK MANUFACTURING

Bulk manufacturing is just that. You order large quantities of a product; for example, 200 of one t-shirt design, spread over different shirt sizes and colours. Bulk ordering with clothes is usually done using screen-printing, and it gives you the highest quality prints. You are looking at about £300 ($400) for 100 t-shirts of one design, and the price drops as the order amount increases.

Other popular items are embroidered baseball caps, beanies, trucker hats, tote bags, mugs (surprisingly, mugs are pretty popular as gifts!), phone cases, vinyl stickers and badges.

If you are buying in bulk, you can typically go to one manufacturing company for all your needs. The best thing you can do is search for your local country or state area for a merchandise company, so it's easier to communicate and get quotes and samples delivered.

If you don't want to hold stock and handle the postage yourself, you want to work with a merchandise company with a 'drop ship' option. This is where they keep the stock and send it out for you on your behalf for a fee.

PRINT-ON-DEMAND

The second option is to go with a print-on-demand company. This is where you have a manufacturer make each product to order. The idea is that you don't have to have any stock filling up your home studio or office. Cafepress was one of the first companies to do this in the early 2000s, and there are now many options available.

Many of these will allow you to 'white label' the service, which means you can integrate it into your website or Shopify store to create a seamless experience for your fans. The Marketing Machine allows you to connect to Printify.com so you can sell POD items directly on your merch shop seamlessly.

So why use bulk when you can use print-on-demand? The main differences are quality and cost.

Most print-on-demand companies tend to produce lower quality merchandise as they typically use print-to-garment (PTG in the industry). This isn't as good quality as screen printing. Quality control can suffer, too, as the companies have hundreds of clients to deal with. Whereas, bulk manufacturing uses screen printing, which is longer lasting and a higher quality print. As you are printing in bulk, the costs come down, which means a bigger profit for you.

When you are starting out, use print-on-demand, and then as you grow, move to bulk manufacturing with dropshipping to give you better quality control and a larger share of the profits.

There are many different print-on-demand companies, each offering slightly different benefits. There is no one-size-fits-all, so it's best to research each one and find one that fits you best. The main companies are:

Printify.com
Integrates well with most types of websites, offers over 300 products and has multiple fulfilment centres worldwide.

Cafepress.com
The original print-on-demand service, worth a mention, but these days there are better options.

Printful.com
They own all their factories (so quality control is good), offer over 200 products and integrate well with Shopify.

Gooten.com
Over 100 products to choose from have multiple fulfilment centres around the world and integrate well with Shopify.

Spreadshop.com
Allows other people to sell your designs, and you get a cut of the sale.

If you do sell merchandise, you are going to need a payment system set up. Shopify is the simplest platform to use and has a considerable amount of support. If you go with Shopify, you can use the website as the main artist page, and some print-on-demand companies integrate directly with the platform.

Otherwise, you can set up an account on Stripe.com and/or PayPal.com – both integrate well with WordPress, Squarespace, and Wix based websites.

VINYL AND CDS

As far as physical products go, vinyl is probably the sexiest merchandise product there is. There has been a revival in the last ten years for vinyl, as fans crave something genuine in the digital world. The same goes for CDs, which are still a great seller for independent album releases.

Vinyl manufacturing is not cheap, and you'll need to press and sell a minimum of around 300 vinyl just to break even. However, you can view this as a marketing cost to validate your release. If it does well and you sell more than 300, you can profit from the release.

There are about eight operational pressing plants around the UK and Europe. North America has about twenty vinyl pressing plants. Because of vinyl's popularity in recent years, your lead time needs to be at least 12 – 16 weeks.

You also need to pay a mastering engineer to get a special master of the music that is suitable for vinyl pressing. Most of the vinyl manufacturing companies have excellent guidelines for preparing music and artwork for a pressing, however.

Recommended vinyl manufacturing companies around the world are

- UK – discmanufacturingservices.com

- Europe – recordindustry.com
- US – urpressing.com

Prices start around $1500 for 300 12" vinyl with one colour print label and a plain cover. Prices go up as you start to add options such as colour labels, colour vinyl or custom-cut shapes, but the overall price decreases as the number of pressings increases.

A new print-on-demand solution for vinyl is now available through elasticstage.com. They offer single vinyl production with no inventory requirements or upfront costs, and their product maintains the authentic look and sound of traditional vinyl. While their manufacturing technology remains proprietary, the results are impressive and effective for small-run releases.

CDs are cheaper to manufacture, and a Google search will give you a range of companies available to press up your batch of CDs. Some digital distributors can do this for you as well, such as CD Baby.

BUNDLES

A popular way to sell merchandise around a specific release is tiers of 'merch bundles' (collections of items sold together).

Typically, you create three tiers of bundles. The first is a download, the second is a download, t-shirt and stickers, and the third is vinyl, t-shirt, stickers and the download.

You should also take advantage of the opportunity for the artists to sign the vinyl; fans love this as it makes it personal. Make each tier level rise in price and fewer of the bigger bundles to create scarcity.

Because of the very hands-on nature of creating bundles, it can be time-intensive but very rewarding and gives lots of behind-the-scenes content to share with fans. When you start doing bundles of more than 300 units, you will be in a good position to contact a specialist fulfillment merch company that can take care of the logistics for you.

Established fulfillment companies we recommend are 8merch.com and topdrawermerch.com.

SAMPLE LIBRARIES

A great income source for artists and labels is to create sample packs. They can also be excellent promotional tools to get your name out there. They are popular with electronic, hip hop and trap artists as sample packs lend themselves to that type of music production.

For some artists, creating a sample pack is a milestone in their career, a point that you have become recognised as a genre's established artist. Deadmau5, Luke Solomon, Carl Cox, Rockwell and DJ Vadim are all artists with their own sample packs.

The typical sample pack is a collection of beats, basslines, vocal hooks, synth pads and lead sounds, providing a musical skeleton to create full tracks around a particular music style.

But you can get creative with sample packs. A unique way to use sample packs is to create some based on the sounds of a particular artist's release and to make it available with the EP. This creates an extra income stream, more promotional material and allows the fans to deconstruct the music and create their own remixes. Following the release, run a remix competition for sample pack buyers.

Another example is selling an EP release as a stem pack. Stems are the individual mix tracks of a song, separated into drums, bassline, and lead vocals, allowing DJs to mix individual parts separately live. The Beatport platform has an entire section of its website for selling stems of tracks. I have done this several times in the past, and the income from the stem sales in the first three months was higher than the EP sales, so it's worth doing for the right release.

Finally, once you have an established roster of artists, you could release a sample pack of the sound of your record label, with each artist contributing a selection of sounds to the project.

When it comes to creating sample packs, production standards and guidelines need to be adhered to.

Ensure all samples are 100% royalty-free. All samples must be supplied in 44.1kHz 24-bit WAV or AIFF format. Ensure all samples are normalised to 0dB.

Loops are typically two bars in length. Any non-tempo based samples can be any length. All loop points must have zero crossing to ensure no clicks on the loop.

Use a uniform naming convention across the sample pack, including name, sounds type, key, and tempo. Some sample packs also contain MIDI loops and presets for popular soft synths such as Massive and Serum.

Once you have constructed your sample packs, you need to sell them. As well as selling directly from your website, there are specialist stores set up for this. The most established ones are:

- splice.com
- loopmasters.com
- loopcloud.com
- modernproducers.com

- primeloops.com
- bigfishaudio.com

They are always open to sign new sample packs to sell, and if your packs have been produced professionally, you won't have a problem signing your sample libraries on each platform.

MUSIC COMPILATIONS

A music compilation is a collection of songs typically from different artists, sold together under a common theme.

Examples are Now That's What I Call Music, Ministry of Sound Annual, UKF Drum & Bass Annual and Bad Boy 20th Anniversary Box Set Edition. A movie soundtrack is also a type of compilation (for example, Guardians Of The Galaxy: Awesome Mix Vol. 1).

As a label, there are two sides to compilations. There are compilations you create from your own label's catalogue, and there are requests from other labels looking to license your music for their compilations.

In the first instance, once you approach milestone releases, you may want to release a compilation album (say for your 25th release) or at the end of the year for a round-up of your most popular singles.

If you release music that is trending, you will get requests from other, sometimes bigger catalogue record labels to license your music. Let's look at this first.

COMPILATION MUSIC REQUESTS

When you get a license request for a compilation, you are usually offered an advance against royalties. If not, ask for it. But how much do you ask for? There is a simple formula to determine what you should be asking for as an advance.

You need to find out (examples in brackets):

- What its wholesale price will be ($3.99).
- What the expected sales will be (20,000).
- The number of tracks (18).
- Royalty percentage you will receive (20%).

Multiply the expected number of sales by the wholesale price, which gives you the total value of the compilation. In this example, $79,800.

Divide this number by the number of tracks to get the value of each track. Which gives you $4,433.

Finally, multiply by the percentage you will receive, which gives a royalties pay-out to expect as an advance for one track. In this example, $886.

This will give you a guide price for an advance on one track, but you need to balance this out with the opportunity to be on the compilation too. If you're launching a new artist with few fans, you won't have the same bargaining power as a track that's from a hot artist.

However, if you are giving the track exclusively to the compilation, always get an advance, even if it's as little as £150 ($200) to cover administrative costs.

When everything is agreed and signed off, you send the mastered uncompressed WAV file and fill out the metadata and once the compilation is published, send an invoice for the advance.

CREATING MUSIC COMPILATIONS

As a label, you may want to release a compilation album once you build a sizable catalogue. As you already own all the music, this can be pretty straightforward. Some distributors even allow you to automatically create complications by simply selecting tracks from previous releases, uploading new artwork and clicking 'distribute now'.

From there, promote the compilation with a marketing plan like any other release. A good time to do this is around the milestones of your record label.

RELEASING A COMPILATION WHEN STARTING A LABEL WITH NO ARTISTS

If you are a music entrepreneur wanting to start a record label, but don't have any artists signed to your label, you need to find music to sign and release. The most common way is to listen to demos on SoundCloud, attend gigs, and get recommendations from peers. This is the traditional way of finding and signing music.

The second way is to licence music that has already been released. This is essentially what music compilations do. You don't sign the copyright; instead, you sign a licensing agreement to sell the music for an agreed revenue share. If you are starting out, this can be a great way to release music to build up a fanbase for the label, so when you do want to sign an artist exclusively, you are a more attractive offer to the artist.

To license music, you simply need to approach the artist or copyright owner of the song (if the song has already been released) with a proposition. You agree to licensing terms and send off an agreement for them to sign. The rightsholder signs the agreement and sends a WAV version of the song, with songwriter information, and you release the track on your label.

It helps to have a product already planned that you aim to license the music for. Common themes include musical styles, the country or city artists are from, or interests like gaming music or running music. This will also give you a jumping-off point for your branding and marketing of the compilation. For example, putting together an indie-folk compilation of Canadian artists, you might use the name: 'Maple Syrup Vol 1 – The sounds of Canadian Indie Folk Music'.

Once you have found the music you want to sign, you have to find out the artists' contact details or those of copyright holders who can sign off. There is no shortcut to this. You just need to research. If the music has been released on a record label, you can Google to find a contact website and email address by looking up the © notes on the track in Apple Music. If the music has been self-released on YouTube and SoundCloud, reach out to the artist via their SoundCloud account or YouTube email address.

It is worth noting that if you decide to license music from another record label, you are more likely to have to negotiate with them a higher compensation rate in the form of a license fee or high royalty share. This is because they have already done the work to promote the artist and music, so there is some value associated with that.

Licensing music that an artist has self-released, you are more likely able to offer a royalty share with no upfront fees. That is not to say don't approach record labels, just be prepared to get a no if you're not offering good compensation.

Next, you want to contact the rights holder, typically via email. If you do have a contact, ask for an introduction, otherwise, send the following email:

Hi (Name),

We are (label name) and will be releasing a music compilation (name of the product) on the (date of proposed release).

We are really into the track (name of track by artist) and think it would be a great fit for the compilation and would like to license it.

We offer 50/50 splits on the royalties, and we will do a full-service promotion to blogs, magazines and a paid social media campaign.
Please let us know if you are interested, and we can send over the paperwork.

If you have any questions, please let us know.

All the best

Name
Record Label Name

When you send the licensing agreement, complete as much of the information you have yourself and highlight the areas they need to fill out that you may not know, such as the writer's legal names and the track's ISRC code. When you get the WAV versions of all the tracks, you are ready to move the compilation into the release schedule.

You can download this email template and a compilation contract by visiting the Book Resources tab on The Label Machine website.

LABELS AND IN-HOUSE PUBLISHING

Setting up as a music publisher allows you to make money from your signed artists' publishing royalties. However, consider the following:

A publisher's role is to make as much money as possible from the composition of the track. They take care of all the administrative publishing work: registering works with rights associations worldwide, collecting the royalties and paying the artists.

Good publishers also create commercial opportunities, such as writing with established recording artists or getting their music into big-budget films or video games.

As an independent record label, can you offer all the above services to justify signing all of an artist's publishing exclusively and know that it's a fair deal for them? Probably not. However, there are some publishing opportunities that benefit the label and an unpublished artist to consider as your label becomes more established.

SINGLE SONG ASSIGNMENT

When a label signs the masters of individual tracks for a single or EP, they can also sign the publishing on those individual tracks, which is becoming more common for smaller indie labels to do. In this arrangement, when the label signs the masters of the track and the artist does not have a publisher, the label signs the publishing on the individual track as a Single Song Assignment.

This gives record labels more opportunities to create revenue for the artist and label by offering the music for sync deals on film, TV, games, and to YouTube gaming streamers that need to clear both the masters and the publishing quickly.

Sometimes the turnaround for placing the music needs to be cleared in just a few days. By having the masters and publishing already cleared, you're more attractive to music supervisors and sync agents as they only have to deal with one company that can offer an 'all-in deal'.

Some artists are wary of signing away publishing, even on a single song. However, you can have a clause in the recording contract that if an artist doesn't have a publisher, the label has the rights to sign off on the masters and the publishing for any tracks secured for a potential sync deal, and revenue between label and artist at 50/50.

Further to this, you can keep this transparent and non-binding by including a clause that states the signing is non-exclusive and that either party can terminate the publishing in writing in 90 days. This allows an artist to still sign the track as part of their catalogue to a publisher should they wish to in the future.

PUBLISHING ADMINISTRATION

Another publishing opportunity for established labels is to set up a publishing administration company. Many indie artists probably won't generate enough publishing royalties for a traditional publisher to want to sign them. However, they still need help in registering and collecting what they earn, which is where a record label side-publishing deal can help.

Many label's side-publishing companies will actually have a deal with a larger publishing company who will actually do most of the royalty collection and administration around the world for them.

So, as your record label grows, consider single song publishing assignments for individual releases and then, as your roster of artists grows, look to offer publishing administration for them as well.

When you want to start signing and managing music publishing, it is best to engage with professionals. Companies that offer publishing administration deals for labels are Songtrust.com, Sentric.com, and KobaltMusic.com

ARTIST MANAGEMENT

A natural progression for established record labels is to move into the management of artists. Likewise, managers can also move into label management if they decide to set up and run labels for the artists they manage.

This is because these two areas traditionally work closely together and are of mutual benefit. When you promote and market a release, you also need the artists to promote it professionally.

Making sure they have a logo, press pics, a well maintained online presence with social media are essential to a successful release. If an artist doesn't have a manager to help manage these aspects, a label will have to arrange this for the artist. After a release, the artist may still need help with managing their career, and an established label is in a great position to help out, especially for younger and newer artists.

If you move into management, you need to agree to your responsibilities and what percentage of the artist's income you will take for your services. The management contract will outline these details, so let's break down a management contract template to understand this.

The term 'Talent' is typically used in management contracts in the entertainment industry for artists, and we will use the words 'talent' and 'artist' interchangeably when discussing management.

Anything in **[square brackets]** indicates sections that need to be updated depending on your agreement specifics.

Management company logo
Management company name
Management company address

This Agreement is made the **[date]** day of **[date]** 20XX.

Parties:

(1) [Manager Name] trading as **[Management Company]** of **[Manager Address]**, ("Manager") and

(2) [ABC] of **[Talent Address]** ("Talent") or [jointly and severally ("Talent")]

1. Type of Agreement: Management Agreement

2. Territory: [World]

3. Term: Six month trial period commencing on the above date following which both parties shall have 30 days to terminate the Agreement by notice in writing to the other party.

If neither party terminates the Agreement the Term shall be deemed extended for a further period of six months and automatically continue thereafter until either party serves a notice in writing on the other party advising that the Term of the Agreement shall expire three months after receipt of notice.

4. Scope: Manager shall act as Talent's sole and exclusive manager in the entertainment industry.

5. Duties: To negotiate any business affairs with third parties on behalf of Talent, such as live booking requests, remix requests, remix fees and interview requests.

Proactively seek out new business opportunities such as production work for film and television.

Provide business advice marketing campaigns and provide assistance with social media such as Facebook, Twitter, and web presence.

Provide business advice and recommendations on Talent's career and public image.

6. Commission: [15%] of all other income or monies worth received by or credited to Talent or on Talent's behalf arising from any of Talent's activities within the entertainment industry during **[and/or prior to]** the Term until such time as Talent earns $150,000 in any one year at which point commission increases to 20%.

VAT or similar taxes, bona fide gifts, video costs, independent press and promotion, payments to third-party producers, Talent's stylists, commission payable to agents, advances due and paid after the Term, and monies payable to Talent by any company in which **[Manager Name]** has a material interest, are non-commissionable.

7. Post-Term: 50% of rate paid to Manager immediately prior to end of Term payable on all income received by or credited to Talent or on Talent's behalf for three years after the Term which arises from Talent's activities in the entertainment industry during the Term including without limitation:

Exploitation of Talent's recordings recorded prior to or during Term and released during Term or within six months thereafter;
Exploitation of Talent's compositions written prior to or during Term and released during Term or within six months thereafter;

Agreements and/or arrangements (other than recording and/or music publishing agreements) entered into by Talent and/or any entity on Talent's behalf during Term and/or entered into within six months after the Term but which were substantially negotiated during the Term together with any replacements of such agreements and/or arrangements.

9. Accounting: Manager shall collect all income commissionable under this Agreement. Manager shall account to Talent in respect of net income (after deduction of commission and expenses) together with payment where applicable quarterly within 30 days from 31 March, 30 June, 30 September and 31 December. Where applicable Talent shall pay VAT on commission payable hereunder.

10. Audit: Talent may audit Manager's books and records relating solely to the Talent's income hereunder once per calendar year. Statements shall not be capable of challenge or objection by

Talent within two years after the relevant statement is rendered. If the audit reveals an underpayment exceeding 10% or $2,000, whichever is the greater, of the amount due to Talent for the audited period, Manager shall reimburse Talent's reasonable costs of such audit (excluding travel, accommodation, and subsistence) up to a maximum of $1,000.

11. Expenses: Manager shall be responsible for office and overhead expenses save for couriers and international phone and fax charges incurred on behalf of Talent. All expenses reasonably and necessarily incurred by Manager in connection with Manager's obligations hereunder shall be repaid to Manager. Manager agrees not to incur any expenses in excess of $500 without Talent's prior approval. Expenses shall be prorated if incurred in relation to other activities.

12. Termination: Manager may terminate Agreement if Talent is in material breach of this Agreement, provided that where such breach is capable of remedy, Talent has failed to remedy the breach by no later than 30 days after receipt of notice from Manager specifying breach.

13. Warranties: Talent warrants, represents and agrees that: Talent has the right to enter into this Agreement and to grant the rights granted in this Agreement;

Talent has the ability to perform the obligations required in this Agreement and shall not enter into any agreements or commitments which shall in any way interfere with Manager's ability to carry out Manager's services hereunder;

Talent is over the age of 18 years and shall be responsible for Talent's own tax and national insurance contributions;

Talent shall immediately refer to Manager all enquiries or offers Talent receives in connection with Talent's activities hereunder including personal endorsements and appearances;

Talent shall carry out to the best of Talent's ability and in sober and punctual fashion all performances, engagements, promotional activities and agreements, obtained or approved by Manager;

Talent shall use Talent's best efforts to further Talent's career during Term and to cooperate with Manager to the fullest extent in the interest of promoting Talent's career;

Talent shall keep Manager reasonably informed of Talent's whereabouts and availability;

Talent shall reveal to Manager all income including without limitation public performance income, and radio and television appearance monies paid directly to Talent; and

Talent has been advised to seek legal advice prior to signing this Agreement.

14. Indemnity: Talent agrees to indemnify Manager against any loss and damages (including legal fees) arising out of or in connection with any claims, actions, or demands by any third party which is inconsistent with any warranties and/

or representations Talent has made under this Agreement. Pending determination of any claim Manager may withhold a reasonable sum Manager deems sufficient to meet such claim.

15. General: Nothing shall prevent Manager from acting for other Talents.

Manager may assign this Agreement to any company owned and/or controlled by or entitled to provide the services of **[Manager Name].** This Agreement shall be binding upon each of the parties and their respective successors and assigns.

This Agreement shall not constitute a partnership between Manager and Talent.

If any provision of this Agreement is held by a court or other body of competent jurisdiction to be void or unenforceable but would be valid and enforceable if a part(s) was deleted or modified, such provision shall apply with such deletion or modification to make the Agreement valid and effective.

[This Agreement shall apply to and bind Artist jointly and severally]

This Agreement is the entire agreement between the parties relating to this subject and may only be varied or modified by a written document signed by both parties.

Notices shall be in writing and deemed served at the time of serving if served in person, the day after posting if sent by overnight express delivery, or two working days following posting if sent by first class prepaid post to the address set out above for the receiving party or such other address as shall have been notified to the sender.

16. Jurisdiction: [This Agreement shall be governed and construed in accordance with the laws of England whose courts shall have exclusive jurisdiction.] OR

[This Agreement shall be governed by the laws of the State of California and any dispute shall be settled in the state or federal courts located in the city of Los Angeles, CA.]

The Parties confirm their acceptance of the above terms by signing below where indicated.

____

[Manager Name]

____

[Talent's full name]

Let's break down and explain each section in detail.

Name and date

This is where you put your own management company label logo, address and the date of the agreement.

Parties

Here is where you detail the legal names of each party the contract is between. The address is the physical address of each party.

For a solo artist, you end it with 'Talent'. If the artist has multiple members, you need to write each of the individual's full legal name and address here and then include the term 'jointly and severally "Talent"' at the end.

Type of Agreement

This states what kind of agreement this is: a Management Agreement

Territory

If the artist you are signing is releasing music worldwide, then use the term World. If you are only signing for one country or territory, amend this section to the appropriate details.

Term

This defines the initial period of the agreement and gives a one month termination notice period in the first 6 months. The second section means that if both parties are happy, the contract extends automatically with a three month termination notice.

Scope

This states that you are the exclusive manager for the artist in the entertainment industry, and you are not responsible for managing activities outside this area, such as personal or private matters.

Duties

These outline the duties that you will be expected to perform in your role as a manager. You may want to edit this to your artist's particular requirements. The number of duties you perform should be reflected in your commission.

Commission

This section details what percentage of the talent's revenue you as a manager take a commission on. Depending on the size of the talent and which genre of the music industry they are in will change this. Typically the range is between 10–20%. There is a commission increase for when the artist passes a earnings threshold, in this example $150,000. This allows management to share in a larger part of the income, and provides an incentive for the manager.

If commissioning on activities before signing the talent include the 'prior to' wording. For example, you would include this wording to cover income from music royalties on previous recordings that the talent has not been paid, and the manager will chase up for payment.

This section also states the non-commissionable income, typically revenue related to expenses and free gifts and services.

Post Term

This section is sometimes called a 'sunset clause'. It outlines the commission the manager receives if the manager and the artist go separate ways, or the artist moves to a new manager or bigger management company. It serves to protect the manager; for instance, if the manager works on a big deal and the artist decides to move to a new manager just before signing the deal, the current manager still benefits from the work they have done.

The '50% of rate paid' means that any deals or revenue streams that the manager was part of during the term, the manager will receive 50% of the original commission post-term. So, if the artist released an album during the term, and the manager was on

15% commission, then after the term, the original manager will receive half of that or 7.5% of the revenue for three years.

The three other sections state that any recordings, compositions and deals made prior to or within six months after the term ends are included in the post-term. Again this is to protect the manager. So, if the artist moves to new management and immediately signs a large recording or publishing deal, the manager benefits from this deal.

The post-term clause may have to be negotiated with the talent depending on what stage the talent is at in their career.

Accounting

This states the manager will collect all income on behalf of the talent and account to them every three months. Sometimes the accounting is for every month, and if the talent has an accountant that invoices on behalf of them, you may have to amend this to reflect that arrangement.

Audit

This clause outlines how the artist can audit the income statements of the manager or management company. This is rarely required between independent talent and managers, but if it is necessary, a specialist accountant is usually assigned to audit the books.

Expenses

Any expenses you as a manager might incur fulfilling your duties can be reimbursed, for instance, paying for the artist's Uber rides, flowers or a photoshoot. Any expenses above $500 needs prior approval before spending.

Termination

This states you can terminate the contract if the talent breaches the agreement, and that you notified the talent of this breach and they did not remedy it within 30 days.

Warranties

This clause states what the talent is expected to do in the role of the artist and in dealings with you as a manager. In summary, the talent agrees they won't enter into any agreements that would interfere with the manager duties, the talent must be over the age of 18, and is responsible for their own taxes, that the talent will send any enquiries or offers to you as the manager, shall act professionally and turn up to gigs, interviews, and act in a sober manner, will cooperate with the manager to advance their career, will keep the manager informed of where they are and when they will be available, share all information about income sources, and that you as a manager has advised them to take legal advice before signing the contract.

Indemnity

This clause states that if the talent does something against what they agreed in the warranties above (for example, trashing a hotel room), the manager has the right to be compensated for any costs associated with dealing with the issue. The manager can hold back an amount of money the manager believes it will cost to cover dealing with a problem.

General

The first clause states that the manager can manage more than one artist. Next, it states that you can assign this agreement to any entity you own or control as a manager. For instance, if you create a specialist management company for a group of artists you manage.

The next clause states that the agreement is not a partnership, joint venture, or employment contract between the manager and the artist. This is to prevent the artist from claiming any legal rights that fall under any of these types of relationships, such as employment rights.

The following clause states that if some of the terms are held to be illegal or otherwise unenforceable, the remainder of the agreement should still apply. For instance, if, for some reason, it became illegal to provide business advice to talent, it would not void the whole agreement. It would be deleted or modified, and the rest of the agreement terms would still apply.

If the artist is more than one person as stated in the parties section, you need to include the clause 'This Agreement shall apply to and bind Talent jointly and severally'. If the talent is only one person, then delete this clause.

The last clause states that if either party wants to change any part of the agreement, it must be agreed by and expressed in a written document signed by both parties.

Jurisdiction

The final clause states in which country the jurisdiction of the agreement lies and which court of law disputes will be settled in. Change this depending on the country or state your management company is based.

The final section is for signing. Edit to state your legal name and the talent's legal name. If there is more than one member for the talent, add each member's legal name.

You can use this agreement template for your own management company, but remember it has been used for educational purposes and should you use it as a template, I recommend consulting an attorney or lawyer to get a stamp of approval on your version before signing any deals.

LIVE SHOWS

Along with selling records, publishing and merchandise, playing live shows is another main income stream for an established artist. It is the main source of income for many independent artists, earning more money than merchandise, music sales, and publishing combined.

If you are a music artist that plays an instrument as a solo artist, as part of a band, or as a producer that DJs, the logical progression from releasing music is to playing regular live shows. It's the dream. Releasing singles and albums and playing to thousands of adoring fans worldwide.

The main consideration of promoters wanting to book artists is their musical output, so it is vital for artists to consistently release great music. It's why many live bands try to work to an album cycle, releasing music in the autumn, to build a buzz so that promoters book them for next year's summer festival circuits.

COVID-19 has permanently altered the live music landscape. Though venues have reopened, artists now face enhanced hygiene protocols, stricter cancellation terms and often reduced capacities. With numerous smaller venues closing permanently, competition for performance slots has intensified.

Brexit has complicated European touring for UK artists, requiring country-specific work permits, equipment carnets and navigating complex cabotage rules affecting merchandise sales. Despite these hurdles, European tours remain vital for expanding your audience.

Post-pandemic, building a strong local following has become even more crucial. A solid hometown fanbase demonstrates your draw potential to promoters whilst providing the foundation needed before tackling the increased costs and administrative complexities of international touring.

There could be a whole book dedicated to the live music scene, and it's different for different music genres. The path to regular live show bookings for bands is different from that of hip hop producers and different again for producer/DJs.

As an artist, your end goal will be to eventually get a booking agent whose job is to handle an artist's live performances. This covers arranging and securing show bookings, negotiating the best deal, collecting the performance fees, pitching the artist to festivals, and arranging logistics such as travel and flights.

Early in an artist's career, when there are fewer shows to deal with, the manager can act as a booking agent and handle most of the above responsibilities. And vice versa, some agents also play the role of manager for some artists.

And before a band has a manager or agent, a band member can arrange those first early shows directly with event and club promoters.

RECORD LABELS ROLE IN LIVE SHOWS

If your label is putting out good music and your artists build a following, then as a label manager, you are in a good position to speak to booking agents to let them know about which artists are on the rise and book for support shows. Having good relationships with booking agents can make your label favourable to new artists looking to sign. They can see that releasing their music on your label can progress to being introduced and signed by a booking agent, leading to potential live shows.

Having a roster of artists on your label that all have booking agents and are playing regular shows is the ideal place to be in when you look to run a label night for your record label. At this point, it's an easy sell to a promoter, as all your artists have a live following and will be popular enough to sell tickets and make a successful sell-out show.

You don't have to wait until all your artists have agents, and if your music genre has a strong local scene, then running label night can be a great way to create a community around your record label and its artists. A great way to start one is to plan an event to celebrate the record label's first anniversary. Putting on local live shows is also an excellent time to sell your first lines of merchandise too.

Putting on label nights can be very rewarding and allows your artists to get together and meet the fans. If your label releases music that supports live artists, you should plan to run label nights as part of your long-term label goals.

THE LIVE SHOW PROCESS

The artist's manager, booking agent, and the event promoter work together to put on a show or tour. You can refer back to Part One of the book for more details on each of their roles. We will look at this from the perspective of an event for an individual artist, as even with a record label showcase, the contracts will still be with the individual artists playing the show, not the record label. The label showcase will be predominantly used as a promotional tool to brand the events.

Typically, the manager will speak to the booking agent about an upcoming album release date, and then the booking agent will reach out to event promoters to see if they will book the artist. This is done at least three or four months in advance of shows being booked.

The event promoter puts together a budget and looks at the event's costs, expected ticket sales and decides if it will make money. The booking agent will also negotiate an artist's performance fee and or a share of ticket sales, depending on the size of the show and the artist's popularity.

Once the booking agent and promoter agree on the artist's performance fee, ticket prices, costs, and the date, a show contract is drawn up. These details are included in the contract along with terms and conditions, and once both parties have signed, the show is booked. If arranging a tour, contracts are sent out to each event promoter who each agree on ticket price, expenses, and venue details.

Another important contract is the artist rider. This document states what the promoter is required to supply the artist with for a show and includes food and booze requests, stage and lighting requirements, and anything else that is needed for the artists to put on a successful show.

It will often include a diagram of how a band's set-up needs to be or, in the case of DJs, how they want the turntables or

XDJs set up. While the show contract is changed for each individual show, the rider agreement is the same for all shows.

If a tour is being arranged for a particular territory (for example, North America), then the booking agent will plan out a tour route, arrange available dates with event promoters and create a spreadsheet with these details to see if the tour will be profitable. Some shows might make a loss, but others make a profit, so having it all in one place to make a judgement call is important.

At this point, even if a tour might look like it will lose money, the manager can approach the band or record label and see if they are willing to put in the money to make up the difference. In the case of a record label, they would agree to recoup this cost from album sales.

CONCLUSION

I hope this book has been insightful and becomes a guide you can refer to frequently through your journey of starting, running and growing your own independent record label.

As you might have guessed at this point, if you want more in-depth lessons, practical guides, and access to a community of artists and managers running their own record labels, then I encourage you to join thelabelmachine.com.

Buying this book also gives you a 50% discount on The Label Machine's online platform. Simply email a copy of your book receipt to book@thelabelmachine.com, and we will send you a special link to sign up. This also includes receipts for buying the book secondhand on Amazon.

There are many other resources I would suggest if you want different perspectives on the topics covered in this book. Below are the ones I have found most helpful.

BOOKS

These books are in-depth resources covering all aspects of the music industry, written from a different perspective.

All You Need to Know About the Music Business – Donald Passman

This is a classic music business book covering music business history from the US perspective of the music industry.

Music: The Business – Ann Harrison
In-depth coverage on contracts and copyright law, from the perspective of the UK music industry.

How to Make It in the New Music Business – Ari Hersand
Great resource of material written from a music artist's perspective and gigging musician based in the US.

YOUTUBE

YouTube is excellent for covering the most recent developments in the music industry, and I find it particularly helpful for looking at modern music marketing trends.

Burstimo
youtube.com/c/Burstimo
Founders Maddy Raven and Alex Jobling provide excellent practical marketing advice for modern digital artists.

Andrew Southworth
youtube.com/user/feltgrape
Music artist Andrew gives great behind-the-scenes guides on using practical advertising techniques to grow your listenership on music platforms such as Spotify.

Damian Keyes
youtube.com/user/Damiankeyes
Rock artist and marketing guru that focuses on various techniques for growing your fan base as a music artist.

All About Helping Musicians
youtube.com/@AllAboutHelping
Ayaz Hussain helps independent artists install smart digital marketing systems that scale their careers without guesswork.

WEBSITES

Most of the websites I use are for keeping up to date on music industry news. Below is a selection of sites I regularly check.

Hypebot
hypebot.com
A music technology and business website that follows music business trends. Articles regularly get over 100K views.

CMU
cmulibrary.com
The Complete Music Update website is a huge online library of articles covering all aspects of the music industry.

DIYMusician
diymusician.cdbaby.com
Online blog brought to you from distributor CDBaby. Lots of great bite-sized articles on all aspects of the business of music.

These links are all available by visiting the Book Resources tab on The Label Machine website.

And, finally, connect with me personally on TikTok and Instagram on my handle @nicksadler.io

ACKNOWLEDGMENTS

Thank you to my Mum and Dad, for raising me to believe that I can do anything. David and Angie, for early support while the first edition of this book was being written at St Leonards Cottage.

Thanks to my fantastic label manager community members, John Eye, Freddie Harb, Scott Sturgis, Markee Ledge, Harry Towell, Rob Gilmore, Phil Cleeves, Vincent Reynolds and everyone else who show up weekly and support each other.

Big shout out out to all the artists I've had the pleasure of working with over the years: Skism, The Prototypes, The Foreign Beggars, Ebow (RIP), Memtrix, Skrillex, Siren, Far Too Loud, MozX, Three Laws, Molly Beanland, Diemetic, Rob Bravery, Eptic, Snavz, The Frederik, Diemetic, Dodge and Fuski, Zomboy, State of Mind, Flux Pavilion, Bar9, 501, Habstrakt, Lazy Rich. Thanks to Lee and Chris at UAA in the early days for showing the ropes of live shows, Francesco at Primary Talent, Kevin Gimble and Steve Gordon at UTA, Rossy Burr and Rob Talbott at Disciple Recordings, Diluk Dias, James Cotterill, and Luke Hood at AEI Group, Tommy Dash and Tom Flanders at Never Say Die Records (RIP), and Leo Corson at Corson Agency.

Thanks to my music writing partners, Michael Christian Unwin, Bruce Gainsford and Mark Paton. Thanks to Original

176 Crew, Rob, Remy, Dave, Molly, Jdubz, Ross, Caro. Thanks my sis Louise, Pavan Mukhi, The Upbeats, Patrick Hawkins, Danny Savage, Adam Relf, Matt & Fran Hodges, Nyrelle Rowan, Rod Hamel, Julz Harrison (YMYD 4 Life), Brad Buckle, Ashley Gallagher, Hemal Shah, Peter Baird, Arielle Fisher, Halina Wielogorska, Jennifer Cochrane, Rebecca Smart Bakken, and Paul Pacifico. Thanks to Kirsty, Phil, Sarah, and the team at Goldfinch for supporting my film endeavours.

Huge thank you to everybody that provided input and feedback on the final manuscript: Matt Ryan, Molly, Luke Hood at UKF, Chris Goss at Hospital Records, Søren Dons Mensberg, James Whitehead, Daniel Gomes, and Pete Callaghan at Promoly.

Huge thanks to my publisher Colin Steven at Velocity Press for his hard work in getting this made into a physical book! Massive thanks to my proofreader/editor Jonny Charles, Paul Baillie-Lane for his typesetting skills, and to Hayden Russell for the fantastic new cover artwork for the book.

Thanks to Daniel Gomes, Rob Singh, Peter Edwards and the extended team at The Label Machine HQ. And shoutout to all the beta members for supporting and feeding back on the original platform.

Finally, thank you to my beautiful wife, my Poppy who supports me no matter what, looks after our two amazing boys, and provided many early proof reads of the first book in its early stages. I love you x

INDEX

SPECIAL THANKS TO EVERYONE WHO PRE-ORDERED THE BOOK

Michael Agar, Jules Alaneme, Julian Ankersmit, Mike Blackwell, Nick Bowman, Ladislav John Brozovsky, Nick Burt, Matthew Butler, Phil Cleeves, Ellyssa Marie Del Maestro, Chris Desmond, Rachel Dreyer, John Eye, Freddie Harb, Johnny Hudson, Philip Klop, Olivier Laurent, Josh Levine, Jeff Mars – Confusion Funky Bat Records, Phil Nobles, K. P., Josh Parkins, Anthony Phillip, Mark Reed, Vincent Reynolds, Aura Riddle, Timo Rotonen, Terence Sharpe, Peri Siolis (aka GLOWKiD), Scott Sturgis, Ryan Sutter, Omar Taveras, Michele Tessadri, Hayden Thomson, Harry Towell, Sebastien Verbraekel, Richard Weeks, Mike Wheeler, Thomas Wouters